MW01165168

CONTEMPORARY JEWISH PHILANTHROPY IN AMERICA

Edited by
Barry A. Kosmin
and
Paul Ritterband

Rowman & Littlefield Publishers, Inc.

ROWMAN & LITTLEFIELD PUBLISHERS, INC.

Published in the United States of America
by Rowman & Littlefield Publishers, Inc.
8705 Bollman Place, Savage, Maryland 20763

British Cataloging in Publication Information Available

Library of Congress Cataloging-in-Publication Data

Contemporary Jewish philanthropy in America /
edited by Barry A. Kosmin and Paul Ritterband.
p. cm.
Includes bibliographical references.
1. Jews—United States—Charities.
I. Kosmin, Barry Alexander.   II. Ritterband, Paul.
HV3191.C56 1991
361.7'5'0973—dc20   91–7661 CIP

ISBN 0–8476–7647–1 (cloth)

5   4   3   2   1

Printed in the United States of America

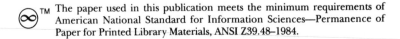

TM The paper used in this publication meets the minimum requirements of
American National Standard for Information Sciences—Permanence of
Paper for Printed Library Materials, ANSI Z39.48–1984.

Contents

Introduction

Paul Ritterband and Barry A. Kosmin

Philanthropy in America is a vast enterprise with an annual turnover in the tens of billions of dollars. Thousands of people have made careers of collecting and disbursing other people's money, and many thousands more volunteer their time in the same enterprise. For these reasons alone, it is appropriate for serious scholars to focus their energies and talents on the study of philanthropy generally and Jewish philanthropy in particular.

The study of Jewish philanthropy has at least two functions. Philanthropy is a major activity in the Jewish community. The authors of the papers included here have taken their responsibility to enrich our understanding of this activity seriously to the end that the community functions more effectively and more efficiently and that it can secure the material needed to achieve its religious, cultural, and humanitarian ends. In addition, Jewish philanthropy is a window on the inner contemporary communal life of the Jews, as well as to their past. Biblical and rabbinic literature is filled with admonitions to care for the poor, the widowed and orphaned, the sick, the indigent bride, and the needy traveler. Beyond admonitions, there is the tale of how the Jewish community devised institutions and patterns of behavior to meet the command of the tradition. Even now, in the midst of what is doubtlessly the most secular period in Jewish history, the ancient commands still resonate as contemporary Jews seek ways of coming to terms with their historic conscience while living their lives in societies far removed from those that spawned their philanthropic ideals.

Whether seeking to settle in New Amsterdam in the mid-seventeenth century or returning to Cromwellian England, the Jews had to promise that not only would they not become public charges, but that they would also take responsibility for the poor among them. From the perspective of the ruling authorities, this was a way of limiting whatever burdens the Jews might be tempted to impose upon the established church and the state. From the perspective of the Jews, taking care of their own did not require a pledge to the authorities. This is what they expected to do, what their tradition demanded and what they understood to be in their own best interests as well.

Communal care of the unfortunate was motivated by a sense of divine command, communal pride, and a deeply felt need to maintain social order. Chaos crouched at the door. The hold of the Jews on their habitation was tenuous. It was important that they not test the patience of their hosts by attempting to shift their burden to the gentile authorities. In the traditional societies, they created brotherhoods or *hevrot*. These would maintain and manage their philanthropic system. Individual *hevrot* dowered brides, saw to the needs of the sick, and took care of itinerants. Chief and most prestigious among these groups, however, was the "Holy Brotherhood" or *hevra kadisha* that buried the dead.

Each of these brotherhoods was made possible by the intimate knowledge that each member of the community had of his fellows. There were no professionals, and in a sense there were no volunteers as we now know them. To participate in the life of a brotherhood was an achievement not open to all. These guild-like bodies recruited the most prestigious members of the community to serve in their midst. One did not volunteer one's time as one might in a contemporary nonprofit organization in order to be a member of a brotherhood. Instead, one was vetted by those already recognized by the community as persons of probity, piety, and in some instances, wealth. To serve in a brotherhood was an honor bestowed rather than a position sought.

During the course of the nineteenth century, a series of events occurred that radically changed the Jewish community and, consequently, the nature of Jewish philanthropy. The Jewish population of Eastern Europe, the home of the largest part of world Jewry, grew enormously in size. Migration followed as a result of the population-induced poverty that was made worse by increasingly severe czarist restrictions on Jewish rights to domicile. The intimate community of the Jewish small town gave way to the impersonality of the big city, particularly among the Jewish migrants to the west. The emancipation and the Enlightenment shattered the Jewish religio-cultural consensus as well as the institutions built upon that consensus.

Enormous waves of Jewish migration came to the United States in particular, a country that allowed for and encouraged voluntarism but did not support the *imperium in imperio* that was the norm for traditional Jews in Europe and the Mediterranean world. The immigrants had to be cared for, but who would do it and with what aims in mind? Hence, the care of the downtrodden increasingly became professionalized and placed in the hands of the newly emerging field of social work. From that point on, there would be donors, professional workers, some volunteers, and clients. All of these factors, along with American notions of efficiency and effectiveness, led to the creation of networks of professionalized, scientifically grounded service agencies with centralized coordination in the cities of the west.

In New York City, the port of entry for most East European Jews, and ultimately the largest Jewish population center ever seen in Jewish history, at least two layers of philanthropic bodies were created. The already established "Uptown" German Jews founded one set of agencies and the "Downtown" East European immigrants founded another. Thus, by the end of the nineteenth century, there were two major Jewish hospitals in New York City, Mount Sinai Hospital (formerly Jews Hospital) founded by the Uptown Jews (1855), and Beth Israel Hospital founded by the Russians (1889). The two hospitals served different populations, had different religious orientations (one was kosher, the other not), and were supported by different donors. The medical situation was emblematic of the larger problem of finding a philanthropic consensus in the American Jewish community. Indeed, there were those who opposed an institutionalized consensus on the grounds that it would violate their notions of a narrowly construed confessional Judaism, a Jewish version of the congregational polity of liberal Protestantism.

Around the country, however, beginning with Boston in 1895, centralized, albeit weak, coordinating bodies were created to aid in the rationalized solicitation of funds and to plan for the social service needs of the Jewish community. The need to respond to the sufferings of European Jewry during the World War I led to further national coordination and limited centralization with the creation of the Joint Distribution Committee. "The Joint," as it came to be known, brought together Jewish organizations with vastly different orientations that agreed on the need to serve their brethren abroad. By the 1930s, a national coordinating body, the Council of Jewish Federations and Welfare Funds, had been established to link and to service the federated Jewish philanthropic cum service bodies that had been created all over the country.

The federalism of Jewish philanthropy on both the local and national levels owes more to the Federalist Papers than it does to the constitutional American Republic. In order to achieve broad consensus, it became necessary to permit authority to remain at the level of the individual agency in the local community and in the hands of the local community at the national level. Consensus required avoiding some issues and focusing on those issues that were grounded in broad agreement. The social work professional norm of "process" and the need to make certain that every one was "on board" made it inevitable that dramatic initiatives would be avoided. The fund-raisers' slogan, "We are one," was in truth a social reality made necessary by the fragile consensus that had been achieved.

By the late 1960s, this consensus was challenged by activist students borrowing methods from the student left to shift the consensus in a more profoundly particularist Jewish direction. Students sat in at the General Assembly of the Council of Jewish Federation (CJF), the weak parliament of American Jewry's voluntary sector, and demanded that funds be allocated for Jewish survivalist cultural and religious purposes. Their task had been made easier by the declining need for funds to support hospitals (now made possible by government and private third-party payments), the embourgeoisment of a community that left behind many of the problems of impoverished immigrants, the rise of ethnic self-consciousness, and the withering away of the melting pot ideal. Symbolically, the CJF dispensed with the "Welfare Fund" half of its appellation. It suddenly was "in" to be "out." Jewish philanthropy now became an instrument of community building instead of that of Americanization and amelioration of the problems of the poor.

It is certainly obvious to note that the Jewish community participating in and served by Jewish philanthropy at the end of the twentieth century is vastly different from that which created the major institutions at the end of the nineteenth century. The differences are usually reflected implicitly rather than explicitly in the papers in this volume. The existence of several papers on the philanthropic behavior of Jewish women reflects the shift from the emphasis on women's divisions to women's participation in main line Jewish philanthropic activity. The papers focusing on the competitive status of Jewish philanthropy reflects the problems engendered by Jewish socioeconomic success and increasing acceptance by and integration into American society. The rise of "new" Jewish philanthropies and their new social base may well reflect the fraying of the consensus underlying federated campaigns as the Jewish community experiences new forms of differentiation and new dilemmas.

We are grateful to our colleagues who have devoted their time to the study of one of the central issues of contemporary Jewish life and have come up with insights advancing our understanding of the modern Jewish condition as evidenced in Jewish philanthropic behavior. The reader is welcome to agree to differ with the formulations published here. We have attempted to meet the standards of academic rigor and theoretical concern while dealing directly with the practical problems of those charged with keeping the community solvent. We hope that the reader will be moved to take the issues further by continued study and analysis.

Part 1

Theory and Background

1

An Economic Analysis
of Philanthropy

Barry R. Chiswick

The dictionary defines "philanthropy" as "goodwill to fellowmen, especially active effort to promote human welfare." Although often thought of in the same context as charity (i.e., financial or other assistance to the poor), philanthropy is far broader and includes the promotion of religion, education, health, safety, and the environment, as well as contributions to artistic and cultural activities that need not directly or indirectly affect the poor. In 1986, reported philanthropic contributions totaled $87.2 billion or nearly 2.1 percent of the Gross National Product (GNP). This figure underestimates the value of all philanthropic contributions because it excludes the value of time volunteered to various philanthropic organizations.[1] Adjusted for inflation, contributions increased at a phenomenal rate of 2.4 percent per year since 1970 (table 1-1).

The vast bulk of philanthropic dollars (about 80 percent) come from individuals and households (table 1-1). The shares provided by charitable foundations and charitable bequests have declined over time, and are now about 6 percent and 7 percent, respectively. Ever mindful of their public image, many corporations make philanthropic contributions. They constitute an increasing share of philanthropic resources from nearly 4 percent in 1970 to over 5 percent in 1986.[2]

3

Table 1–1. *Philanthropic Contributions by Source and Allocation, 1955–86*

	1955	1970	1980	1986
Total Funds (Billions)				
Dollars	7.7	21.0	48.8	87.2
1986 Dollars[a]	31.5	59.3	64.9	87.2
Source (Percent)				
Living Individuals	87.7	77.0	83.4	82.2
Personal Bequest	3.1	10.1	5.9	6.7
Gifts by Foundations	3.9	9.0	5.7	6.0
Gifts by Corporations	5.5	3.8	4.9	5.2
Total	100.0	100.0	100.0	100.0
Allocation (Percent)				
Religion	—	44.3	45.6	46.9
Health	—	16.2	13.8	14.1
Education	—	15.7	14.2	14.6
Human Service	—	13.8	10.1	10.4
Arts, Culture	—	3.3	6.6	6.7
Public, Society Benefit	—	2.4	3.1	2.8
Other	—	4.3	7.2	4.6
Total	—	100.0	100.0	100.0

Note: Detail may not add to total due to rounding.

[a]Converted to 1986 dollars by the Consumer Price Index (CPI).

Sources: Virginia Ann Hodgkinson and Murray S. Weitzman, *Dimensions of the Independent Sector: A Statistical Profile,* Washington, D.C.: Independent Sector, 2nd ed., 1986, tables 3.1 and 3.2, 52–53

U.S. Bureau of the Census, *Statistical Abstract of the United States, 1988, 108th Edition,* G.P.O., 1987, table 600.

Over the past two decades nearly half of all philanthropic dollars were devoted to the promotion of religion and religious institutions (table 1-1).[3] Health and educational philanthropic resources have increased even after adjusting for inflation, but as a fraction of total resources they have each fallen from about 16 percent to about 14 percent. Antipoverty programs—what most refer to as charity—are but one component in the human services category. The resources in the human services area have fallen from 13.8 percent to 10.4 percent over the period. The share specifically devoted to the poor has declined even further. The arts, cultural, and human activities have seen their share of resources double over the period to 6.7 percent of the total.

In the context of this paper, philanthropy will be understood to mean the *voluntary unrequited transfer of resources for the benefit of others*. If the transfer were requited—that is, if the resources were transferred in exchange for a benefit from the recipient or some third party—it would be a transaction, not philanthropy. If the transfer were involuntary it would be taxation when done by the government or theft when done in violation of the law.

Regardless of the form or the timing of philanthropy, the question arises as to why "homo-economous," economic man, would make voluntary unrequited transfers of resources. At first glance this might seem to be irrational behavior outside the realm of economics. On closer inspection, however, the economist's approach can explain philanthropic behavior and provide a rich set of insights regarding this behavior.

This paper discusses the evolution of thinking in economics regarding philanthropy. Three approaches are considered. The first, which I shall refer to as the "neoclassical" approach, views philanthropy as a consumer good. The second, referred to as the "altruism" approach, focuses on "inter-dependent utility functions." Both of these approaches provide useful explanations for much behavior, but are limited in their implications and lack intuitive appeal for explaining philanthropic behavior. The third approach, developed for this paper, is based on the New Home Economics and views the observed philanthropic activities as inputs in "club" membership, and it is the club membership that the donors are acquiring. The club membership approach expands the realm of insights regarding philanthropy. This paper reviews each of these approaches and cites some of the relevant literature.

The Neoclassical Approach

The neoclassical approach to consumer behavior views individuals as seeking to maximize an unmeasurable item called "utility" by consuming goods and services such as housing, food, and movies. It is the finiteness of resources, in terms of both money (as income) and time, that constrain or limit consumption.

Using this approach, economists have viewed philanthropy as a consumer good (e.g., Schwartz 1970, Feldstein and Taylor 1976, Boskin and Feldstein 1977). Frequently, without addressing the question as to why it should be so, it is assumed that philanthropic contributions increase the donor's utility or economic well-being.[4] The constraint, of course, is that by giving one dollar in philanthropy the consumer has fewer resources for other goods or services. Because of the tax deductibility of most philanthropic contributions, the "price" to the donor of a dollar of philanthropy is $(1 - t)$, where t is the appropriate tax rate. To the extent philanthropy is tax deductible, the higher the tax rate in the person's tax bracket, the greater the tax savings from a dollar of philanthropy and hence the lower the cost of the donation. For example, if a donor is in the 30 percent tax bracket, every $100 donation actually costs $70 because the donor's taxes are reduced by $30. Empirical research has indeed found that philanthropic contributions vary directly with the tax rate. A 10 percent increase in the tax rate tends to increase donations by about 14 percent for those who itemized their deductions (Feldstein and Taylor 1976) and by about 25 percent among low-income and middle-income households (Boskin and Feldstein 1977).

These studies, and others, provide ample evidence that the reduction in tax rates in the 1980s had the perhaps unintended consequence of sharply reducing the incentives for philanthropic contributions. There was, therefore, an inherent inconsistency in the Reagan administration's joint objectives of expanding the voluntary sector and simultaneously reducing the federal government's taxes and expenditures on social services, the arts, and related activities.

The neoclassical approach can also be used to analyze the effect of increases in income or wealth on philanthropy. Philanthropy is likely to be viewed as a "good," that is, wealthier people would give more than those who are poorer. It is less certain whether the *proportion* of income or wealth allocated to philanthropy rises with the level of income or wealth. Some studies show that whereas the dollar value of contributions increases with the level of income, the share of contributions in income declines. For example, studies suggest that a 10 percent higher level of income is associated with 7 to 8 percent greater donations when the price effect, the tax rate, is held constant (Feldstein and Taylor 1976, Boskin and Feldstein 1977). Bequests to philanthropic organizations appear to have a greater responsiveness to wealth than transfers given during the donor's lifetime.

The data in table 1-2 on contributions in 1984 suggest that except for the poorest of households, many of whom have temporarily low incomes, philanthropic contributions rise as a proportion of income as the level of income increases.[5] Contributions to religious organizations do not vary as a proportion of income (about 1.8 percent across income groups). Contributions to nonreligious charities, on the other hand, rise sharply as a proportion of income from 0.4 percent in the $10,000 to $20,000 category, to 0.7 percent in the $40,000 to $50,000 category, to 1.2 percent for households with income in excess of $50,000. Another index of the effect of income is the proportion of households devoting less than one-half percent or 3 percent or more of their income to philanthropic causes. The former proportion declines and the latter proportion rises with the level of income.[6]

Although a useful starting point, the neoclassical approach has two failings. One is conceptual. It does not provide an appealing explanation as to why the voluntary reduction in one's own consumption for the benefit of others can, up to a point, increase a person's perception of his or her well-being. From the point of view of the donor, it is not clear how this differs from "waste," that is, consuming fewer resources than one has available. Indeed, it presumably differs from waste from society's perspective in that it provides benefits for others.[7]

The second problem is the limited range of testable hypotheses. The two key hypotheses derived from the model are that donations respond negatively to a higher price (lower marginal tax rate) and positively to

Table 1–2. *Philanthropic Contributions by Age and Income, 1984*

Age and Household Income	Amount (mean)	As Percent of Income		
		Total	Religious	Other
Total	$ 650	2.4	1.7	0.7
Age (years)				
18–29	380	1.6	1.2	0.3
30–34	500	1.7	1.2	0.5
35–49	910	2.6	1.9	0.7
50–64	880	3.0	2.0	1.0
65 and over	400	2.7	2.3	0.5
Household Income				
Under $10,000	170	3.0	2.3	0.5
$10,000–19,000	340	2.3	1.9	0.4
$20,000–29,000	520	2.1	1.6	0.5
$30,000–39,000	820	2.3	1.8	0.6
$40,000–49,000	1,060	2.4	1.7	0.7
$50,000 and over	1,940	2.9	1.8	1.2

Source: Hodgkinson, Virginia Ann, and Murray S. Weitzman, *Dimensions of the Independent Sector: A Statistical Profile,* Washington, D.C.: Independent Sector, 2nd ed., 1986, tables 3.7 and 3.8, 58–59.

a higher income. Now that these propositions have been well established, we seek a richer model for philanthropy that can explain these and other behavior patterns.

Altruistic Approach

An alternative approach to philanthropy, which addresses in part the conceptual problem in the neoclassical approach, is to assume that people view their well-being as having increased if the well-being of others increases (Becker 1974). Suppose the utility of Dick were dependent on his consumption of goods and services and the utility of Jane. Jane's utility is a function of her consumption and may or may not be reciprocal by also including Dick's. Up to a point, the transference of consumption resources from Dick to Jane can increase Dick's utility.

In this framework the unrequited transfer of resources from one person to another is a form of self-interest. For example, altruistic parents have lower direct consumption but receive indirect benefits from the higher level of consumption of their children.

The altruistic approach is very powerful for explaining resource transfers within a family among members of the same generation (between spouses, among siblings) and across generations (between parents, children, and grandchildren).[8] It also has testable implications. The transfers will be greater: (a) the lower the price (e.g., the greater the efficiency of the recipient in convecting transfers to his or her own use), (b) the smaller the group (e.g., the recipient can take greater account of the interests of the donor), (c) the closer the relationship between the recipient and the donor (e.g., siblings rather than cousins), (d) the higher the income of the donor and the lower of the recipient.[9] Transfers among family members are not treated as charitable contributions under the tax law so the price effect (marginal tax rate) discussed above would not be applicable.

The altruism approach to philanthropy is not, however, without its pitfalls. There is the "free-rider" problem. In the example given above, Dick can benefit from the philanthropic contributions made by others to Jane, so there is little incentive for Dick to reduce his consumption to help Jane.

The impact of the recipient's utility on the utility of the donor can be viewed as a "collective good" from which other similarly inclined donors cannot be prevented from benefitting. For example, all older siblings benefit when the youngest one receives a transfer from any sibling, and any sibling's benefit does not detract from that of the others. When there are collective goods and excludability is not possible (e.g., fireworks displays, national defense), the private sector undersupplies the good. So, too, would be the case with philanthropy beyond the immediate family.[10]

It is also clear that the degree of interdependence among individuals would depend on the "distance" between the donor and recipient. Within a generation, siblings would presumably be closer than cousins (stronger positive effect of siblings' than of cousins' well-being), and cousins' well-being would be stronger than that for strangers. This would presumably be a direct characteristic of utility functions, but it may also arise indirectly as donors would have less influence over the behavior of recipients.[11] Some charities (e.g., "Christian Children Fund") make explicit recognition of the effect of "distance" on donations by creating nonbinding foster-child relationships between donors in the United States and recipients in less developed countries and by emphasizing the exchange of letters and pictures as an attempt to reduce this distance.

In summary, the altruism model can provide a useful framework for the analysis of unrequited transfers within a small, close group where one can conceptualize interdependent utilities and the "free-rider" problem is minimized. It can also explain the emergence of taxes and public income transfers for the poor to correct for the imperfections generated by the free-rider problem.[12] Yet it is less compelling for explaining philanthropy—unrequited transfers—outside the small group (e.g., to the anonymous poor) and to activities that are primarily for the benefit of the nonpoor (e.g., education, health, opera, art museums, and antidrunk driving organizations).

The "Club" Model

A model of philanthropic behavior should be able to account for the wide range of types of philanthropies (e.g., charity, cultural, environmental), should enable one to observe donations in spite of the potential "free-rider" problem discussed above, and should offer a richer range of implications, including implications for the size and form (e.g., cash versus volunteering of time) of philanthropic contributions. The model to be developed in this section satisfies these requirements.

Using the approach of the New Home Economics, consider a model in which individuals maximize utility or economic well-being by consuming "commodities."[13] Commodities are produced by the household by combining goods and services purchased in the market and the household member's own time. For example, eggs, juice, coffee, gas and electricity, and certain consumer durables (frying pan, stove, etc.) are combined in the home with time to produce the commodity "breakfast." One set of commodities is membership in philanthropic groups or clubs.

Club membership can be viewed as a commodity that is produced by combining time (including volunteer activities) and market resources (e.g., monetary donations). Whereas altruism implies identification with the recipient, club membership implies identification with other donors. A sense of group membership or group participation (beyond merely the immediate nuclear family) appears to be a widespread and longstanding human need.[14]

The club membership view of philanthropy is consistent with much behavior of philanthropic organizations. At least one such organization, the Sierra Club, is quite explicit in its name. Many others have "membership cards" or provide patrons with specially marked pens, address labels, stickers, and other items to attest to one's participation. The so-called "charity ball" is a well-established institution through which club membership is publicly acknowledged and demonstrated. Many philanthropies prominently announce their club memberships (and the intensity of this membership) in public meetings, mailings, booklets, or "playbills."[15]

In this approach to philanthropic behavior, club membership (a real or imagined sense of participation in a group) directly enters the utility function. The production of this commodity by the household involves combining market goods (donations in cash or in kind) and the donor's own time. Then the *full* price of a unit of this commodity is the sum of the money price and the value of the time inputs.

In this framework it is easily shown that the higher the money price of philanthropy (i.e., the lower the tax rate) the higher is the price of club membership, and hence the smaller will be the amount of club membership and philanthropy. It can also be shown that the greater is the level of income or wealth, the greater will be the demand for club membership and philanthropy in terms of donating money and time. A lower price and a higher income imply a larger aggregate amount of philanthropy to be distributed between greater donations for continuing clubs and the addition of new clubs to a person's philanthropies.

Additional implications not obtained from the previous models can also be developed. The price of club membership is higher the greater the value of time, as measured perhaps by the wage rate, holding the market price component constant. Individuals with a higher value of time will tend to join clubs that require little input of their own time, and within clubs to be relatively less generous with their own time and more generous with other resources. Thus, those in high income households, who themselves have a low value of time in the labor market, are more likely than others to be volunteers. The premier example would be the nonworking wives of high income individuals.[16]

Because of scale economies in philanthropies, it would be expected that the absolute number of philanthropies would increase as the population of a community grows, but that the number of philanthropies per 100,000 population would decline. In larger communities the average household would be a member of a smaller proportion of all of the philanthropies in the community (i.e., lower probability of joining any one "club"), and donate less per philanthropy, but would be a member of a larger absolute number of philanthropies.

Communities of the same size may differ in the demographic characteristics of their populations. Consider one community that is homogeneous, and another that is heterogeneous with respect to, say, religion, ethnicity, income, or other relevant characteristics. The community with greater heterogeneity will have a larger number of clubs for two reasons. One is the establishment of particularistic clubs. In an extreme case, if a heterogeneous community with a population size of one million is composed of say ten noninteracting groups, it can be viewed as if it were ten communities each with a population of one hundred thousand. The aggregate of the number of clubs in the ten communities of 100,000 exceeds the number of clubs in a community of one million.

A second effect of heterogeneity is that some "public goods" provided by the local government in the homogeneous community may be relegated to the private philanthropic market in communities in which particularism is more rampant. That is, the greater ease of public provision of certain public goods in a homogeneous community reduces the extent of the private philanthropic provision of these activities (Roberts 1984). Thus, the greater the heterogeneity of the population, the greater will be the number of clubs, and the smaller the donations per club, even if aggregate donations are larger.

Some philanthropic membership may be viewed as a substitute for extended family ties. Individuals with greater extended family networks may join more within-family clubs and fewer extrafamily clubs.

If so, the decline of the extended family should be associated with an increase in philanthropic activities—both the number of clubs joined and the person's aggregate expenditures of time and money.

This approach to philanthropic contributions is consistent with the findings in the study by Silberstein et al. (1987) on the extent of contributions by Jews to the local Jewish federation campaign. In a study of one hundred Jewish communities across the country, the proportion of the Jewish community that makes a contribution to the federation campaigns (one club) is significantly lower the larger the size of the Jewish community in the metropolitan area and the larger the percentage of the population that is Jewish. The observed significant negative effect on the proportion who are donors of a larger percentage increase in the Jewish population may be reflecting a "newcomer" effect. Newer entrants to an area are less likely to be known or identified by the local federation campaign, and having been directly approached for a donation is an important determinant as to whether a donation is given and its magnitude.[17]

Summary

This chapter has discussed several models economists have developed to understand the seemingly "uneconomic" behavior called philanthropy. The altruism and club approaches are the most compelling for understanding why individuals would voluntarily reduce their own consumption to increase that of others. The altruism approach requires identification with the recipient and can be effective for understanding behavior within small close groups such as the family. The club model implies identification with other donors and is more compelling for understanding what is generally referred to as philanthropy.

The economists' approach provides a range of hypotheses about philanthropic behavior, only some of which have been explicitly tested. Donations are larger when they are less costly (higher marginal tax rate) and when the donor's income is greater. The club model offers additional implications that have not yet been subject to rigorous testing. Philanthropic behavior would be expected to vary systematically with the size and heterogeneity of the community, nonphilanthropic substitutes for group membership, and the relative value of time. Further theoretical and empirical analyses are needed if we are to develop a fuller understanding of philanthropic behavior.

Notes

1. Volunteer labor services can be provided to philanthropies at no money wage or when the wage is below the person's labor market alternatives for a comparable nonphilanthropic job.

2. For analyses of corporate philanthropic contributions, see Nelson (1970).

3. The importance of religion in philanthropic contributions suggests the need for more research on the determinants of religious affiliation and participation. Some path-breaking research on this topic has been done by Iannaccone (1986 and 1988).

4. Some authors try to provide a conceptual framework. Ireland (1969), for example, refers to a "Kantian Motive," a desire to perform good acts. Long (1976), on the other hand, emphasizes social pressure as the cause of philanthropic contributions.

5. Table 1-2 suggests that the simple "income elasticity" for philanthropy appears to be greater than unity. By income elasticity is meant the responsiveness of changes in amount given to amount of income. This arises because the price of a philanthropic contribution is lower the higher the level of income (i.e., the tax bracket).

6. The percent distribution of philanthropic contributions by household income in 1984 was:

Household Income	Less Than 0.5 Percent	1 to 2 Percent	3 or More Percent	Total
Under $20,000	40	41	19	100
$20,000–39,999	27	46	27	100
$40,000 and over	17	45	38	100

Source: *Statistical Abstract* (1987), table 601, p. 359.

7. One would expect the "waste" of material goods (e.g., buying more prepared foods, replacing rather than repairing durables) to rise with the value of time and the level of income.

8. Becker (1976) shows how evolutionary forces (natural selection) could have favored the genetic fitness of altruism. He does note, however, that the survival value of altruism depends on "physical and social interaction: kin have had much more interaction with each other because they have usually lived with or near each other. Since the economic model requires interaction, not common genes, it can also explain the survival of some altruism toward unrelated neighbors or co-workers" (Becker 1967, p. 826).

9. The last implication arises because under altruism transfers are generally made from higher income to lower income individuals.

10. Douty (1972) has an interesting discussion of cooperative behavior among those sharing disasters (e.g., flood victims). He suggests that this is

based on a sense of collective (joint) experience. This may be an example of what Coleman (1987) calls "social capital." The cooperative activity of the victims of the October 1989 San Francisco Bay area earthquake seems to be another example.

11. Becker (1974, 1976) emphasizes this point as a limiting feature of private transfers.

12. There is evidence that private donations for the poor (charity) have decreased in relative amounts and real dollars in response to the rise in public income transfer programs. For a study of this effect with regard to the nursing home market, see Chiswick (1976), and with regard to welfare and social insurance programs in general, see Roberts (1984).

13. This approach to consumer behavior was developed in Becker (1965).

14. Perhaps in the evolution of the species this trait had special survival value, and it is imprinted in the genes of the modern-day descendants of prehistoric man.

15. Many philanthropies distribute widely an annual list of donors specifying each donor's contribution, usually in broad intervals (e.g., "patron," "donor," etc.) but sometimes to the dollar.

16. The incidence of volunteer activities appears to rise with education and household income. The percent of adults doing volunteer work (1985) by:

Education		Household Income	
Years	Percent	Amount	Percent
0 to 8	28	Under $10,000	40
9 to 11	38	$10,000–$19,999	42
12	46	$20,000–$39,999	52
13 to 15	61	$40,000 or more	60
16 or more	65		

Nearly one-half (48 percent) of those fourteen and over reported at least some volunteer work in the previous year in religious organizations. For some other volunteer activities the proportions were: education (27 percent), recreation (21 percent), and health (19 percent).

The data on volunteerism are from *Statistical Abstract* (1987), table 599, p. 359.

17. Using 1964 data on donations to health-oriented philanthropies, Long (1976) shows that donations are greater when the solicitation is face-to-face rather than by mail, and when the solicitor is known rather than a stranger.

Bibliography

Becker, Gary S. "A Theory of the Allocation of Time," *Economic Journal* 75 (299) (1965): 493–517.

———. "A Theory of Social Interactions," *Journal of Political Economy,* 82 (6), (1974): 1063–93.

———. "Altruism, Egoism and Genetic Fitness: Economics and Sociobiology," *Journal of Economic Literature* (1976): (September), 817–26.

Boskin, Michael J., and Martin Feldstein. "Effects of the Charitable Deduction on Contributions by Low-Income and Middle-Income Households: Evidence from the National Survey of Philanthropy," *Review of Economics and Statistics* (1977): (August), 351–54.

Chiswick, Barry R. "The Demand for Nursing Home Care: An Analysis of the Substitution Between Institutional and Non-Institutional Care," *Journal of Human Resources* (1976): (Summer), 295–316.

Coleman, James. "Social Capital in the Creation of Human Capital," mimeo, Department of Sociology, University of Chicago, 1987.

Douty, Christopher M. "Disasters and Charity: Some Aspects of Cooperative Economic Behavior," *American Economic Review* (1972): (September), 580–90.

Feldstein, Martin, and Amy Taylor. "The Income Tax and Charitable Contributions," *Econometrica* (1976): (November), 1201–22.

Iannaccone, Lawrence R. (1986). "An Economic Model of Religious Participation," mimeo, Department of Economics, Santa Clara University, November 1986.

———. "A Formal Model of Church and Sect," *American Journal of Sociology* (1988): vol. 94, supplement, 241–68.

Ireland, Thomas R. "The Calculus of Philanthropy," *Public Choice* (1969): (Fall), 23–33.

Long, Stephen H. "Social Pressure and Contributions to Health Charities," *Public Choice* (1976): (Winter), 56–66.

Nelson, Ralph L. *Economic Factors in the Growth of Corporate Giving,* New York: National Bureau of Economic Research, 1970.

Roberts, Russell D. "A Positive Model of Private Charity and Public Transfers," *Journal of Political Economy* (1984): (February), 136–48.

Schwartz, Robert A. "Personal Philanthropic Contributions," *Journal of Political Economy* (1970): (November), 1264–91.

Silberstein, Richard, Paul Ritterband, Jonathan Rabinowitz, and Barry Kosmin. *Giving to Jewish Philanthropic Causes: A Preliminary Reconnaissance,* North American Jewish Data Bank (1987): (Reprint Series no. 2), Graduate Center, CUNY.

U.S. Bureau of the Census. *Statistical Abstract of the United States 1988, 108th Edition,* Washington, D.C., 1987.

2

The Dimensions of Contemporary American Jewish Philanthropy

Barry A. Kosmin

Dr. Samuel Johnson once stated that "In the absence of counting everything floats in the mind without clarity." While this may not be true for the innumerate, undoubtedly we need to know the dimensions of our subject within the context of philanthropic giving, that is, the measurement of its extent, capacity, and importance. Furthermore, we must narrow the scope of the subject matter since contemporary American Jewish philanthropy is a vast topic. It involves—among other things—the costs of raising money, styles and targets of solicitation, the time period of campaigns, and the size and numbers of dinners, awards, and plaques.

My interest is in following the flow of dollars that enables the whole variously named independent, voluntary, nonprofit, or third sector of the American economy to function. I shall not discuss, however, taxation policy or the effects of business cycles in this chapter.

Philanthropy encompasses more than what is commonly known as charity, or economic transfers to the poor and suffering. It also includes support of institutions providing services of merit. True gifts imply an asymmetric relationship without reciprocity; the term generosity, then, better describes mixed, rather than purely altruistic, motives of donors.

Our complex social and economic environment leaves little, even in the voluntary sector, that remains pure for long. Philanthropy itself operates with a mix of revenues from sales or fees as well as donations of cash and time. Many services that are targets of private generosity also obtain funds from taxation via public sector support. Not only are the sources of support diverse, but the recipients of services are not necessarily Jewish. The best example of this dynamic at play is the "once charitable and Jewish" hospital in many large cities. Some Jewish community centers in small communities also have a substantial non-Jewish clientele. On the other hand, some money from non-Jewish private gifts finds its way to Jewish causes through United Way support for Jewish agencies or through Christian generosity toward Israel-based philanthropies such as the Jewish National Fund's forests. For example, the overall proportion of funds for sixteen major Jewish federations (excluding New York) in 1986, which were received from United Way campaigns, was 4.3 percent, and the total amount was $26.7 million (CJF 1987). Further complications arise when one tries to analyze which types of communal services have a producer and which a consumer subsidy.

Although these issues are beyond the scope of this chapter, it is a widely held belief that sources of revenue relate strongly to an organization's output. Hence, if philanthropic organizations want to communicate effectively with givers, then some of these wider issues have to be addressed and explained.

My own reading of the literature on the independent sector leads me to conclude that contemporary philanthropic giving is simply that which the U.S. Internal Revenue Service (IRS) accepts as a tax-deductible donation. Philanthropy to Jewish causes largely fits under the rubric of religious giving in national statistics even though little of it can be defined as "sacramental." In fact, many Jews regard their political contributions to Political Action Committees (PACs), parties, and causes as part and parcel of their philanthropic support of worthy causes such as Israel or human rights. It is thus part of the Jewish community's political agenda and social concerns. Frequently, this activity often results in supplemental governmental support to these causes. Thus, political activism and private giving often complement each other.

Not all giving by Jews is "ethnic" or so-called religious giving, however. American Jews are part of a larger society in which more than ninety-seven out of every one hundred of their fellow citizens are not Jewish. Moreover, Jews are now more accepted and accessible in

American society than they ever were. Nevertheless, the relationship between the Jewish minority and the wider American society is asymmetrical so that the larger society has a bigger impact on the Jews than they have on America. Let us turn to Tonai's (1988) California survey of givers to demonstrate the point.

Tonai studied a group of second and third generation Americans with a high median household income of $53,000 a year. Eighty-two percent were college graduates, and 55 percent were professionals. Yet for Americans they were surpisingly secularized: 37 percent claimed to be nonreligious. Despite their wealth and high social status, 65 percent claimed to be members of the Democratic Party. On average they donated 2.7 percent of their income to philanthropy of which 57 percent was what might be termed "ethnic giving." They also gave to political campaigns out of proportion to their voting numbers. They liked to be solicited by people they knew. Family tradition and support for family was positively related to their giving patterns. It confirms what we know about American Jewry. However, this was a survey among Chinese- and Japanese-Americans in San Francisco.

If we had a working hypothesis that suggested that ethnic succession occurs in philanthropy so that Jews copy white Protestants and Asians mimic Jews, then Tonai's study demonstrates its reliability. Her data also suggest that there may be an essentially national pattern that overlays the whole, which would allow us to both map and predict trends.

Unfortunately, there has yet to be an attempt to measure the dimensions of the Jewish nonprofit sector along these lines, although Hodgkinson and Weitzman (1986) have examined the entire independent sector in this regard. They showed that for the nonprofit sector as a whole, 27 percent of funds come from contributions and 6 percent from endowments as against 38 percent from dues, fees, and charges and 27 percent from the state. The *American Jewish Year Book,* until fiscal year 1975, recorded the Jewish community's gross national product (Goldberg 1978). Then the Jewish communal GNP was calculated at $2.8 billion, but the Jewish hospitals comprised half that amount. The Filer Commission on Private Philanthropy and Public Needs used Goldberg's figures for 1972 (Filer Commission 1977). Then the total Jewish religious and communal GNP was assessed at $2.21 billion. Individual gifts accounted for $736 million. The pattern of giving varied across causes; for instance, the top 10 percent of gifts accounted for 86 percent of total dollars in federation campaigns but only 25 percent of dollars in synagogues.

However, the real importance of this figure of $736 million is that it
totaled 3.3 percent of all giving to any U.S. cause, which amounted to
$24.48 billion or 2.1 percent of the GNP in 1972 (AAFRC 1987, 13). If
we assume that in the early 1970s two-thirds of Jewish philanthropic
dollars went to Jewish causes and one-third to general or secular
causes, then Jewish giving amounted to around $1.1 billion. Therefore,
5 percent of all U.S. philanthropy originated from Jews. Since Jews
composed only 2.5 percent of the population, this means that Jewish
generosity was twice the national norm.

Let us turn now to the current picture. AAFRC (1987, 13) reports
that the percentage of GNP given over to philanthropy, which fell in
the late 1970s, is now again at around 2 percent. This means that total
giving in 1985 was $79.72 billion, and in 1986 it was $87.22 billion. The
dollars of private individuals accounted for over 82 percent of this
total. Bequests accounted for nearly 7 percent, foundations for 6
percent, and corporations for 5 percent of all giving. If we assume that
Jewish support of Jewish causes was maintained at the same rate as in
1972, then we would expect that, minus the corporate gifts, Jews gave
3.3 percent of $75 billion in 1985, or $2.5 billion so we are looking to
account for $2.5 billion of ''ethnic giving.''

I have tried to locate these dollars. Federation/UJA campaign gifts
and new endowment monies totaled $1.128 billion in 1985. Undoubt-
edly the market has changed adversely for the umbrella campaign since
1972. For a start there has been a net reduction in the number of gifts
since 1974. Its market share has been eroded by institutional and
capital campaigns and designated giving to schools, hospitals, old-age
homes, Israel-based educational institutions, and Jewish political activism.

Yet the federation campaign is still the dominant force in Jewish
fund raising. In 1985, the main Israel-based institutions, the ''friends''
groups, Hadassah, Jewish National Fund (JNF), etc., raised under
$200 million. The Israeli yeshivot, Lubavitch, American-Jewish univer-
sities, seminaries, and synagogues probably raised between them several hundred million dollars.

No assessment or analysis of giving to communal capital campaigns
exists, but the edifice syndrome still thrives among American Jewry.
The Jewish Welfare Board claims that community centers are in the
midst of the biggest building boom since the 1950s (Mowlem 1987).
Twenty-six center buildings were completed in the years 1983–87, and
fourteen more are presently under construction at an average price of
around $5 million. Overall, this only accounts for $30 million a year of

new money. Of course, day schools, synagogues, homes for the aged, and camps are also being built so the total figure for capital projects must be several times the centers' noble endeavors.

The community relations and defense organizations—the Anti-Defamation League, American Jewish Committee, American Jewish Congress, and the Simon Wiesenthal Center—have done well in recent years, and in 1985 they raised a little over $40 million between them. Since 1972 other new organizations have emerged such as the Center for Learning and Leadership (CLAL), which raises about $2 million a year. However, if one adds up the figures and estimates, it is very difficult to get even close to $2 billion of philanthropic giving to Jewish causes, never mind the $2.5 billion for which we are searching. Therefore, my conclusion, is that relative to the growth of U.S. philanthropy giving to Jewish causes has fallen since the early 1970s. This relative decline has occurred despite the obvious success of project-oriented giving and the flourishing endowment funds of many community federations.

It could well be that since Jews are now an overwhelmingly native-born population, we should increasingly expect them to behave like other Americans and reduce their level of generosity. Moreover, the Jewish population total has remained stable since 1972 and so has fallen to 2.4 percent of a growing American population. If these factors hold true, then total Jewish giving at 2.4 percent of the gross in 1985 should have been $1.8 billion. This figure is, of course, close to our actual estimate of giving to Jewish causes.

The problem is that Jews are not like other Americans on most economic indicators. They *are* much better educated, and as a result have on average higher status occupations. Jews are acknowledged to be "the most successful group in American society" (Greeley 1976, 39; see also Silberman 1985; Sowell 1981).

Table 2-1 shows that the latest evidence suggests that Jewish incomes are 50 percent above the national median. Now in some ways this is an exaggeration since the Jewish population is geographically biased toward the large metropolitan areas of the two coasts, that is, to states and areas with above average costs of living.

One could also argue that the cost of living Jewishly, not only for religiously observant Jews but also for others who wish "to belong" in terms of membership fees and other costs, results in a comfortable middle-class Jewish status starting much higher up the income ladder than other Americans. Winter and Levin (1985) calculated that an affiliated young family with an income of $50,000 in 1983 would be

Table 2-1. *Income Statistics of U.S. Jewish Households (Cumulative %
Frequencies)*

Income Per Annum	Data Bank 9-City File, 1984	NFO, 1986	Market Facts, 1985–86
Under $7.5K	7.7	–	–
Under $12.5K	17.6	–	–
Under $20K	24.1	23.6	17.2
Under $30K	44.3	40.8	37.0
Under $40K	64.9	58.3	51.0
Under $50K	71.8	71.2	63.4
Under $60K	80.0	–	–
Under $80K	89.9	–	–
Under $125K	95.1	–	–
Over $125K	100.0	100.0	100.0
Proportion Over $75K	12.0%	12.1%	14.5%
Median Income (1986 equivalent: $36,000)	$33,200	$35,000	$38,000
U.S. Total Population	$22,400*	$24,000	$26,700
U.S. White Population	$23,600*	–	–
% of Jews refusing to answer income question	33.1%	–	18.4%
Sample Size	14,193	5,814	675

*Official U.S. government figures for 1984.
Source: Kosmin 1988, 18.

unable to make a significant philanthropic contribution after paying for the costs of religious and communal services, tuition, and fees in addition to maintaining a normal suburban standard of living.

Thus, this evidence combined with that in table 2-1 suggests that substantial givers should be found mainly among those with household incomes in excess of $75,000 in 1986. This segment would account for about 13 percent of the 2.3 million U.S. Jewish households, or around 300,000 units. The Yankelovich, Skelly, and White (1986) study showed that major contributors who gave over 2.5 percent of their incomes had annual incomes above $50,000. The Bureau of the Census shows that in 1986, 16.8 percent of all households and 17.9 percent of white households had annual incomes exceeding $50,000 (*Statistical Abstract* 1987, 422). Table 2-1 suggests that the proportion among Jews was approximately twice this at around 28–36 percent.

Nevertheless my reading of the situation is that the potential pool of major Jewish donors does not exceed 300,000 households. This is because of some unique characteristics of American Jewish society in the 1980s.

The Jewish income distribution is not as sharply pyramidal as the national profile. One ironical result of this is that many apparently affluent Jewish households have a psychological sense of relative deprivation as they measure themselves against even more successful relatives and neighbors. They are faced by the escalation of real housing costs and college tuition for their children. Some of their costs are self-imposed by their life-style: they subscribe to the ethos of you are what you drive, or to the high entertaining costs of Jewish *simchas,* which are a unique expense in themselves.

Nevertheless, in a society where yesterday's luxuries are today's necessities, the amount of discretionary income available often cannot keep pace with even the increasing cash flow of two-earner Jewish households. Whatever the claims of economists or even moralists, many of these people feel financially strapped. This situation is crucial to any understanding of Jewish fund raising potential. A significant finding of the Yankelovich et al. study (1986) was that giving was highly correlated with feeling that one had enough money for one's needs, and had no worries about having enough money in the future.

This scenario does not appear to bode well for Jewish fund raisers, but does this make sense in practice? Let us analyze the largest Jewish communal fund raising effort—the federation annual campaigns.[1] In 1987, the federations raised $710 million; $420 million was raised from 13,000 gifts. Another 853,000 gifts accounted for the remaining $290 million. If we translate gifts into households, which probably slightly exaggerates the level of overall participation, then we can calculate that 1,400,000 Jewish households gave zero dollars to the annual campaign. Among those that actually gave, 452,000 donated less than $100. So 1,850,000 Jewish households from a total of 2,300,000 with a median income of $36,000 a year, gave less than $100 to the community's main fundraising arm.

If we take our 300,000 high-income households as a pool, then we can assume that probably one-third gave a quality gift to the annual campaign since altogether across North America there were 100,000 gifts of over $1,000. This scene seems to play itself out at the microlevel as well. Bubnic's (1988) survey of medical practitioners, 30 percent of whom were Jewish, showed that the Jewish doctors gave at the national norm. They gave more than Catholics but less than Protestants. The

Jewish shortfall was mainly due to the fact that they gave less than Protestant doctors to "religious causes" that accounted for only 32 percent of their philanthropic dollars.

Am I correct then in assuming that Jewish giving is in relative decline? Is that why meetings of Jewish fund raising organizations increasingly seem like meetings of the petroleum industry? It's not that "the well has run dry," but that all the easy oil has already been found. Moreover, as the market softens the competition has grown especially over the last twenty years. It is a national problem across the United States. There are now "124,000 non-profit groups vying for donors, and two-thirds of these did not exist in 1960" (Edmondson 1986).

Now it may be that our 300,000 high-income households are in fact differently distributed to wealthy Americans in general. Certainly if the Forbes list of the "reported" 400 wealthiest American individuals is used, then the pattern is highly skewed. Bubis[2] has identified 40 percent as Jews among the top forty names and 23 percent among the list as a whole. *The Foundation Directory* (1987) details 5,148 private foundations with either assets of over $1 million or annual giving of over $100,000. These 5,148 cover 97 percent of all foundation assets and 92 percent of foundation giving in the United States. If *The Foundation Directory* is analyzed, it reveals that there are 355 entries for foundations that specify Jewish giving, comprising around 7 percent of all foundations. These 355 entries for Jewish giving can be contrasted with 437 entries for Protestant giving and only 155 entries for Catholic giving. In proportion to the total population, Jews are twenty-three times as likely to establish a foundation dedicated to, among other causes, Jewish giving as Catholics are to their religious group, and Jews establish foundations at about twelve times the rate for Protestant religious givers.

In ethnic terms Jewish entries can be contrasted with nine entries for native Americans. Entries for Jewish welfare are as common as medical research as a target of American foundations. Furthermore, there are seventy-five entries for Israel compared with thirteen for all of Africa, four for Italy, three for Poland, six for France and two for Scotland, as well as fifty-seven for foreign Christian missionary programs. Even more intriguing is the finding that the geographical distribution of foundations by state correlates very highly with the unique distribution of American Jewry, with high concentrations in the Middle Atlantic States, the East North Central region, California, and New England.

Yet when one examines the list of the one hundred largest founda-tions in terms of assets, led by the massive Ford, Getty, MacArthur, Kellogg, Lilly, Rockefeller, Carnegie, Pew, and Mellon Foundations, then only one Jewish targeted foundation can be found, and there is none in the list of the one hundred largest foundations in terms of total giving.

The reason for these rather conflicting findings may, of course, be that Jews have not had their wealth long enough to build up massive assets or that they do not distribute their individual wealth in the same way as the other American elites. They are also probably less willing to give up control of their philanthropy to bureaucrats. Here we are still dealing with the issue of capability or potential for giving, but at this level we should probably be more interested in intent.

The creation of foundations is itself demonstrative of serious phil-anthropic intent. It is the most cost-effective way of giving for an individual so the number of serious Jewish givers does seem to be above the average. My impression is that there is a core minority of moderately wealthy Jewish families who are highly imbued with the spirit of *tzedakah*. The Jewish fund raisers work very cost-effectively with these individuals. The fund raisers have taken to heart Irving Warner's dictum: "You raise money when you ask for it, preferably face to face, from the smallest possible number of people, in the shortest period of time, at the least expense" (Warner 1975, 19).

The real problem for the Jewish community organizations today is the division of the philanthropic dollar between Jewish and general causes. Among the Jewish masses a large majority, over 60 percent of households, ignored the United Jewish Appeal (UJA) campaign, yet in surveys close to 90 percent of Jews claim to give. Therefore, we must assume that most of their dollars go outside the Jewish community to the United Way, Red Cross, cancer fund, etc. This is especially likely for the middle class and "yuppies" because the historic standards of quality giving inside and outside the community are so different.

Yankelovich et al. (1986) defines $500 as a large donor nationally, whereas in federation circles it is $10,000. Obviously there is more recognition for less money outside the Jewish community than within it. Many Jewish fund raising institutions would not regard this as important unless this trend is also occurring at the top among the wealthy Jewish donors. A 1981 study of UJA giving patterns (Yanke-lovich et al. 1981) showed that 93 percent of very large donors of over $50,000 gave to general causes as well as Jewish ones. In fact, their giving patterns were quite dispersed. One of the trends recorded by

Silberman (1985) is that Jews and their money are now readily acceptable in the higher echelons of American society. Everyone knows that
ivy league colleges that discriminated against Jewish applicants only
thirty years ago are now willing to raise funds from and name their
buildings after the same people.

Other findings on general American philanthropy also suggest that
"ethnic giving" has declined among Jews. Seventy percent of giving
by individual Americans is to religious institutions and causes, but this
giving is highly related to attendance at religious services. Jews are
more secularized than other Americans. Thirty percent do not even
identify with a Jewish denomination, and only 40 percent are synagogue members (Kosmin 1988, 15). The even-lower-than-average rates
of affiliation and religious worship in Los Angeles and the new developing centers of the west such as Phoenix and Denver are highly
correlated with nongiving. Weekly attendance at services by Jews is
well below that for the Christian denominations.

We also know that nonreligious charities do better as incomes and
education levels rise. Therefore, we would expect secular or general
giving to be above average among Jews. Certainly Bubnic (1988)
showed this trend with medical doctors in the San Francisco Bay area.
Even the large Jewish foundations exhibit this tendency, most of them
divide their dollars equally between Jewish and general targets. A
typical case is the Koret Foundation of San Francisco: "By Board
policy the Foundation plans to allocate some 50 percent of its distri-
butable resources to the general community; some 40 percent for Bay
Area Jewish purposes; and some 10 percent for efforts in Israel"
(Mogulof 1987, 286). Interestingly, the major Jewish foundations in
Britain, Heron and Wolfson, have a similar policy.

Jews—as evidenced by their high rates of intermarriage—are increasingly drawn into the mainstream of American society, but this
draw is at a certain level. Jews significantly support "high culture" in
America. Their support of hospitals, museums, symphonies, and universities across the country now appears disproportionate not only to
their numbers but also to their proportion of the wealthy. For example,
if one looks at the names of the founders on any plaque and then the
list of the current trustees or donors, one sees the striking change that
has come about.

Part of the reason for the fall-off in the attraction of Jewish causes is
their lack of interest in analysis and market research. Sklare (1962)
remarked upon this oversight and weakness among the leading Jewish
fund raising institutions early on. Their awareness of the need for

research and development has not increased much since then. Further-more, despite the legions of accountants and MBAs in the Jewish community, no financial analysis is done of communal resources at the regional or national level. Basic questions of measurement go unasked and what published material exists is largely ignored due to the short-term horizons and the annual cycles that concern most Jewish fund raisers. There is little realization that American Jews now constitute a diverse set of subgroups, and the community is in reality many com-munities with different political, social, economic, and religious agen-das. In other words, the Jewish market is segmented, and secular causes are often better placed for marketing in this new situation.

The arcane world of Jewish fund raising is impenetrable to most American Jews—a large proportion of whom according to federation-sponsored survey—have no idea what a federation does. These surveys also show that the "don't knows" predominate on service questions about Jewish agencies and services in a market place where we know that personal involvement as a volunteer or personal knowledge and family experience as a client is highly correlated with giving.

If two-thirds of the Jewish philanthropic dollar went to Jewish causes in 1972, all the evidence suggests that this has been reduced to around half in the late 1980s. Could such a shift in the pattern of Jewish philanthropy have developed in a mere fifteen years? My final piece of evidence suggests that the rapid rate of demographic and compositional change in American Jewry made it very likely. The North American Jewish Data Bank has aggregated the findings from recent community surveys to produce a composite profile of the Jew most likely to give to the federation campaign and the Jew most likely to give to a secular charity. The results indicate that the ideal type for a federation cam-paign is a person with a high income, aged fifty-five to sixty-four, who is a second-generation American. He or she is a Conservative syna-gogue member with a high degree of ritual observance, attending synagogue once a month, and all of his/her friends are Jewish. On the other hand, the best Jewish prospect for a secular philanthropy is a high-income individual aged forty-five to fifty-four, who is a third-generation American. He is not a synagogue member but identifies with Reform Judaism. He never attends a synagogue but attends a Seder and has some Jewish friends.

The Jewishly oriented philanthropist is older both in age and gener-ation. His or her social and religious characteristics may be reproduc-ible, but the generational experience and outlook is not. The older Jew born in the 1920s remembers the Depression, the inner-city Jewish neighborhood, Yiddish being spoken, and World War II. The Jew who is ten years younger is largely a product of the more unthreatening and assimilating environment of a prosperous post-war America, its suburbs, and its more tenuous ethnic ties. If Jewish traditions such as *tzedakah* are retained, then they are more likely to be applied on a larger and more universalist stage.

What then is the impact of the growth in the number and amounts of endowments to Jewish causes? Essentially this is not new money to the extent that it comes from a restricted pool from within our "upper 300,000" households. Most of the endowments are given by known and long-time givers, "ideal federation" types. However, endowments probably serve to attenuate the loss of dollars to Jewish philanthropy because they "stop the clock" in a particular generation. My own informal research suggests that many endowments are expressly given in order to ensure that non-Jewish descendants cannot interfere with the giving patterns of the donor, that is, the family's money and giving will remain Jewish even when the next or a future generation of the family is no longer Jewish. This type of giving therefore appears defensive not only in terms of taxation but also socially. However, such a strategy can only slow down trends, not reverse them.

The Jewish philanthropic dollar seems to be increasingly secularized. It is distributed in a pattern unlike that of the average individual American, but in fact in a similar manner to that of philanthropic giving in total. The total dollars in 1986 were distributed among the philanthropic sectors this way: 50 percent to religion, 15 percent to education, 14 percent to health, 11 percent to human services, 7 percent to arts, culture, and humanities, and 3 percent to public/society benefit (AAFRC 1987). My final estimate is that around 4 percent of all U.S. giving is by Jews, that is a grand total of $3.1 billion in 1985 and $3.5 billion in 1986. To place these figures in context, the generosity of American Jews thus exceeds the GNP of entire Third World countries such as Nepal and Madagascar and the military budgets of Cuba or Turkey.

Clearly, we need to research this topic in more detail and with a higher level of precision, to tease out such intriguing dimensions as the real split between local, national, Israel, and other overseas philanthropy both for and by Jews. As a result of this comprehensive examination hopefully some of the unhappy findings for Jewish philanthropy presented here may even be proved wrong.

Notes

1. The sources of the campaign data are the Council of Jewish Federations (CJF) series of annual *Campaign Reports*.
2. Private communication from Professor G. Bubis, director, School of Jewish Communal Service, Hebrew Union College–Jewish Institute of Religion, Los Angeles.

Bibliography

[AAFRC]. *Giving USA*. New York: AAFRC Trust for Philanthropy, 1987.

Bubnic, A. *The Charitable Behavior of San Francisco Bay Area Physicians.* (Working Paper no. 5). San Francisco, CA: University of San Francisco, Institute for Non-Profit Organization Management, 1988.

Council of Jewish Federations. *Special Tabulations for 17 U.S. Large City Federations Comparing 1977 and 1986 Statistical Returns to CJF.* New York: Research Department, Council of Jewish Federations, Sept. 1987.

Edmondson, B. "Who gives to charity?" *American Demographics 127* (November 1986).

[Filer Commission Report.] *The Commission on Private Philanthropy and Public Needs* (vol. I) 1977: 426–49. Washington, D.C.: Department of the Treasury.

The Foundation Directory (11th ed.). New York: The Foundation Center, 1987.

Goldberg, S. P. "Jewish Communal Services: Programs and Finances." In *American Jewish Year Book,* (vol. 78). New York: American Jewish Committee and the Jewish Publication Society, 1978.

Greeley, A. M. *Ethnicity, Denomination and Inequality.* Beverly Hills, CA: Sage, 1976.

Hodgkinson, V., and M. S. Weitzman. *Dimensions of the Independent Sector.* Washington, D.C.: Independent Sector, 1986.

Kosmin, B. A. *Understanding Contemporary American Jewry: Implications for Planning.* (Occasional Papers no. 4). New York: CUNY Graduate Center, North American Jewish Data Bank, 1988.

Mogulof, M. "Foundations: Their Actual and Potential Influence on Jewish Communal Life." *Journal of Jewish Communal Service* (Summer 1987).

Mowlem, M. J. (ed.). *Program Services and Budget 1988.* New York: Jewish Welfare Board, 1987.

Silberman, C. E. *A Certain People: American Jews and Their Lives Today.* New York: Summit Books, 1985.

Sklare, M. "The Future of Jewish Giving." *Commentary*, 6 (November 1962).

Sowell, T. *Ethnic America*. New York: Basic Books, 1981.

[Statistical Abstract.] *Statistical Abstract of the United States 1988*. Washington, D.C.: U.S. Department of Commerce, Bureau of Census, 1987.

Tonai, Rosalyn M. *Asian American Charitable Giving*. (Working Paper no. 4). San Francisco, CA: University of San Francisco, Institute for Non-Profit Organization Management, 1988.

Warner, I. R. *The Art of Fundraising*. New York: Harper & Row, 1975.

Winter, J. A., and L. I. Levin. *The Cost of Affiliation and Participation: Implications for Federations, Agencies and Communal Organizations*. (Social Policy Report). New York: Council of Jewish Federations, January 1985.

Yankelovich, Skelly, and White Inc. *A Study of Giving Patterns to the United Jewish Appeal*. New York: United Jewish Appeal, 1981.

———. *The Charitable Behavior of Americans*. Washington, D.C.: Independent Sector, 1986.

Part 2

General Philanthropy

3

The Relationship Between Jewish Identity and Philanthropy

Mordechai Rimor and Gary A. Tobin

Abstract

The present study investigated the relationship between Jewish identity and philanthropic behavior. The data for this case study was extracted from the MetroWest, New Jersey survey. Our work focused on three main issues. First, we analyzed the pattern of philanthropic behavior, which revealed that philanthropy is characterized by whether or not a person contributes to a campaign as well as the amount contributed. Second, analyzing the pattern of behaviors pertaining to Jewish identity, three factors emerged: behaviors pertaining to religious identity, behaviors pertaining to civil Judaism, and in-between behaviors. Third, a regression analysis on the independent variables that express Jewish identity, with contribution and amount contributed as dependent variables, showed that synagogue attendance and organizational membership associate directly with whether one contributes or not; synagogue and organizational membership and visiting Israel represent the sole predictors for the amount contributed. Religious practices, denominational affiliation, having Jewish friends, and years of Jewish education, by contrast, are not associated directly with philanthropic behavior. Rather, their association is largely explained by the other four main variables of Jewish identity. Major operational implications of the results for fund raising are discussed.

Introduction

The work investigates the degree of relationship between the pattern of variables representing Jewish identity and the pattern of variables representing philanthropic behavior. It is generally assumed that a stronger Jewish identity is highly associated with greater participation in Jewish philanthropy. The purpose of this chapter is to examine that relationship in more detail. Jewish identity is characterized by a number of variable components, including ritual observance, synagogue attendance, friendship patterns, and support for Israel, to name a few. Jewish philanthropy is understood by noting both the act of contribution and how much fund raising support organizations receive. Our aim in this study is to examine which Jewish identity variables are associated with which contributing variables. The overarching relationship between an amorphously defined "Jewish identity" and a non-rigorously defined "Jewish philanthropy" is not very useful in either helping planners understand the phenomenon or in developing fund raising strategies.

While a substantial general literature exists discussing philanthropy in economic, or, more specifically, in mathematical or organizational terms (e.g., Andrew 1950; Olson 1965; Phelps, 1975), as well as in psychological terms (e.g., Milgram 1970); Mussen and Eisenberg-Berg 1977), they are not specific enough for our purposes. Sociologists collecting data describing Jewish philanthropy in Jewish communities (e.g., Cohen 1978, 1980, 1983; Ritterband and Cohen 1979; Sklare 1962; Tobin 1984, 1986, 1987a, 1987b) have focused mainly on one aspect of the issue—giving. There are, of course, many works that have dealt with Jewish identity (e.g., Himmelfarb 1975; Herman 1989), but they dealt solely with another side of the issue, namely, behaviors indicating Jewish identity. Other sociologists who have explored the philanthropic behavior of the general American population (Andrews 1950; Hodgkinson and Weitzman 1986; Yankelovitch, Skelly and White 1986) did not focus on the Jewish community specifically.

Preliminary works presenting philanthropic behavior according to main demographic and Jewish identity variables (e.g., Rappeport and Tobin 1987; Silberstein, Ritterband, Rabinowitz and Kosmin 1987; Tobin 1987b) compared contribution behavior of different Jewish communities with some background variables and with ritual observance. These sources showed that philanthropic behavior tends to be associated with certain demographic variables and with religious identity variables. Data from other Jewish communities, including Baltimore, Rochester, New York City, Worcester, Massachusetts, Washington, D.C., and San Francisco, demonstrate the high association between strong Jewish identity and increased giving to Jewish philanthropies (Tobin 1984, 1986; Tobin and Fishman 1988a; Tobin and Fishman 1988b; Tobin and Sassler 1988). Our work builds on these prior discussions by analyzing patterns of philanthropic behavior, patterns of Jewish identity behaviors, and the pattern of relationship existing between these two sets of variables.

Few areas of discussion other than the aforementioned concern the Jewish community more seriously. The organizational and institutional structure that binds the Jewish community together, as well as the financial and political support of Israel and Jewish communities around the world, rest in the ability of Jewish fund raising organizations to provide revenue. Therefore, the factors that facilitate or hinder fund raising efforts are of extreme importance to the Jewish community. Furthermore, the tradition of *tzedakah* is one of the most basic components in Jewish communal and religious tradition. Philanthropy patterns mirror the relative health of the contemporary Jewish community in the United States in many ways.

As a case study for our investigation, we use the data gathered from the survey polling the Jewish community of MetroWest, New Jersey in 1986 (Rappeport and Tobin 1987; Tobin 1987b), sponsored by the United Jewish Federation of MetroWest. (MetroWest refers to Morris and Essex Counties, New Jersey.) The study randomly sampled 1,665 households (representing more than 45,000 households) via an in-depth survey (181 questions) and covered a wide range of issues relating to Jewish demography, religious identity, and communal behaviors. More than twenty questions raised the issues of Jewish identity and philanthropic behavior.

We selected the MetroWest survey to comprise our data base because this community study was one of the earliest to devote an extensive section of its survey instrument to questions concerning philanthropy. Subsequently, communities such as Worcester, Massachusetts, Rochester, San Francisco, and Dallas have built upon the questions initially formulated in MetroWest (Tobin and Fishman 1988a, 1988b). Among other issues pertaining to philanthropy, the survey also included questions on giving motives.

While we do not contend that Morris and Essex counties fully represent the American Jewish community, this geographic area provides a useful case study for the following reason. Both Jewish identity variables and philanthropy variables from other community studies fall within the middle range of the MetroWest frequency distributions. Similar analyses such as the one contained in this case study would very likely yield similar results in other Jewish communities.

Note that we are looking for the relations between two behavioral areas, philanthropic behavior and Jewish identity, which well may belong to the same hypothetical construct; philanthropic behavior may well belong to the area of Jewish identity. The differentiation we pose may be more logical than real. We do not claim that the model we present is a causal model. At most, it is a correlational model, intended to answer the following question: What comprises the association between Jewish identity and philanthropic behavior?

We look, first, at the philanthropic behavioral data and their pattern. Second, we look at the main indices of Jewish identity and their pattern. Third, we explore the relationship between these two sets of variables.

Philanthropic Behavior

Do people who give to one campaign tend to also give to other campaigns? Is it true that a large gift to one campaign predicts that the donor will give substantially to other campaigns? Or maybe it is the other way around—we contribute to one campaign only, thinking that "it is enough," and "let the others contribute to the other campaigns." Is there a one overall measure for philanthropy, or many submeasures?

In the survey, there were eight questions measuring general contributing behavior to the main campaigns.

1. Do you or any member of your household make outright contribution or gifts to Jewish philanthropies or charities? [CONT J PHIL]
2. Total contribution of your household in this year to all Jewish philanthropies in ranges of dollars. [AMT CONT J PHIL]
3. Did your household make a contribution to MetroWest Federation's United Jewish Appeal this year? [CONT TO FED]
4. Total contribution to the federation, in ranges of dollars. [AMT CONT FED]

5. Did your household make a gift to the Women's Division last year? [CONT WOM DIV]
6. Total contribution to the Women's Division in ranges of dollars. [AMT CONT WOM DIV]
7. Does your household contribute to any non-Jewish philanthropies? [CONT NON J PHIL]
8. Total contribution to non-Jewish philanthropies in ranges of dollars. [AMT CONT NON J PHIL]

We also added a question relating to voluntary behavior to the analysis of these questions; namely, "How many hours per month do you (/your spouse) volunteer on behalf of Jewish organizations?" The question has a face validity for philanthropic behavior. We expected that if a strong relationship between voluntary behavior and contribution exists, it would provide us with an added measure of philanthropy.

As was known and expected, major background variables—such as income, age, and length of residence—correlate significantly with contribution. In order to partial out their effect on contribution and to investigate the pattern of the interrelations of the philanthropy variables without the confounding effects of the background variables, a partial correlation matrix was computed, controlled by income, age and length of residence. The results are presented in table 3-1.

The table shows that most of the correlations are positive, and that a pattern exists among the variables. Far and above the socioeconomic factors, contribution to Jewish philanthropies correlates with other contributing behaviors, and the amount contributed to Jewish philanthropies relates to amounts given to other causes.

These relations may seem obvious and partly tautological: people who give to the federation or the Women's Division will probably report that they give to Jewish philanthropies as well; people who give a certain amount to the federation or to the Women's Division will probably report this amount as given to Jewish philanthropies as well. However, the high correlations between giving to Jewish causes and giving to non-Jewish causes and between giving to the federation and to the Women's Division (0.29 and 0.39, 0.27 and 0.37 for contribution and amount contributed respectively) indicate that there is a real tendency of philanthropic behavior to be generalized across institutions and amounts (see Rimor and Tobin 1989).

The data indicate that the tendency to give, whether to Jewish philanthropies in general, to the federation, or to non-Jewish philanthropies, all correlate. In general, the largest givers are likely to

Table 3-1. *Correlation Matrix of the Variables on Philanthropy*

	(1) CONT J PHIL	(2) AMT CONT J PHIL	(3) CONT FED	(4) AMT CONT FED	(5) CONT WOM DIV	(6) AMT CONT WOM DIV	(7) CONT NON-J PHIL	(8) AMT CONT NON-J PHIL
AMT CONT J PHIL	ns							
CONT TO FED	.49	ns						
AMT CONT FED	ns	.50	ns					
CONT WOM DIV	.19	.21	.27	.31				
AMT CONT WOM DIV	ns	.25	ns	.37	ns			
CONT NON-J PHIL	.29	ns	.26	ns	ns	ns		
AMT CONT NON-J PHIL	ns	.39	ns	.29	ns	.20	ns	
VOL TIME	ns	.18	.16	ns	.16	ns	ns	ns

$p < .001$
ns = not significant
range of n's: 218–1475

Source: Cohen Center for Modern Jewish Studies, 1989.

participate in a broad range of Jewish philanthropic activity, including the federation.

One could hypothesize that in a fixed pool of philanthropic dollars, Jewish philanthropies are competing for contributions with non-Jewish philanthropies (see Ritterband in this volume). One could argue as well that the pool of philanthropic dollars *expands* depending on both motivating factors and agencies involved. The latter illustrates that philanthropists give to a wide variety of causes, both Jewish and non-Jewish, and the amount given is not necessarily dependent on the decision to give to a Jewish versus a non-Jewish cause. If the donation pool, that is the amount given, is somewhat fixed, then non-Jewish philanthropies have serious competition from Jewish philanthropies. If the pool expands, depending on the case made and the motivation that is provided, the amounts given tend to reinforce one another rather than be competitive. In either case, giving to any set of philanthropies correlates highly with giving to other philanthropies.

Table 3-1 also shows that the average volunteer time of the household (respondent and spouse) correlate modestly with some of the philanthropic behaviors. Note the relatively low values of the significant correlations. The strength of the association does not compare to that of the amounts contributed to both Jewish and non-Jewish philanthropies. This may indicate, as will be investigated below, that volunteering may belong to another factor within the behavioral bundle of philanthropy (see Goldstein in this volume).

One may conclude that major contributions may be achieved without high levels of involvement as measured by volunteer time. Building contributing behavior need not focus on increasing volunteer efforts. Certainly volunteers are necessary for a wide variety of organizational and institutional needs. For some issues, the association between voluntarism and contribution to Jewish philanthropies is significant (e.g., volunteering and contribution to the Women's Division) but the correlations are not high, so as to suggest that other means of promotion of involvement may not be as successful or more successful than integrating individuals into the volunteer tracks.

A factor analysis (Principal Components, Varimax Rotation) summarizes the correlation matrix and is presented in table 3-2.

The table shows three main factors that underlie the contribution variables. The first two factors—contribution and the amount contributed—mean that if one contributes to a campaign, it is more likely that s/he will contribute to other campaigns as well, non-Jewish included. The same is true for the amount contributed. This suggests that Jewish

Table 3-2. *Factors of Contribution Behavior*

{*eigenvalue*}	Factor 1 (2.6)	Factor 2 (1.8)	Factor 3 (1.0)
Amount Contributed to Federation	.83		
Amount Contributed to Jewish Philanthropies	.76		
Amount Contributed to Women Division	.70		
Amount Contributed to non-Jewish Philanthropies	.64		
Contribution to Jewish Philanthropies		.79	
Contribution to non-Jewish Philanthropies		.76	
Contribution to Federation		.70	
Contribution to Women Division			.70
Voluntary Time			.59
Variance %	29	20	11
	Amount Contributed	Contribution	Voluntarism & Specific
Total Variance		60%	

Source: Cohen Center for Modern Jewish Studies, 1989.

fund raising should be concerned with market share (see Ritterband in this volume).

Contributions to a Women's Division of a federation and volunteer time show a definite association within the third factor. This suggests that the more traditional pattern of promoting contributions through more active participation in volunteer activities in the organization holds true for the Women's Division. Women who are not actively involved in the Women's Division are less likely to make a contribution to it. Note that volunteer time is relatively independent, and is associated only with contribution to the Women's Division. This means that volunteer time, as an area of contribution, relates more to specific campaigns. Needing an encompassing and direct measure for contribution, we did not use it subsequently as an index for philanthropic behavior.

Thus we are left with two general factors for contribution: contribution and the amount contributed. From each of the two factors we chose one variable—the most general and abstract one—to represent it: contribution to Jewish philanthropies, and the amount contributed to Jewish philanthropies. These two variables served us as measures for philanthropic behavior.

The next step was to check if these two measures differentiate various aspects of Jewish identity. The relationship of the two representative philanthropy variables, controlled by income, age, and length of residence, with some major variables representing Jewish identity—religious practices, synagogue attendance, and visiting Israel—is presented in table 3-3.

Religious practices are a combined (Likert) scale of eleven items, on which the households were rated regarding the frequency of occurrence from "always" to "never" (see also Himmelfarb 1975; Cohen 1988): lighting Sabbath candles, participating in a Passover Seder, staying home from work, school, or alter normal activities on the High Holidays, fasting on Yom Kippur, not having a Christmas tree, buying only kosher meat for home use, not driving or riding on the Sabbath, keeping two sets of dishes for purposes of keeping kosher, reciting kiddush on Friday night, building a Sukkah, putting on tefillin daily. Synagogue attendance is a seven-point scale measuring attendance at Jewish services from never, never except for weddings and bar mitzvahs, only during High Holidays, a few times a year, a few times a month, weekly, to several times a week or more. Visiting Israel is a dichotomous (yes/no) variable.

Generally, the correlations in table 3-3 of religious practices, synagogue attendance, and visiting Israel with giving and amount given to Jewish causes are positive and mostly significant indicating the sound association between Jewish identity and philanthropic behavior.

The pattern of the correlations in table 3-3 shows a differentiating picture between the two measures of philanthropy. Partialing out income, age, and length of residence, the two correlations of the act of

Table 3-3. *The Correlation of Contribution and Amount Contributed with Religious Practices, Synagogue Attendance, and Visiting Israel*

	Religious Practices	Synagogue Attendance	Visiting Israel
Contribution to Jewish Philanthropies	.25	.24	.19
Amount Contributed to Jewish Philanthropies	.21	.22	.25

$p < .001$
range of n's: 260–1615

Source: Cohen Center for Modern Jewish Studies, 1989.

contribution with two indices of Jewish identity—religious practices and synagogue attendance—are higher than the correlations found between the amount contributed and the two indices of Jewish identity. For visiting Israel this pattern is reversed: the amount contributed is more strongly correlated with visiting Israel than the mere act of contribution. Similar systematic patterns were found between the philanthropic variables and the other Jewish identity variables (not shown in the table).

The amount contributed to Jewish philanthropies correlates with visiting Israel. Since federations are a major fund raising arm for contributions to Israel, this association should come as no surprise. Nevertheless, the systematic differences between this identity variable (visiting Israel) and the two religious identity variables (religious practices and synagogue attendance) should be noted. Traditional religious practices and synagogue attendance do not necessarily translate into higher philanthropic behavior when amount is considered.

Trips to Israel, on the other hand, are a definite plus for federations. The data may suggest that missions programs and other organized efforts to bring people to Israel have strong benefits for the fund raising efforts of federations. The causal relationship between whether or not people who are more inclined to go to Israel are more inclined to give to the federation in the first place is less relevant than the association itself. The data suggest that any mechanism that can encourage people to visit Israel will have positive effects on the amount given, while increasing religious practices or synagogue attendance in themselves will have benefit on the act of contribution more than on the amount given.

Jewish Identity

We now examine whether the variables constituting the hypothetical construct of Jewish identity associate in a meaningful pattern. We chose the items that have a content validity of relating to this construct and that were used in works such as Cohen's (1988) and Goldscheider's (1986). We had a list of at least ten items that serve as indices of Jewish identity:

1. How many of your best friends are Jewish? None, one, two, three, all. [J FRIENDS]
2. Years of Jewish education. [J ED]

3. Receiving *The Jewish News*. [J NEWS]
4. Frequency of performing eleven religious practices (a combined additive scale, as discussed in the results of table 3-3). [REL PRAC]
5. Denominational identification: Orthodox, Conservative, Reform, "just Jewish." [DEN]
6. Synagogue membership (yes/no). [SYN MEMB]
7. Synagogue attendance from "never" to "several times weekly" on a seven-point scale (see in the results of table 3-3). [SYN ATT]
8. Visiting Israel (yes/no, or "number of times"). [VIS ISRL]
9. Organizational membership (yes/no). [ORG MEMB]
10. Supporting Israel, an attitudinal variable, from "very important" to "opposed to Israel's policies," on a four-point scale. [SUP ISRL]

With one exception, each item in the above listing represents a behavioral index. We looked for the pattern in the variables that constitute Jewish identity as expressed in their interrelations. The correlation matrix is presented in table 3-4.

The correlations in the table are positive and significant, indicating a unifying construct underlying these behaviors. In addition, the table indicates that a pattern exists among the variables. For example, while religious practices strongly correlate with other religious variables,

Table 3-4. *Correlation Matrix of Jewish Identity Indices*

	J FRIENDS	J ED	J NEWS	REL PRAC	DEN	SYN MEMB	SYN ATT	VIS ISRL	ORG MEMB
J ED	ns								
J NEWS	.25	ns							
REL PRAC	.21	.19	.19						
DEN	.15	.10	.14	.51					
SYN MEMB	.15	.10	.25	.44	.35				
SYN ATT	.17	.16	.21	.56	.39	.54			
VIS ISRL	.12	.15	.16	.26	.14	.20	.18		
ORG MEMB	.16	ns	.24	.36	.22	.37	.35	.21	
SUP ISRL	ns	ns	ns	.17	.11	.15	.15	.13	.12

$p < .001$
ns = not significant
range of n's: 260–1471
Source: Cohen Center for Modern Jewish Studies, 1989.

they correlate less with "having Jewish friends" or "receiving *The Jewish News,*" or, unlike religious practices, "having Jewish friends" or "Jewish education" correlate only modestly with most of the variables. Note that the attitudinal variable (support for Israel) correlates rather modestly or nonsignificantly with the other Jewish identity variables. Theoretically it contrasts with the variables that all represent behaviors. It is known that attitudinal variables do not relate directly to their behavioral indices (Wicker 1971; see, however, Snyder, Tante and Berscheid 1977). Note also that the direct behavioral index for Israel area—visiting Israel—does correlate significantly with the other variables. The attitudinal variable, therefore, was not included in the following analysis.

In order to present the pattern described above in an orderly and concise fashion, we used factor analysis (Principal Component, Varimax Rotation) on this matrix. The results are presented in table 3-5.

The factors in the table summarize the prior matrix. Three main areas constitute what we termed Jewish identity. The labels are written below the factors. The first area is mainly the religious area and consists of four variables: religious practices, denominational affiliation, synagogue membership, and synagogue attendance. The second area is what may be called "civil" Judaism and consists of three variables: having Jewish friends, receiving *The Jewish News,* and organizational membership (see also Woocher 1987). The third area is not as clear: Jewish education and visiting Israel. Theoretically this

Table 3-5. *Factors of Jewish Identity*

[eigenvalue]	Factor 1 (3.0)	Factor 2 (1.1)	Factor 3 (1.0)
Religious Practices	.77		
Denomination	.71		
Synagogue Membership	.73		
Synagogue Attendance	.79		
Jewish Friends		.70	
Jewish News		.74	
Organization Membership		.37	
Jewish Education			.83
Visiting Israel			.64
Variance %	34	12	11
	Religious	Civil	Israel
Total Variance		57%	

Source: Cohen Center for Modern Jewish Studies, 1989.

category may fluctuate between the religious and the civil areas. Thus we have three broad areas of Jewish identity expressed by nine indices. Having described the pattern of variables within the area of philanthropic behavior and the area of Jewish identity, we are ready to explore the relations between the two areas. Before proceeding, however, a further, partly methodological, question remains. We differentiate between contribution behavior and Jewish identity indicators. Our aim is to find their interactive pattern. But are we justified in dividing these two areas? Is contribution behavior a factor independent in the realm of Jewish identity? One way to test these questions is to analyze the pattern of interrelations of all the variables: both the Jewish identity and the philanthropy variables. We used factor analysis on the correlations of the eighteen variables (the nine indices of Jewish identity and the nine indices of philanthropic behavior). We expected to find an independent factor for contribution behavior, and thus to have also an empirical justification for the proposed differentiation. The results are presented in table 3-6.

The data indicate that the main factor representing Jewish identity clusters around religious aspects (Factor 1): religious practices, synagogue attendance, denominational affiliation, synagogue membership, and voluntarism. The other variables cluster around three factors of organizational civil Judaism: the factor of the amount contributed (Factor 2), the factor of various philanthropic behaviors, receiving *The Jewish News,* and organizational membership (Factor 3), and the factor of friendship patterns, years of Jewish education, visiting Israel, and contribution to the Women's Division (Factor 4).

Voluntarism is more likely to be associated with religious identity in terms of ritual practice and synagogue life than with the amount contributed to Jewish philanthropies, with various philanthropic behaviors, or generally with civil Judaism. Given that people volunteer more so for a synagogue or temple than for any other Jewish organization, the finding is not surprising. Reading a Jewish newspaper and organizational membership cluster with contributing to a philanthropy, be it a federation or a non-Jewish philanthropy. The amount given clustered independently when accessibility is considered. This finding is also not surprising. Those who read Jewish newspapers and those who belong to some organization are more likely to receive phone calls or mailings from Jewish fund raising organizations. Their contribution reflects organizational solicitation as well as greater proclivity to give. This survey, as well as others, found that the single largest reason

Table 3-6. *Factors of Jewish Identity and Contribution Behaviors*

[eigenvalue]	Factor 1 (4.2)	Factor 2 (2.1)	Factor 3 (1.5)	Factor 4 (1.1)
REL PRACTICE	.81			
SYN ATTENDANCE	.76			
DENOMINATION	.70			
SYN MEMBERSHIP	.70			
VOL TIME	.42			
AMT CONT FED		.82		
AMT CONT J PHIL		.80		
AMT CONT NO-J PHIL		.68		
AMT CONT WOM DIV		.60		
CONT J PHIL			.76	
CONT NON-J PHIL			.72	
CONT FEDERATION			.71	
REC J NEWS			.48	
ORG MEMBERSHIP			.32	
JEWISH EDUCATION				.66
CONT WOM DIVISION				.44
JEWISH FRIENDS				.39
VISITING ISRAEL				.32
Variance %	23	12	8	7
	Religious	Amount Contributed	Contribution & Civil	Civil Israel
Total Variance		50%		

Source: Cohen Center for Modern Jewish Studies, 1989.

Jews gave for not contributing to a Jewish philanthropy is that nobody asked them to contribute (Tobin 1987b).

Basic to our point, the table shows that contribution is expressed mainly as two independent factors within the realm of Jewish identity— amount contributed is purely independent (Factor 2) and contribution is largely independent (Factor 3). The data indicate that it is justified to see contribution as a subarea, partly independent, within Jewish identity.

The Association Between Jewish Identity and Philanthropy

In this section we examine the pattern of association between the indices of Jewish identity and the two measures of philanthropic behavior; we look for the degree of association between the independent variables of Jewish identity and the two dependent variables of contribution.

In the following analysis we used only seven independent variables. Jewish education was not used for two reasons: first, this background variable does not fit theoretically with the other variables that describe current behaviors related to Jewish identity; second, its ties with the Jewish identity variables are rather low (as was seen in table 3-4); and third, and more statistically important, its ties with all the contribution variables, as seen from table 3-7 are low.

Table 3-7 shows that the correlations of years of Jewish education with the amount contributed to Jewish philanthropies, federations, or the Women's Division are modest, and with contributing to a Jewish philanthropy, federation, Women's Division, non-Jewish philanthropies, or voluntarism are nonsignificnt.

Interestingly, these low correlations remain low when major background variables, such as sex and denomination are controlled (not shown in the table), for one may raise the argument that Jewish women, especially in more traditional denominations, are less exposed to Jewish education, thus lowering the overall association with Jewish identity.

These findings should encourage an examination of the efforts made to use years of Jewish education as a measure for Jewish identity (including philanthropic behavior). The number of years respondents receive Jewish education did not correlate strongly with Jewish identity (table 3-4) or with contribution (table 3-7). A better indicator than a

Table 3-7. *Correlation of Years of Jewish Education with the Philanthropic Variables*

	Years of Jewish Education
Contribution to Jewish Philanthropies	ns
Amount Contributed to Jewish Philanthropies	.13
Contribution to Federation	ns
Amount Contributed to Federation	.10
Contribution to Women Division	ns
Amount Contributed to Women Division	.17
Contribution to non-Jewish Philanthropies	ns
Amount Contributed to non-Jewish Philanthropies	ns
Voluntary Time	ns

$p < .001$
range of n's: 560–1460
Source: Cohen Center for Modern Jewish Studies, 1989.

quantitative one (years) may be a qualitative one (type). Therefore we would have to examine the kind of Jewish education and its effect on Jewish philanthropy, or when that Jewish education was received. The data would indicate the need to examine what is being taught in terms of philanthropy and *tzedakah* in the formal education systems as well. This debate is beyond the scope of our paper (see Bock 1975 versus Himmelfarb 1977). Since the data show the strong association with visiting Israel on increased giving to federations and Jewish philanthropies, more "hands on" experiences in the short term may be a most immediate and pressing need. One may speculate that efforts to raise Jewish consciousness through missions, specialized events, and more targeted appeals are likely to have more positive effects on fund raising efforts than long-term investments in preadolescent Jewish education. Nevertheless, since Jewish education does touch the great majority of Jewish children, incorporating greater emphasis on philanthropic behavior, *tzedakah,* and communal responsibilities may be essential.

We also did not include receiving *The Jewish News* in the analysis for its association with contribution is partially redundant. In addition to its subscribers, all contributors of $10 or more have a subscription to this paper. Thus we are left with seven independent variables whose relations with contribution behavior we now explore.

Checking the relative importance of each of the seven independent variables that predict contribution behavior, while all the others are held constant, that is, while controlling for the other variables, we found that only four variables are important in predicting contribution behavior. The results are presented in table 3-8 and derived from a multiple regression analysis.

The four variables appearing in the regression equations best explain contribution behavior. For contribution, these are (in a descending order of importance) synagogue attendance and organizational membership. For the amount contributed, they are (in a descending order) synagogue membership, visiting Israel, and organizational membership. The relation of the other variables—religious practices, denominational affiliation, and having Jewish friends—with contribution is largely explained by the prior four main variables.

One may speculate that synagogue attendance and membership—which relate to the religious area of Jewish identity—are more basic to giving than, for example, religious practices, because they represent the active participant and communal aspects of Judaism and are also not limited to religious practices that can be performed more individually or at home. However, from the religious identity perspective, they

Table 3-8. *Summary Table of Forward Regression of Jewish Identity Variables with Contribution and Amount of Contribution*

Dependent Variable: Contribution

$R^2 = .26$	Standardized B Coefficient	t-test
Synagogue Attendance	.26	**
Organizational Membership	.20	**

Dependent Variable: Amount of Contribution

$R^2 = .29$	Standardized B Coefficient	t-test
Synagogue Membership	.14	**
Visiting Israel	.14	**
Organizational Membership	.13	**

**p < .001

Source: Cohen Center for Modern Jewish Studies, 1989.

are related (as was previously shown in the factors of Jewish identity). Organizational membership and visiting Israel—which relate to civil Judaism—may be thought of as reciprocal with giving.

Note that the four independent variables cover the gamut formed by the three factors found as prominent in the Jewish identity pattern (table 3-5): the religious, the civil, and the third area. Organizational membership and visiting Israel are related to the civil areas (second and third factors). Synagogue attendance and membership are related to the religious area (first factor).

While synagogue attendance and organizational membership associate more strongly with contribution, organizational and synagogue membership and visiting Israel associate more strongly with the amount contributed. This suggests that increasing organizational and institutional involvement might increase both contribution and the amount contributed, as well as increase the positive effect visiting Israel has on contributing amounts. That is, while the philanthropic Jew is also communally active, he may not necessarily be religiously active. Thus, while all these behaviors are interrelated, focusing more on behaviors relating to civil Judaism will affect fund raising efforts positively.

The association between the four indices of Jewish identity with contribution is illustrated in the cross-tabulations of the four Jewish identity variables with contribution in tables 3-9 and 3-10.

Table 3-9. *Contribution to Jewish Philanthropies by Four Identity Variables*

	Contribution	No Contribution
Synagogue Attendance		
Never	47	53
Weddings or Bar Mitzvah only	70	30
High Holidays only	84	16
Few times a year	86	14
Few times a month	90	10
Weekly	94	6
Several times/week or more	94	6
Organizational Membership		
No	69	31
Yes	91	9
Synagogue Membership		
No	70	30
Yes	89	11
Visiting Israel		
No	74	26
Yes	93	7

Source: Cohen Center for Modern Jewish Studies, 1989.

Table 3-10. *Visiting Israel by Amount Contributed*

Amount of Contribution	Visit	No Visit
Up to $500	37	63
$500–$1,000	65	35
$1,000 +	69	31

Source: Cohen Center for Modern Jewish Studies, 1989.

Tables 3-9 and 3-10 show the direct and monotonic association between synagogue attendance, organizational membership, synagogue membership, and visiting Israel with contribution, and the direct and monotonic association between visiting Israel and the amount contributed. In table 3-9 note the monotonic relationship between synagogue attendance and contribution. Note the higher percentages of givers of those who are synagogue and organizational members, and of those who visited Israel. In table 3-10 note that monotonic relationship between the amount given and visiting Israel.

The other three variables constituting Jewish identity—religious practices, denominational affiliation, and having Jewish friends—had no direct association with contribution behavior. Their relation, as mentioned above, is explained by the four main variables. As an illustration, see the following cross-tabulation in tables 3-11 and 3-12.

Table 3-11 shows an apparent monotonic relationship between the number of Jewish friends and contribution to Jewish philanthropies. It seems that the more Jewish friends one has, the more s/he is likely to contribute. However, when one holds organizational membership constant, the effect disappears, as seen in table 3-12.

Table 3-12 does not show the prior clear monotonic relation between number of Jewish friends and contribution: neither for those who are members nor for those who are not members. The percentages fluctuate without order. Yet, there is a clear overall association between organizational membership and contribution (95 percent for those who are, versus 69 percent of those who are not).

It seems that the four variables—synagogue attendance, organizational membership, synagogue membership, and visiting Israel—are more basic in explaining contribution behavior than having Jewish friends, religious practices, and denominational affiliation.

Table 3-11. *Contribution to Jewish Philanthropies by the Number of Jewish Friends*

Number of Jewish Friends	Contribution	No Contribution
No Jewish Friends	51	49
1 Jewish Friend	69	31
2 Jewish Friends	80	20
3 Jewish Friends	85	15
All Jewish Friends	88	12

Table 3-12. *Contribution to Jewish Philanthropies by the Number of Jewish Friends for Organizational Members Versus Non-Members*

Number of Jewish Friends	Organizational Membership		Not Organizational Membership	
	Contribution	No Contribution	Contribution	No Contribution
No Jewish Friends	100	—	40	60
1 Jewish Friend	100	—	70	30
2 Jewish Friends	94	6	65	35
3 Jewish Friends	86	14	81	19
All Jewish friends	97	3	79	21
Overall	*95*	*5*	*69*	*31*

Subjective Reasons for Giving

As a final note, we look at the results of the philosophical question about giving and what people say when asked why they contribute. Earlier, we tried to explain contribution by examining the unverbalized behavioral indices of Jewish identity; their association with contribution may represent an unconscious act by the individual. It is interesting, therefore, to check the respondents' open verbalized answers to the following question: "Please try to describe for me your overall philosophy regarding your donations to various organizations."

Will their answers reflect what we found in the prior results? The categorized answers are presented in table 3-13.

As expected, answers varied greatly and therefore were not easy to categorize. That 34 percent of the answers were "not applicable or no reason" supports that it is not easy for people to articulate their reasons for giving (although, note, that these are the same persons who are the "givers"). However, we can note a general trend in responses when we use content analysis to analyze them.

Table 3-13 shows that most state that they contribute for altruistic reasons such as: "just try to help others," "to help the needy," without specification, either religious or organizational. These reasons are much more closely tied to civil Judaism; they reflect a sense of general commitment to philanthropy. The second most common answers do relate to Jewish causes and *tzedakah* as a religious imperative; "anything to help Jews," "to maintain Judaism," "obligation to give" or *"tzedakah."* These reasons are tied more to the religious area. The rest are reasons that relate to specific organizations, disease cures, and personal reasons.

Such results may reflect, in an intuitive fashion, our higher order results. Earlier we saw that three out of the four variables explaining contribution and amount contributed were related to civil Judaism.

Table 3-13. *Reasons for Giving*

Reasons	Percentage
General Altruism	33
Jewish Causes and Tzedakah	14
Specific Organizations	8
Disease Cure	7
Personal Reasons	4
Not Applicable & No Reason	34

The same was found in the reasons stated for giving: if one counts only the first two reasons, altruistic reasons, which relate more to civil Judaism, they outnumber the strictly religious reasons by similar ratio. A strong commitment to traditional Jewish life, as expressed by religious practices, plays a secondary role.

Conclusion

The data suggest that religious identity is associated with patterns of philanthropy. Building Jewish identity over a long time period certainly will have positive effects on Jewish philanthropy. Obviously the association works in both directions, so that building commitment to Jewish philanthropy also supports and increases Jewish identity. Both a long-term and a short-term strategy, building religious identity through increased synagogue attendance and membership ultimately will have strong effects on fund raising campaigns. As our results point out, the religious aspects of Jewish identity are highly associated with one another as are the civil aspects of Jewish identity.

Similarly the data suggest that short-term strategies that build upon civil Judaism, especially organizational membership and visiting Israel, will have a strong and positive effect on Jewish philanthropic behavior.

While long-term strategies of promoting Jewish education and building religious life have a general positive effect on philanthropic behavior, amounts contributed are most affected by visits to Israel and organizational and synagogue membership. Trips to Israel are related strongly to the amount contributed to a campaign, over and above income, age, and length of residence. More immediate and targeted efforts, therefore, are suggested. Building more mission programs, informal and formal events, and targeted programming will most likely increase participation in Jewish philanthropies. The effects of greater ritual observance and having Jewish friends are only realized when they are supported and enhanced by visits to Israel or other bolstering factors. While religious identity correlates with patterns of philanthropy, the strength of that association rests with intervening variables that raise Jewish consciousness and commitment immediately, as reflected in organized communal behaviors.

Notes

We thank Drs. Larry Sternberg and Sylvia Barack Fishman for their very helpful comments on the chapter. A consise version of this chapter was

presented at the Conference on Jewish Philanthropy, Graduate School and
University Center, City University of New York, June 15–16, 1988.

Bibliography

Andrews, F. M. *Philanthropic Giving.* New York: Russell Sage Foundation,
1950.

Bock, G. *The Jewish Schooling of American Jews: A Study of Non-Cognitive
Educational Effects.* Unpublished doctoral dissertation, Harvard University,
1976.

Cohen, S. M. "Will Jews Keep Giving? Prospects for the Jewish Charitable
Community." *Journal of Jewish Communal Service,* 50 (1978): (1) 59–71.

———. "Trends in Jewish Philanthropy. *American Jewish Yearbook, 1980.*
New York: American Jewish Committee, 1980.

———. *American Modernity and Jewish Identity.* New York: Tavistock Publications, 1983.

———. *American Assimilation or Jewish Revival.* Bloomington: Indiana University Press, 1988.

Goldscheider, C. *Jewish Continuity and Change: Emerging Patterns in America.* Bloomington: Indiana University Press and Center for Modern Jewish
Studies, Brandeis University, 1986.

Himmelfarb, H. S. "Measuring Religious Involvement." *Social Forces,* 53
(1975): (4), 606–18.

———. "The Non-Linear Impact of Schooling: Comparing Different Types
and Amounts of Jewish Education. *Sociology of Education,* 50 (1977): 114–
29.

Hodgkinson, V. A., and M. A. Weitzman. *The Charitable Behavior of Americans.* Washington, D.C.: Independent Sector, 1986.

Milgram, S. "The Experience of Living in Cities." *Science,* 167, (1970): 1461–
68.

Mussen, P., and N. Eisenberg-Berg. *Roots of Caring, Sharing and Helping:
The Development of Prosocial Behavior in Children.* San Francisco, Calif.:
Freeman, 1977.

Olson, M. *The Logic of Collective Action: Public Goods and the Theory of
Groups.* New York: Schoken Books, 1968.

Phelps, E. S. (ed.). *Altruism, Morality and Economic Theory.* New York:
Russell Sage Foundation, 1975.

Rappeport, M., and G. Tobin. *A Population Study of the Jewish Community of MetroWest, New Jersey.* East Orange, N.J.: The United Jewish Federation of MetroWest, 1987.

Rimor, M., and G. Tobin. "Jewish Giving to Jewish and Non-Jewish Philanthropy." Paper presented at conference on Philanthropy and the Religious Tradition, Independent Sector, Chicago, March 10–11, 1989.

Ritterband, P., and S. M. Cohen. "Will the Well Run Dry? The Future of Jewish Giving in America." *Response, 12* (1979): 9–17.

Ritterband, P., and R. Silberstein. "Generation, Age and Income Variability. In *Jewish Philanthropy in Contemporary America.* (Information Series no. 2). New York: City University of New York, North American Jewish Data Bank, 1988.

Silberstein, R., P. Ritterband, J. Rabinowitz, and B. Kosmin. *Giving to Jewish Philanthropic Causes: A Preliminary Reconnaissance.* (Reprint Series no. 2). New York: City University of New York, North American Jewish Data Bank, 1987.

Sklare, M. "The Future of Jewish Giving." *Commentary* (November 1962).

Snyder, M. L., E. D. Tanke, and E. Berscheid. "Social Perception and Interpersonal Behavior: On the Self-Fulfilling Nature of Social Stereotype." *Journal of Personality and Social Psychology, 35* (1977): 656–66.

Tobin, G. *An Analysis of the Fund Raising Campaign of the United Jewish Appeal Federation of Greater Washington.* Washington, D.C.: United Jewish Appeal Federation of Greater Washington, D.C., 1984.

———. *Analysis of the Fund Raising Campaign of the Associated Jewish Charities and Welfare Fund of Baltimore.* Baltimore, Md.: Associated Jewish Charities & Welfare Fund, Inc., 1986.

———. "We Are One, We Are Many: Reaching Potential Givers." Paper presented at the International Leadership Reunion of the United Jewish Appeal and Keren Hayesod, 1987a.

———. "Patterns of Philanthropy in the MetroWest, New Jersey Jewish Community." East Orange, N.J.: The United Jewish Federation of MetroWest, 1987b.

Tobin, G., and S. Fishman. *Analysis of the Fund Raising Campaign of the Jewish Community Federation of Rochester.* Rochester, N.Y.: Jewish Community Federation of Rochester, NY, Inc., 1988a.

———. *Analysis of the Fund Raising Campaign of the Worcester Jewish Federation.* Worcester, Mass.: Worcester Jewish Federation, Inc. 1988b.

Tobin, G., and S. Sassler. *Analysis of the Fund Raising Campaign of the Bay Area Jewish Community.* San Francisco, Calif.: Jewish Federation of the Greater East Bay, Jewish Community Federation of San Francisco, and Jewish Federation of Greater San Jose, 1988.

Wicker, A. W. "An Examination of the Other Variables Explanation of Attitude-Behavior Inconsistency." *Journal of Personality and Social Psychology, 19* (1971): 18–30.

Woocher, J. *Sacred Survival: The Civil Religion of American Jews.* Bloomington, Ind.: Indiana University Press, 1987.

Yankelovitch, Skelly and White, Inc. *The Charitable Behavior of Americans.* Washington, D.C.: Independent Sector, 1986.

4

The Determinants of Jewish Charitable Giving in the Last Part of the Twentieth Century

Paul Ritterband

May He bless those who consecrate synagogues for prayer and those who come to pray, those who provide light for them, wine for blessing the coming and the going of the Sabbath, food for wayfarers, and charity for the poor. Yea, may He bless all those who faithfully concern themselves with communal needs.

—from the Sabbath morning liturgy

Philanthropy in America is a growth industry. Edmondson (1986) reports that amounts given to charity by Americans doubled between 1978 and 1985. The increase in the rate of giving has exceeded the rise in the rate of inflation in every year since 1981. Our best estimate is that between 80 percent and 90 percent of American households generally and Jewish households specifically reported giving an annual charitable gift during the 1980s. For an industry that "sells" a luxury item, not necessary to survival, one would have to say that philanthropy in America is a thriving enterprise. While reaching a smaller fraction of households than do butchers and bakers, philanthropies in America do better than do candlestick makers, car dealers, and a host of other industries. Major Jewish philanthropies, however, are a less

57

happy lot. Between 1973 and 1986, the number of gifts to Federated Jewish campaigns fell 27 percent from 1,200,000 to 875,000 (UJA 1986). From 1987 to 1988 the total amount collected by the United Jewish Appeal fell by 5.7 percent in nominal dollars, amounting to a loss of approximately 10 percent when inflation is taken into account.

Elsewhere in this volume we have detailed reports of the macropicture. We are presented with information on the state of Jewish campaigns in relation to others and in relation to themselves over time. In this chapter I shall move to the level of individual households to portray and analyze the "socioeconomics of the firm," the nature of the decision-making process that determines if and how a charitable gift is given to Jewish and non-Jewish causes as a consequence of characteristics of the households, and of the charitable institution.

A little over a decade ago a colleague and I published a paper titled "Will the Well Run Dry?" (Ritterband and Cohen 1979). There we found portents of decline in the Jewish charitable enterprise. We hypothesized that the decline of Jewish charity was linked to other changes in the Jewish community, some of which we shall examine here. The well has not yet run dry, nor is it likely to, but the flow has certainly decreased. The burden of this chapter is to determine empirically and theoretically why this is now the case.

Hence, the question of giving is really several questions. Should one give at all? How much should one give? How should one divide the household's charitable dollar? Should the gift be visible and if visible, to whom? To whom should one give? To give at all and how much to give are influenced by U.S. income tax laws. The American tax system, with its credits for charitable donations as well as its progressive rates, encourages giving, particularly large gifts by the well-to-do. Still, it must be remembered that under current tax laws and regulations, no gift is free, nor can donors make profits on their charitable gifts as in the past. Why then should the donor give and to whom shall he give? If Jews are about as likely to give as are non-Jews, the question for the Jewish community is why do Jews seem to be giving less of their charitable dollar to Jewish causes? Even when they give to Jewish causes, why are they moving away from mainstream Jewish causes? The answers to these questions lie in the changing nature of American Jewry and in the unchanging nature of the campaigns.

How do potential givers decide to give at all, and how do they choose among the enormous number of worthy causes presented to them? Everyday's mail brings an appeal from one or another worthy cause, most of which are ignored by the recipients of the mail. Why give to combat this disease and not another? Why do some people of substantial means give to universities, art museums, and other institutions of high culture? How does one choose? As guiding principles, we shall suggest five issues of choice: identification with the recipient, moral commitment to give, identification with the community of givers, accessibility to the campaign, and dividing the pie. Identification with the recipients is the social-psychological analogue of what Chiswick (see chapter 1) terms "altruism." Person X gives to person Y when X derives some satisfaction from Y's satisfaction. While Chiswick argues that altruism, or what I have termed identification, does not extend beyond the small group (usually the family), evidence from the Jewish experience suggests otherwise: altruism extends beyond the conventional family. The campaign literature of Jewish campaigns stresses the quasi-familial relationships among Jews and appeals to family ties to elicit gifts.

Identification is not enough. One must have a sense of moral obligation toward those with whom one identifies. Jewish tradition contains a vast literature that assumes the transcendent obligation to give, an obligation that includes the poorest among us. The nature of that obligation and the ways that it works through the life of the individual and family is clearly present in the Orthodox community as described in this volume by Heilman. Liberal religion, with its emphasis on freedom of choice among the commandments, does not and cannot create a sense of transcendent obligation once the existence of a transcendent reality that has the right to command and demand is no longer present. When one gives charity, the tradition does not require the recitation of a benediction as is the case with so many other positive commandments since it is assumed that the obligation to give is based upon someone else's need to receive. We do not thank God for another's discomfort. Despite the lack of formal ritual attached to giving, there are many ritualized contexts in which giving is expected, indeed demanded. It is difficult to demand with a sense of moral rectitude when both the solicitor of the gift and the potential donor know that giving is a voluntary act. Hence, we would expect that as Jews become secularized and lose their sense of *mitzvah* or divine commandment, it would become increasingly difficult to get them to give. The overwhelming evidence is that over time, Jews have become far more secularized than has been the case for Protestants and Catholics (Abramson 1975, 253–57; Lenski 1963, 45). Consequently, we should find their secularization linked to a decline in giving to Jewish causes. An irony should be noted. Observers of the American

scene such as Alexis deTocqueville or Max Weber have commented on
the extent to which Americans are religious believers. Anticlericalism
is all but unknown in the United States. However, as Jews have become
more American (and less Jewish) in their style of life, they have
become less American on another level, that is, the religious plane.

If altruism involves identification with the recipient and transcendent obligation gives motive force, then identification with fellow givers
supplies a significant contextual force in determining giving and the
level of giving. Identification with fellow donors (what Chiswick terms
membership in the club) can work in many ways. Donors give to the
muscular dystrophy campaign not only because they identify with the
afflicted and because they feel a moral obligation to give, but also
because they identify with the soliciting process, they identify with
"Jerry's kids," with Jerry and with the "pseudo-Gemeinschaft" created during the campaign. They identify with the celebrity solicitor
and their identification increases as the fund raising marathon continues and the solicitor becomes visibly exhausted. If the principle applies
to small gifts to a mass campaign, it applies even more to the large and
visible gifts of the wealthy few. Large and visible gifts certify to the
place of the donor among the charmed circle of the enlightened or the
"gliteratti." One not only chooses the beneficiary of one's largesse,
one chooses one's colleagues, one's club. The more distinguished the
club, the more distinction is offered the giver. This, in part, accounts
for the cliché that the rich get richer. When a well-endowed, distinguished university solicits gifts, the donor knows that his gift will find
its place on a roster of the elite. Thus for Jews, their new money is
given a patina of old money by virtue of its patrician associates and
neighbors.

The fourth factor to be considered is the accessibility of the potential
donor to the campaign. There is no "Yellow Pages" of worthy causes.
The donor does not check "D" for diseases and then looks for an
appropriate or attractive affliction to which he might send his contribution, nor does he look up "R" for religion or "P" for poverty.
Someone solicits his gift. In order that he might give, in the vast
majority of cases, the potential giver must be reached by a solicitor.
For some causes, solicitation comes through the place of work, others
through the home. Some seek a broad constituency while others appeal
to a small group. For a broad-based, omnibus charity such as the
United Way, solicitation is a minor problem. For Jewish philanthropies,
even the Federated Jewish campaigns, accessibility is a hurdle they
must leap.

The last factor this paper will consider is that of dividing the pie. The typical middle-class household receives many requests for help. Given the array of requests, the household must have some criteria (usually implicit) to decide how it will divide the pie. The various causes soliciting funds can be understood as merchants selling their goods. The merchant's prosperity is linked to the general state of prosperity of his industry and is also a function of his market share. For individual causes, including Jewish causes, the key question is market share or dividing the pie. There is probably little they can do to get Jews to increase their total charitable contributions. Their struggle is to get Jews to give a larger fraction of their charity dollar to Jewish causes, to increase their market share, to cut the pie so that more remains within the Jewish community.

The factors noted—identification with the recipient, moral obligation, membership in the club, accessibility, and dividing the pie—are far more variable in the modern world in which Jews now find themselves. At the time when the mass of Jews believed that "Charity saves from death" and that only Jewish charities had a legitimate call upon their means, and further that their social position within the Jewish community depended upon their gifts, the fact that Jews gave in concert with, to, and for fellow Jews, was self-evident, not calling for comment. In the American context however, Jewish giving to Jewish causes loses its self-justifying and self-evident character. Jewish philanthropies now function in a competitive market. Some sort of particularist motive now is required to give to a Jewish cause, and some positive act is often required to become accessible to Jewish causes. For solicitation to take place, one must associate with other Jews (at home or at work) through formal (affiliation with Jewish organizations) or informal ties, through a network of friends and business or professional contacts. The old-fashioned *meshulah*, the messenger-collector representing a yeshiva, who would knock on every door in a Jewish neighborhood, is all but totally absent from the current American scene.

These factors suggest that a comparative approach to the study of Jewish giving would be fruitful. We are not interested solely in the fact that Jews do (or do not) give to Jewish causes; we are interested in their giving to Jewish causes in the context of their philanthropic activity more generally. This chapter then will place Jewish giving to Jewish causes next to Jewish giving to general or non-Jewish causes. Using two sets of survey data, we shall first examine the two sorts of giving in parallel, that is, we shall treat the Jewish and general philanthropic activity as alternative campaigns with alternative strategies and appeals with our emphasis on accessibility. The second part of the analysis will assume that the amount of giving is fixed, but that the proportions given to Jewish and non-Jewish causes is variable, and the way that Jews cut the pie will be our concern. In both parts of the analysis, we will be concerned with the individual's motives to give (and how he allocates his gifts), and the campaign's solicitations strategy and its access to potential donors.

Accessibility

Elsewhere in this volume, Rimor and Tobin report that the most frequently given response to the question "Why don't you give?" is "No one asked me." In this section we will work at understanding who is asked, that is, who is accessible to the campaign. Two factors—generation and income—give us our initial insight into the differential access to potential givers and the alternative strategies of campaigns. Let us examine first the question of generation (see table 4-1). Generation is the engine that drives the processes of acculturation and secularization among Jews. With each generation in America, Jews become more involved in the larger American community and less involved in the Jewish community. With passing generations, religious observance (and belief) declines, synagogue attendance becomes less frequent, the moral hold of the tradition becomes weaker, the individual's friendship circle includes fewer Jews and more non-Jews, and the propensity to affiliate formally with the Jewish community lessens. As a consequence of these social changes, all of the factors that we have identified as being part of the cluster that supports the Jewish charitable sentiment and make the individual and the household accessible to the campaign become increasingly attenuated. The potential donor feels less compelled to give, is less moved by the psychic rewards for giving in the Jewish community, and indeed become less visible and accessible to the fund raising apparatus.

The greatest propensity to give is to be found among second-generation Jews. These Jews are nurtured by Old World memories and traditions related by their parents but are sufficiently westernized to appreciate the need for the style of large-scale, bureaucratized philanthropy. With each generation after the second, the probability of giving to the Federated Jewish campaign declines. For the general campaign, as would be expected, generation in America has a slight depressing

Table 4-1. *Giving to Federation Campaign and Non-Jewish Campaigns by Generation and by Income Using the Nine-City Sample*

A. Generation	Generation			
	1	2	3	4
% give to Federation campaign	51	60	42	34
% give to non-Jewish campaign	63	71	74	71
% give to Federation campaign if asked	79	83	73	69

B. Income	Income less than (in thousands of dollars)										
	7.5	12.5	20	30	40	50	60	80	100	125	125+
% give Fed.	30	43	36	42	47	53	62	67	78	75	81
% give non-Jewish	59	58	66	68	71	71	74	76	76	78	78
% give Fed. if asked	65	74	71	74	82	84	85	84	86	93	87

effect on the first generation but after that, there is no significant effect at all.

The generational effect has two sources: motivational and structural. Third- and fourth-generation Jews tend to be less committed to Jewish tradition and less moved by the moral imperatives of the Jewish religious tradition. They are also less likely to be formally affiliated with the Jewish community and thus less accessible to Jewish charitable campaigns. Simply stated, third- and fourth-generation Jews are less likely to be asked to give. Being asked to give is obviously critical. When we restrict our analysis to those who have been asked to give, we find a much weaker generational effect. In addition to its direct effect on motive, generation in America tends to make the Jew less visible and accessible to the campaign. When we examine giving among those who have been solicited by the campaign, we find that the effect of generation is reduced by almost half. In part then, the problems of the Federated campaign flow from the weakened motive to give and in part from the weakened visibility and accessibility of the third- and fourth-generation potential giver.

In contrast to generation, income has an effect both on the Federated Jewish campaign and on the secular campaigns. In both instances, we find that households with lower incomes are less likely to give. That finding comes as little surprise (though even the poor can give small amounts). What is more significant is that the Federated Jewish campaign is much more susceptible to the income effect than are non-Jewish campaigns. In the Federated Jewish campaign, 30 percent of the lowest income group reports giving a gift as compared with 81 percent of the top income group. By contrast, in the non-Jewish campaigns, 51 percent of the lowest income group reports having given a gift as compared with 79 percent of the highest income group. The difference in fund raising strategies lies at the core of the difference in income effects. Less than half of the lowest income Jewish households report having been asked to give to the Federated Jewish campaign, while in contrast four-fifths or more of the higher income households report having been solicited by the campaign. Here, too, the effect of solicitation is dramatic. Among the lowest income Jewish households, the probability of giving among those solicited is more than twice that of the low income group more generally.

The motivational effects of income on giving are self-evident. Those with less are less likely to give. The structural effect, which shows a significant difference between the Federated Jewish campaign and non-Jewish philanthropies, is based upon a strategic decision to be "efficient," to go after the potential big givers, and to largely ignore or at least invest relatively little in a broad-based campaign that would include households of modest means.

This decision results in the distribution of gifts that we find reported in Fruehauf's paper, chapter 11. His data show us that 1.2 percent of the gifts account for 60 percent of the income. Low-income households are potentially as accessible as higher income households, but they are clearly far less likely to be able to manage a "quality gift," that is, one exceeding $10,000. Low-income households are significantly less likely to be invited to become members of the club of federation givers. While this might make sense from the point of view of efficiency, it makes little sense when considered from the perspective of community building. Increasingly the latter is asserted as one of the chief concerns of Jewish communal fund raising. The major givers also want to know that they are not alone in their support of the Federated campaign. The public face of the campaign is one of a broad-based appeal while the reality is somewhat different. Clearly, practice has not yet caught up with ideology.

To get a fuller understanding of the process of solicitation, we turn to an analysis of the New York Federation campaign. In the New York data collection of 1981 (one of the constituents of the nine-city file), detailed questions were asked about who solicited a gift. In all, we have information on the solicitation of a gift by someone from the householder's synagogue, a friend or neighbor, people from work, and a stranger. To simplify the analysis, the solicitations were added together so that each household may have a score running from zero (no solicitation) to four (solicitation by a fellow congregant, friend, neighbor, co-worker, or stranger). The assumption of the analysis is that people are not randomly accessible. In some way, they make themselves known to the campaign staff or volunteer, and someone thinks it is worthwhile to contact them and ask for a gift. In the analysis based upon table 4-1, we contented ourselves with the impact of being asked to give.

In this section we look at who is being asked to give, and what is the impact of being asked as well as other relevant social characteristics in determining whether or not a household does, in fact, report a gift to the campaign (see table 4-2).

The determinants of solicitation fall into two broad categories: sociodemographic characteristics and Jewish behavior/identification. Among the sociodemographic characteristics, generation is the "primordial" factor. It is a critical determinant of the processes of acculturation that can be expected to lead to changes in accessibility to the campaign as well as response to the campaign. The strategy of the

Table 4-2. *The Determinants of Solicitation and of Giving to the New York Federation Campaign (New York Population Study, 1981)*

	A	B
	No. of Solicitations	*Give to Campaign*
Generation 2[1]	*	.046
Generation 3[1]	*	*
Generation 4[1]	*	*
Years in residence	*	.034
Age	.119	.139
Log income	.172	.132
Orthodox synagogue member[2]	.107	*
Conservative synagogue member[2]	.172	.076
Reform synagogue member[2]	.155	.032
Member Jewish organization outside of synagogue	.118	.095
Number of 3 closest friends who are Jewish	.032	.077
Number of solicitations	——	.383
R^2 =	.146	.328

[1]Reference category = generation 1.

[2]Reference category = not synagogue member.

*Coefficient does not reach .01 level of significance.

——Variable not included in the equation.

campaign is to seek out those with greater means; thus, we introduce household income as a second predictor. (Since the distribution of income is highly skewed, the distribution is normalized by transforming it into its logarithm.) Other research has shown that geographic mobility tends to disrupt Jewish communal connections leading to a lower rate of participation in the campaign (Silberstein, Ritterband, Rabinowitz, and Kosmin 1987). To test for the effects of geographic mobility, we have introduced number of years in current residence. The last of the "secular" considerations is age. In part, age is introduced because of its frequent confusion with generation. Over and above its methodological significance, age is a factor taken into account by the campaign. There is a "young leadership" division through which there is a program of outreach to the younger members of the Jewish community. The main leadership of the campaign tends to be older, reflecting having spent years coming up through the ranks as well as having had the time to have "made it" in their careers. The existence of the young leadership program bespeaks a concern among federation leaders that they are not reaching the young through the networks that work for the older population. The question then is to what extent are the young inaccessible to the campaign?

Federated Jewish campaigns are centralized bodies that work through local Jewish addresses. Chief among these are synagogues and Jewish voluntary organizations. One out of five households in this survey have reported a campaign contact from a fellow member of their synagogue. It is not at all clear however, that the three major denominational bodies are equally likely to participate in the campaign. Thus, each of the denominations is treated individually with nonmembership defined as the reference category. The large number of Jewish voluntary organizations has made it impractical to detail the effects of each of them individually so the household is scored dichotomously as to whether it is affiliated with a nonsynagogue Jewish membership organization. A Jewish friendship circle is the last factor to be considered. Approximately one in eight of the households reports a solicitation from friends or neighbors. Presumably, the more Jewish friends one has, the more likely one is to be solicited by the campaign.

The results of this first analysis are presented in column A of table 4-2. As we expected, generation has no direct effect on solicitation. The effect of generation is mediated through affiliation with synagogues, Jewish voluntary organizations, and Jewish friendship. In addition, residential stability has no direct effect since it is mediated through the Jewish affiliational variables. Age and income both have significant direct effects, suggesting that despite the efforts of the campaign, it is still not effectively reaching the younger Jewish population. It is not reaching the lower-income population, which is consistent with its efforts.

Among the Jewish variables, formal affiliation, either through synagogues or organizations outside of the synagogue, has a far more significant effect than do Jewish friendship circles. Jews associating with other Jews for specifically Jewish purposes are major vehicles for general Jewish communal fund raising. Among the varieties of synagogues, those associated with the Conservative movement are the most likely to participate in pan-Jewish campaign efforts while many of the Orthodox maintain and support specifically Orthodox charities (religious schools, homes for the aged, health organizations, etc.), some in exclusion of nondenominational Jewish philanthropies. The Jewish household most likely to be solicited is older, affiliated with a Conservative synagogue and with other Jewish organizations as well, and earns a high income. Accessibility to the campaign is in part a function of the nature of the campaign leadership itself calling upon its age cohort. This is, in part, a strategic decision of the campaign to go after those whose means make it most likely that they will give and a function of the motivated willingness of the rank and file of Jews to be solicited through formal affiliation with the organized Jewish community.

The second part of this analysis (presented in table 4-2, column B) examines the success of the campaign net of solicitation; that is, by using solicitation as one of the control variables, we predict giving to the campaign as a function of the same variables used to predict solicitation. As would be expected, solicitation itself is the most powerful predictor of giving. This simply underscores our continued assertion that without asking there is no giving. Among the secular variables, both age and income have significant effects over and above having been solicited.

The effect of age is not peculiarly Jewish. In their analysis of general American patterns of charitable giving, Hodgkinson and Weitzman (1986, 30) note that "religious giving tends to increase with age both in the amounts given and as a percentage of income, indicating a sustained level of generosity even if, for example, average total income drops after 65 years of age." Among the Jewish variables, Conservative synagogue members are the most likely to give and Orthodox the least likely. Members of non-synagogue Jewish organizations give as well as Jews whose intimate friendship circle is largely or totally Jewish.

In sum, those who are most likely to respond positively to a solicitation to the campaign are older, higher-income members of Conservative synagogues who are members of other Jewish organizations as well, and whose friends are Jews. These are the people who form the backbone of the campaign, upon whom participation in the campaign can be depended. Insofar as the Federated campaign and its associated organizations form the government of American Jewry (though a weak government), these are the citizens who carry the burden. These are the folks that traditional Jewish language calls *Amkha*, the People! They are the rank and file of the campaign and probably the rank and file of many other pan-Jewish communal efforts.

Dividing the Pie

In the previous section we presented parallel analyses of Jewish and non-Jewish campaigns and then dwelt on the determinants of solicitation within the Jewish campaign. Our emphasis was on the determinants of the act of solicitation. We included in our analysis givers and nongivers. In this section we turn to another aspect of Jewish philanthropy, the question of dividing the pie or market share. If Jews have continued to donate money as they have in the past, but the receipts of the major Jewish campaigns are down, then clearly they are dividing the pie differently. Jewish market share is slipping.

The question we turn to here is how to account for Jewish market share. The dependent variable is the proportion of total contributions made that are given to Jewish charities. This would include the Federated campaign as well as any other Jewish philanthropy. The analysis is restricted to those households that reported giving some charitable gift during the previous twelve-month period (see table 4-3). (Because of the skewed nature of the distribution, the logarithm of proportion given to Jewish philanthropies is taken as the dependent variable.)

Much of the outcome offers little surprise. Those who are most involved in Jewish life give most of their money to Jewish causes. The Orthodox, who were laggards in the Federated campaign, are the most likely to give to Jewish campaigns, generally followed closely by the Conservatives, with the Reform adherents far behind. Members of Jewish organizations and Jews with Jewish friendship circles are the most generous to Jewish causes. Age ceases to have direct effect, and

Table 4-3. *Dividing the Pie—Proportion of Philanthropic Dollar Given to Jewish Causes (New York Population Study, 1981)*

Generation 2[1]	*
Generation 3[1]	*
Generation 4[1]	−.068
Years in residence	*
Age	*
Log income	−.210
Orthodox synagogue member[2]	.157
Conservative synagogue member[2]	.141
Reform synagogue member[2]	.056
Member Jewish organization outside of synagogue	.091
Number of 3 closest friends who are Jewish	.129
R² =	.133

[1]Reference category = generation 1.
[2]Reference category = not synagogue member.
*Coefficient does not reach .01 level of significance.

the negative zero order relationship with the fourth generation is reversed, that is, the negative effect of generation four is a function of the distance of the cohort from Jewish communal involvement. When this generation is involved, they do give. Neighborhood residential stability, which made people accessible to the Federated campaign, has no effect on the division of the pie.

The most intriguing, surprising, and disconcerting finding is the strong negative effect of household income. The higher the income, the lower the proportion of the household's total charitable contribution given to Jewish causes. It is also the case, as Hodgkinson and Weitzman report, that since 1981, the very rich have been cutting back on their total charitable giving. The Jewish charities then, with their dependence upon big givers, face a twofold loss: (1) they participate in the general decline of giving characteristic of the American rich, and (2) they lose a significant fraction of their gifts to non-Jewish campaigns.

At several points we noted the Federated campaign's decision to go after the high-income households. It turns out that other philanthropic bodies work with the same strategy, and on balance they win. The Jewish philanthropies collectively are losing their potentially largest contributors to non-Jewish causes. While we have no certain explanation for this phenomenon, one theoretical line at least has the ring of plausibility, that is, the effect of "club membership."

Large gifts are noted in public ceremonies, are memorialized by public plaques, and are attached to esteemed professorships. When it comes to large gifts, the Jewish community has to compete with the powerful public relations apparatus of the concert hall, the opera house, the university, the research library. It was not that long ago that few university buildings or museum pavilions were associated with Jewish names. Now a walk through America's great cultural institutions is a walk through a Jewish hall of fame. What can the Jewish community offer by way of distinctions and honors comparable to those offered by the venerable cultural institutions? While few Jews can point to distinguished colonial lineage, they are now in a position to associate themselves with those who can. The ubiquitous annual dinners mounted by Jewish causes with their distinguished "honorees" are poor competition for the elegant occasions sponsored by the major secular cultural institutions. Honorary degree ceremonies, redolent with their studied pseudo medieval costume, marches, medals, now domesticated mace, and escutcheon, are a difficult act to follow. To be honored by one's alma mater, when one was barely tolerated there as a young undergraduate, offers enormous satisfaction and vindication.

Does this mean that the Jewish community should not go after "quality gifts" and big givers? Probably not. What it does mean is that competition for the attention of these givers is keen and in all likelihood will get keener. As the ever more attractive world of high-culture giving becomes accessible to Jews, the relative attractiveness of Jewish causes becomes less and less attractive. With the pie not expanding, the Jewish piece of the pie contracting, the future for major Jewish gifts becomes ever more clouded.

Some Reflections

Without cynicism, one can think of charitable giving as a kind of conspicuous consumption. It is a socially useful sublimation of egocentricity in which the surrender of goods leads to the gaining of the esteem of one's fellow and the grace of one's God. As the primary relations of the clan and village give way to the impersonality of the city and the nation-state, charity loses its face-to-face intimacy and becomes institutionalized in large-scale organizations designed to solicit funds and then turn them over to others to use for some public good.

Responding to social change, the Jewish community has produced a dense network of charitable bodies whose purpose is to maintain Jewish communal institutions and serve the religious, cultural, health, and welfare needs of the Jews. For the most part, no longer able to depend upon traditional religious sentiment and increasingly exposed to competition from non-Jewish causes, the community has found it necessary to devise strategies to solicit funds and to compete in the charitable arena. Jewish charities must find Jews and then motivate them to give.

The Jewish community is caught up in a self-contradiction. It fights for a neutral society in which Jews pay no price for being Jews at the same time that it argues for the legitimacy of Jewish particularism. There is an obvious tension between these goals, a tension that, over time, becomes resolved in favor of universalism. As Jewish communal affiliation weakens and Jewish involvement in the commonweal grows, the accessibility of Jews and their particularist generosity become ever more problematic.

One solution to this problem is the creation of Jewish philanthropies that have a particularist base of givers (Jews) with recipients chosen on universalist grounds: the poor. This sort of solution underlies some of the new Jewish philanthropies described by Silverman elsewhere in this volume.

Another solution lies in the federations' realization that their contributors are likely to be their clientele (see chapter 14). Jewish philanthropy has a self-interested stake in Jewish community building for it is those who are involved with the community who take on the burden of voluntary taxation that Jewish philanthropy has become. The well may not be running dry but its sources have become increasingly distant.

Appendix: The Nine-City Sample

In the absence of an up-to-date study of American Jewry, a sample of metropolitan Jewry was constructed using studies conducted on the nine largest Jewish communities in the United States. These include New York, Boston, Philadelphia, Baltimore, Miami, Cleveland, Chicago, Los Angeles, and Washington, D.C. Where comparable questions were posed, it was possible to merge the data sets. Where this was not possible, the New York data set was analyzed and reported here.

References

Abramson, Harold. "The Religio-Ethnic Factor and the American Experience: Another Look at the Three Generation Hypothesis." *Ethnicity*, 2(2), (June 1975).

Chiswick, Barry. "An Economic Analysis of Philanthropy." In *Contemporary Jewish Philanthropy in America*, edited by Barry A. Kosmin and Paul Ritterband, 3–15. Savage, Md.: Rowman & Littlefield, 1991.

Edmondson, Brad. "Who Gives to Charity?" *American Demographics* (November 1986).

Feldstein, Don. "The Changing Client System of Jewish Federations. In *Contemporary Jewish Philanthropy in America*, edited by Barry A. Kosmin and Paul Ritterband, 219–29. Savage, Md.: Rowman & Littlefield, 1991.

Fruehauf, Norbert. "The Bottom Line: Major Gifts to Federation Campaigns." In *Contemporary Jewish Philanthropy in America*, edited by Barry A. Kosmin and Paul Ritterband, 173–85. Savage, Md.: Rowman & Littlefield, 1991.

Heilman, Samuel C. "Tzedakah: Orthodox Jews and Charitable Giving." In *Contemporary Jewish Philanthropy in America*, edited by Barry A. Kosmin and Paul Ritterband, 133–44. Savage, Md.: Rowman & Littlefield, 1991.

Hodgkinson, Virginia Ann, and Murray S. Weitzman. *The Charitable Behavior of Americans*. Washington, D.C.: Independent Sector, 1986.

Lenski, Gerhard. *The Religious Factor* (Revised ed.). New York: Doubleday Anchor, 1963.

Rimor, Mordechai, and Gary A. Tobin. "The Relationship Between Jewish Identity and Philanthropy." In *Contemporary Jewish Philanthropy in America*, edited by Barry A. Kosmin and Paul Ritterband, 33–56. Savage, Md.: Rowman & Littlefield, 1991.

Ritterband, Paul, and Steven M. Cohen. "Will the Well Run Dry?" *Response*, (Summer 1979): 9–17.

Silberstein, Richard, Paul Ritterband, Jonathan Rabinowitz, and Barry A. Kosmin. *Giving to Jewish Philanthropic Causes: A Preliminary Reconnaissance*. (Reprint Series no. 2). New York: CUNY Graduate Center, North American Jewish Data Bank, (November 1987). (Originally published in *Spring Research Forum: Working Papers*, Washington, D.C.: Independent Sector and United Way Institute.)

Silverman, Ira. "The New Jewish Philanthropies." In *Contemporary Jewish Philanthropy in America*, edited by Barry A. Kosmin and Paul Ritterband, 205–16. Savage, Md.: Rowman & Littlefield, 1991.

Part 3

Special Philanthropy

5

Tradition and Transition in Jewish Women's Philanthropy

Madeleine Tress and Barry A. Kosmin

The 187 area-based Jewish federations are the major focus of contemporary Jewish communal philanthropy in the United States and Canada. In 1986, there were 816,747 individual contributions to the annual campaign and some 1,500,000 people received services from the more than 1,300 social agencies these gifts support. The aggregate cost of services in the Jewish voluntary sector, including federation allocations, government and third-party payments, client fees, etc. was about $4 billion in 1986.

The federation is both a fund raising and allocating institution. Around half its annual campaign dollars are sent to Jews in need around the world through its partnership with the United Jewish Appeal. However, it is the local level and particularly women's role in it, rather than the associated national and international activities of federations that is the focus of this chapter. At the local level the federation is both a charitable and an operative decision-making body touching upon local services usually including a hospital, a family and children's service, institutional and other programs for the aged, community centers, and Jewish educational and vocational agencies.

The impetus for this philanthropic endeavor and the moral basis for federations lies deep in Jewish values and history. It is epitomized by the biblical concept of *tzedakah*, which can be translated as charity but also as righteousness or justice. The traditional universalist Jewish concerns for the dignity of human beings, social justice and the importance of community appear to harmonize with the contemporary American context whereby a significant role is afforded to the non-profit and voluntary sector in the social and communal realms of society.

The requirement that both males and females should engage in charitable behavior and good deeds was recognized by Jewish leaders from medieval times. Their modes of participation, however, were differentiated in *halakha* (Jewish law), where women were exempt from the obligation to perform the commandments or *mitzvot* having communal requirements at specific times. Hence, they were excluded from religious activities, including study, which occurred in the public sphere (Baskin 1985) and, by extension, the public sphere itself.

A woman's activity was confined to the private realm of home and family since she spent a good part of her adult life giving birth to and raising children. In contrast, a man's function was in the public sphere of business and politics. Rosaldo (1974, 22) suggests that it was the gender relations of traditional societies that resulted in a "differentiation of domestic and public spheres of activity." *Halakha*, then, was a reflection of this situation rather than a determinant of it. Indeed, it is because of a woman's "natural" function that the rabbinic literature credits her with more compassion and concern for the unfortunate than men (Baskin 1985, 6).

The rise of mercantile capitalism raised the position of Jewish women in Europe during the Renaissance period. As print capitalism developed, a distinctive literature for women emerged (e.g., *Mitzvat Nashim* published in Venice in 1552; *Seder Nashim* published in Prague in 1629; and *Mitzvat Ha'Nashim* published in Hanau in 1677), creating an "imagined community" (Anderson 1983) of Jewish women united by language and common cause of caretakers. However, most contemporary authorities now discount the exaggerated claims of almost universal female literacy in Hebrew made by Roth (1934).

All of these "women's" books emphasized their gender-related charitable obligations. Schultz (1987) reports that the most famous of these was *Ze'enah Ure'enah*, a Yiddish language companion book first published in Lublin, Poland in 1590 and written by Rabbi Jacob ben Isaac Ashkenazi. It was a best seller for three hundred years and went through 210 editions including translations into Latin, Italian, French, Hungarian, German, English, and Hebrew. It is significant that in this religious "guide book" communal interests are foremost when the rules of social behavior are emphasized. For instance, not only is the reader told that giving charity extends one's life expectancy, but in the earliest extant edition of 1622 the *Eshet Chayil*, or worthy woman, "is prepared to work day and night or to trade day and night to maintain her home, and to give charity to the poor from what she has produced or earned (*was sie desarbet oder gewint*)."

The early economic roles of Jewish women, such as trading, transcended their "natural" function as caretakers. Finkelstein reports that the sixteenth-century Jewish legal movement toward women's rights "had its origins and compelling force largely in the fact that women began to occupy a prominent position in the economic world" (379; see also Falk 1966). While she had more movement than non-Jewish women, she was still limited as a European Jew in the period preceding the French Revolution.

The Napoleonic code notwithstanding, there was a regression in Jewish gender roles during the nineteenth century. The post-1850 *Eschet Chayil* only "works day and night to maintain her home and gives charity to the poor" (cited in Carlebach 1987, 43).

Nevertheless, women were entering the labor force during that period in both the "feminine occupations" such as teaching or nursing, and office worker and consumer goods production as well. Simply stated, her work in the private sphere had become socialized so that she was engaged in many of the same things she had done in the household, albeit in a new locale and under new conditions (MacKenzie 1986, 86).

The women's movement in the last third of the twentieth century represents, then, not only a demand for equality or parity in the public sphere, but also—in the case of Jewish women—a reassertion of the earlier sixteenth-century political agenda.

Given the combination of a long-standing endorsement of an explicit women's role in communal philanthropy as well as women's entry into the public sphere, however limited it may be, the early establishment of women's divisions in federations is not surprising. The united Jewish community campaign came into its own in the late 1930s and by the late 1940s women's divisions were common. By 1976, women were raising $52.7 million or 11.2 percent of the total. In 1986, 105 women's divisions raised $93,422,753 or 12.2 percent of the regular campaign total. However, women's gifts numbered 273,588 or 33.5 percent of the total number of gifts (CJF 1986). Since not every federation has a women's division and many women donate through other divisions such as professional or business groupings, these figures actually underestimate the input of women. No figures are available on federation volunteers for Super Sunday, phonathons, or other forms of mass solicitation, but if other areas of Jewish social activity and other general observations are to be believed, then women are the majority of volunteers in general fund raising. Certainly they often chair such events. In addition, in fifty-four cities in 1986, women pledged $1,529,127 toward the Project Renewal Campaign, which assists underprivileged neighborhoods in Israel by twinning them with local federations.

The relationship between women and voluntarism has been a strong one since modern philanthropy's early days. Gold (1971) argues that women were disengaged from the public sphere "with their own eager cooperation" in the form of voluntarism (533) and that its role was as much social and psychological as it was for helping those less fortunate than they.

The archetypical volunteer was a suburban woman, married to a professional or executive, with school-aged children. If she had worked before marriage, it was in a "helping" profession such as teaching, nursing, or social work. It was more likely, however, that she had no real skills with which she could support anyone, including herself. She felt isolated and anonymous in her milieu, suffering from the "suburban sadness" (Gold 1971, 537) that would impel Friedan (1963) to write *The Feminine Mystique*.

Suburban Jewish women formed structures such as Women's Division so they could fulfill their own social needs for adult contact even though they claimed they were acting out of an obligation to the Jewish community. Personal need notwithstanding, they were financially successful in their endeavor. For example, in 1986, the eight-county New York Women's Division raised over $13.5 million. More than $4 million was raised by Chicago, Los Angeles, and Miami. The best per capita performance ($47 per Jewish individual in the population) was in Detroit, where women raised over $3 million with an average gift of $462. In parts of South Florida, where elderly retired women are a large part of the Jewish population, the Women's Division raises over 30 percent of the local total. In fact, as can be seen from table 5-1, women are generally a much more significant force in small communities.

Though money is raised by federations from a reasonably large fraction of the Jewish population, probably from around a third of all households, in general most of the funds come from relatively few

Table 5-1. *Women's Divisions 1986 Regular Campaign Totals*

Population	No. of Feds. Reporting	Total Pledged	Per Capita Gift (Total Jewish Pop.)	% of Total Campaign From Women's Divisions
Large cities	19	$60,116,253	$ 1.27	12.2
Large-Intermediate	25	20,324,089	26.36	19.7
Small-Intermediate	28	8,899,583	34.37	18.3
Small Cities	33	4,082,828	45.03	22.1
	105	$93,422,753	$17.51	12.2

people. Around 1 percent of the gifts account for 40 percent of the total funds raised while 3 percent account for around 70 percent of the money donated. Women's divisions are generally must less polarized or dominated by a handful of "big givers" than the regular campaign, though there are special national groups for women "big givers," that is, the Ruby Division for $10,000 and over and the Lion of Judah for donors of over $5,000.

In real terms, allowing for inflation and economic growth, the general campaign has been flat over the last ten years. That one area showing major real growth in federation philanthropy has been endowment funds. These grew from under $200 million in 1975 to $1.4 billion in 1986. Unfortunately, no figures are available by gender on the endowment sector. Nevertheless, in the mid-1980s federations began to take seriously the increasing importance of business and career women as well as the wealthy widow as potential significant donors. They have initiated women's endowment seminars and courses using evocative titles such as "A Woman and Her Money: Pride, Priorities, Power."[1]

However, as the above figures illustrate, it is in the area of personnel power rather than economic power that women's contribution is largely acknowledged. Given the high level of residential mobility among American Jews, the need to recruit and involve newcomers to communities is constant (see Kosmin, Ritterband and Scheckner 1987 for data on the high volume of geographical movement). Over 80 percent of volunteers in federation outreach or "Shalom" programs are women. Certainly in the larger cities the women's divisions were quicker to see the potential of the suburbs and peri-urban areas than the federation leadership as a whole. The women volunteers' greater social awareness has resulted from their much earlier move away from mere solicitation toward the concept of "community building" composed of year-round education and social programming as well as recruitment and campaign planning. Again, there is in these programs much more infusion of local issues and concern for the local community. This contrasts with the traditional men's leadership whose primary concern has been Israel.

We believe that much of the local emphasis is due to the more potentially isolating circumstances of women vis-à-vis the public and private spheres. However, there is an area beyond pure philanthropy and social activities that is more controversial and difficult, especially in Jewish society. This, of course, is the area of power and politics. The place of women, as defined by the rabbinical tradition, is much more circumscribed in the political field largely because most of the medieval authorities, such as Maimonides, emerged from Islamic societies.

Maimonides, also known as the Rambam, gave a ruling that "all appointments to positions of authority in Israel" were restricted to men (*Hilkhot Melakhim* 1:5). (For a comprehensive treatment of this theme, see Biale 1986.) Contemporary modern Orthodox thinkers have expanded this a little to suggest that it is acceptable in *halakha* (Jewish law) for women to have an influence on decision making; that is, they can be voters or even advisory members of decision-making groups, but not leaders per se. As recently as 1987, Dr. Sir Immanuel Jakobovits, the British chief rabbi, had declared that, in the Orthodox communities under his jurisdiction, "if what the women want is full participation, they can and will have everything. If what they speak is equal rights in a spurious quest for 'women's liberation,' they will have nothing" (Jakobovits 1987, 5).

Given this historical and political background and the federation concern for consensus in the Jewish community, it took a long time for the issue of women in leadership roles to emerge. This was despite the fact that not only do Orthodox Jews comprise less than 10 percent of American Jewry, but indeed the Orthodox have traditionally been underrepresented in federation leadership.

Women volunteers were the functional equivalent of serious community-service professionals. Working on the periphery, they emphasized an anonymous collective approach, more comfortable with private discussions than speaking up at a board or staff meeting (Daniels 1988; Martin 1989). Hence, through the 1960s, women leaders were largely unknown.

Women's political issues did eventually emerge at the 1972 Council of Jewish Federations' (CJF) General Assembly. Jacqueline Levine, then president of the Women's Division of the American Jewish Congress, called for women to be given access to "higher levels of decision- and policy-making." At that time there were very few women board members, and there were no women presidents. This situation was to change quite rapidly in the 1970s as shown in table 5-2. In 1986, there were forty-three women presidents of federations and the council itself elected a woman president, Shoshana Cardin, in 1984. Moreover, over two of the three most recent presidents of the massive New York federation have been women.

This rapid breakthrough was of course related to the women's movement, which made Jewish women increasingly assertive within their own communities. One result was a movement toward monitoring women's participation. This led to three surveys of female representation in the governance of federations.

The 1986 survey upon which we shall report in some detail gained responses from ninety-two federations, mostly the larger ones with professional staffs. Among these ninety-two individual respondents, forty-two were women and fifty were men (Kosmin 1989; see Kosmin and Scheckner 1986, for the complete findings). The most dramatic changes recorded in the period since 1975 have been the growth of women presidents and treasurers. There are now three times as many women presidents in 1975 so that today one in five of federation presidents is a woman. As table 5-2 demonstrates, the growth in the number of women treasurers is even more dramatic. They have increased more than eight times and now represent a quarter of all holders of this office. The board position with the highest percent of

Table 5-2. *Percentage of Women as Board Members and Officers by Year*

	1975	*1979*	*1986**
Officers/Board members	17.3%	24.7%	28.8%
Presidents	6.2	17.1	20.0**
Vice Presidents	21.4	23.4	28.0
Treasurers	3.1	18.4	25.3
Asst. Treasurers	na	na	29.0
Secretaries	43.1	39.5	54.4
Asst. Secretaries	na	na	37.1
Executive Committee	16.5	22.7	27.6
Board of Directors	na	na	28.5

*Number of completed surveys was 92.

**For the Office of President we have information from 187 federations.

women is that of secretary (54.4%), where a majority are now women. Overall, the proportion of women in the governance of federations, the combined total of officers and board members, has increased by two-thirds from 17.3 percent of all board members in 1975 to 28.8 percent in 1986.

The 1979 findings show that the number of women in leadership positions had increased substantially over 1975. However, it also indicated that women were still largely confined to the traditional roles of secretaries and members of social-welfare committees. The follow-up study covering 1986 found that the gradual entry of women into key federation posts, which was a feature of the 1970s, is continuing.

Women's general rate of participation reflects more their percentage of all donors rather than the lower level of campaign in 1986. Since many people sit on more than one committee, our survey asked for the total of individuals on committees. Here women are slightly more likely to "wear several hats" than men. As table 5-3 indicates, women on all other miscellaneous committees are 50.5 percent. This high percentage is due in part to the inclusion of women's committees in that category.

As chairpersons of the key committees women have been well represented. It was difficult to determine this accurately since many committee chairs are shared by two or more people, and many key committees are divided into subcommittees in some communities. Nevertheless, approximately 43 percent of the key communities have at least one woman chairing each of the key committees.

On the individual committee level women are still poorly represented in the areas of finance and endowment. Only 15.3 percent and 17.9 percent respective of those committee members are women. Nevertheless, on the committee level, the greatest jump has recently occurred in campaign committees. In 1975, only 12.1 percent of the committee members were women; in 1979, the figure was 19.8 percent; but in 1986, it was 28.3 percent women. In the area of campaign some federations reported separate women's divisions and thus could not effectively state the number of women on the campaign committee. Our survey had the campaign and overall campaign listed separately. However, many communities with no separate campaign divisions simply combined the two.

Of the key committees, both social planning and community relations are about 38 percent female. Here it must be borne in mind that some communities combined allocations with social planning. In the other communities, those dealing with social issues like aging, youth,

Table 5-3. *Percentage of Women on Federation Committees by Year*

	1975	1979	1986
Key Committees:			
Campaign	12.1	19.8	28.3
Overall Campaign	na	na	26.4
Allocations	23.4	28.4	34.2
Social Planning			38.6
Community Relations	34.0	37.2	38.3
Total of Key Committees	na	27.6	33.0
Other Committees:			
Human Resource/Leadership Dev.	na	na	47.8
Endowment			17.9
Finance			15.3
Education			42.2
Social Services			49.1
Youth			49.1
Singles			40.9
Aging			51.7
All Others			50.5
Total Committee Members	na	30.3	36.3
Total Individuals on Committees	na	na	35.6

and social services all report about a 50 percent membership of women. This does not include women's committees that are, by definition, almost 100 percent women.

Taken together, the data indicate that even in the volunteer sector, women's role is confined mostly to the traditional realm. Hence, the committees in which they serve still indicate a socialization of the private realm, albeit with new parameters, viz., a committee structure.

In the attitudinal areas of the survey there were some interesting results: 100 percent of those responding agreed with the statement "Women can be effective on all levels and areas of federation leadership." Only 31 percent agreed with the statement "Women can be more effective in certain federation leadership posts than in others."

For those agreeing with the statement, we asked in which position they felt women could serve more effectively. Leadership development, major gifts, and education were most often cited. The areas in which the respondents felt women could serve less effectively were finance, budget, and business. Difference of opinion still exists over this issue since "major gifts" appeared on this negative list as well.

One respondent felt tokenism was a problem and that women were less effective "when put in a position because it's time for a woman as opposed to the best person for the job."

In assessing the current climate with regard to women's participation, most respondents felt it was improving, but there were still certain pockets of resistance. Some felt the "old boys" network was the chief hindrance while others thought women themselves do not seek out top leadership positions with any frequency. Some respondents equate money with power and felt as long as that held true women could only rarely achieve top positions or solicit major gifts. However, it is difficult to ascertain how much of the money that women do contribute is their own and how much is their husbands'.

Before the advent of the women's movement, middle-aged women, whose husbands were professionals or executives, carried out the expectations of their class through noblesse oblige. They were a Jewish aristocracy in a federation community court, helping those Jews who were less fortunate than they, but not, of course, sharing in their fate. Their philanthropic efforts—then and now—support the status quo in which they have held relatively privileged positions (despite their dependence on "male" wealth). More drastic social change for themselves as women, as well as their clients, was simply out of the question (Daniels 1988; Gold 1971; Martin 1989).

Nevertheless, women who responded to our survey demonstrated tendencies toward a feminist/activist perspective. While at times citing subtle examples of sexism, these women felt that federations as a whole were not doing enough to speed the process of increasing the number of women in high positions, yet the area of recruitment of women seems increasingly problematic particularly because of their changing world and career patterns. In addition, questions remained as to whether women would redefine the federation mainstream once they entered it.

The difficulties seem greatest at the large and the large intermediate city federations. The small city and especially the volunteer-directed federations show greater attention to women's roles. In some very small communities, every capable adult, regardless of sex, is needed for the federation to operate effectively.

The issue of the place and role of married couples has often been regarded as an important factor in federation work. Our survey included a question explaining this issue: "Does the role of the husband affect the role of the wife?" Of course, there are cases where one spouse has objected to the other's heavy commitment to federation.

Increasingly changing social patterns offset this effect somewhat since, with the delay in marriage age seen over the past two decades, there are some single women taking leadership roles. This is in addition to the number of divorced women and widows who are involved.

Nevertheless, most federation activity is still directed toward women who have men in their lives, and families as well. A review of the CJF Women's Division *Ideas Bazaar*, since its initiation nearly a decade ago, indicates that many activities still occur during standard business hours and that the social/fund raising galas are geared toward heterosexual couples. Despite the existence of gay and lesbian congregations in most major cities as well as Jewish gay and lesbian societies on most major college campuses (Fishman 1988), Women's Division lesbians are still "in the closet," that is, they simply do not exist.

Hence, women's role in federations are largely effected by that of their husbands' although this effect should not be mistaken for influence. Many of our respondents report women achieving higher status than their husbands in federation with the husband's activity or inactivity having little effect. This may be due, in part, to their husbands subsidizing their "careers" as federation volunteers. Others state that the high status of the husband is most responsible for bringing women up through the ranks, and conversely women have helped their husbands along. There now appear to be some situations where women are, in effect, competing against their husbands for board seats in much the same way that women compete against other women.

One significant finding from the data was that the hierarchy or rank order of women's representation in terms of officers and committees is not influenced by the size of the community. In all types of communities, women are more likely to be secretaries than presidents, and on human resource rather than finance committees. Nevertheless, there is a relationship between community size and women's leadership roles. The conclusion from the evidence is that the smaller the community the greater the likelihood that women will be involved or incorporated into the leadership level of the federation. Communities of under 15,000 population are likely to be short of potential candidates for positions, which makes the entry of women much easier. Within the category of large federations, the female proportion of the leadership does not vary greatly by area, nor is there any differential due to the influence of the age or wealth of the federation.

Our general conclusion from the 1986 survey was that there appears to be a consensus in the federation movement over the place of women in leadership roles alongside a low acceptance of a growing role for women. We are now perhaps ready to look at some of the realities and dilemmas facing federations as they try to deal with the new balance of gender roles. One obvious reality is that women are as differentiated by age, income, and outlook as men. Women's divisions have to balance the requirements of professional and business women on the one hand with those in less prestigious or lower paid occupations and of both groups with the interest of homemakers. The obvious areas for conflict are over meeting times—evenings versus lunches—and over pricing policies and volunteer assignments.

Federations are aware that they are not too successful with younger women and have tried to rectify this through programming as evident in the content and range of programs presented in the CJF Women's Division *Ideas Bazaar*. If one analyzes the average leadership development group, two clear themes emerge. One is an emphasis on the "shared heritage," an educational component related to Israel and Jewish history. Another theme is personal development through courses on the techniques of facilitation, solicitation, meeting and communication skills, public speaking, delegation, and time management. Obviously this is meant to enhance women's abilities in key leadership areas such as negotiation, budgets, and committee work so that they can participate fully in decision making after they gain admittance to the inner circle of power.

In the area of substantive topics, the speakers and discussions are heavily biased toward intergenerational change, mother-daughter relationships, family life, or to "the emerging Jewish women," and "changing lifestyle of women." A network of Jewish feminist speakers, including a few associated with the publication *Lilith*, are increasingly featured on the women's division lecture circuit.

From the traditional male fund raiser's viewpoint, women's divisions are useful in that they provide "plus-giving," an add-on amount over and above what the husband gives. This assumes that among couples such financial decisions are not jointly made. Moreover, given the fact that even when women go out to work they still earn lower wages and salaries than men, the fund raisers assume that the dominant economic partner makes the household philanthropic decisions. Yet there is little research on how such decisions evolve and who makes them in the modern two-earner dual-career household, with only a handful of federations showing some awareness of such issues (e.g., Los Angeles

1983). In addition, there is little accommodation toward single-parent households in this regard.

The initial response to this attitude in the 1970s in some women's circles was to try to abolish separate women's divisions on the basis that separate can never be equal. Approximately ten federations actually abolished their women's divisions, but nearly all were reinstated during the 1980s. Moreover, professional and business women tended to establish their own groups within the women's divisions rather than join trade campaign divisions. Part of the move toward reinstatement was a realization common among most minority groups that they need to build up self-confidence and solidarity within their group before they can go out to compete equally in the world, hence the type of educational programs described above. Indeed, in practice, many potential women leaders found it easier to emerge from the women's division. This secure base facilitated their efforts to enter the power nexus by breaking the old-boy network's monopoly of key nominating committees.

What then has the new power and influence of women in federation decision-making achieved beyond token resolutions in favor of the Equal Rights Amendment? A short illustration of the development of one women's issue, day care for children, can provide us with some idea of the real impact on the pattern of federation-funded services. The issue of child care was traditionally seen in the United States in a welfare model as assistance for the poor and unfortunate. The Jewish community—with its emphasis on family ties and values—regarded working mothers as an unfortunate necessity for the casualties of life rather than as a preference. Certainly, when the issue of day care for middle-class, married, career women first emerged in the 1970s, there was a feeling in many circles that this was not a priority concern for the Jewish community. Nor was it to be encouraged and certainly not subsidized except for the poor. However, many of the leading women in federations had emerged from the National Council of Jewish Women (NCJW) that pioneered day care in the general community. NCJW sponsored both the first national publication on day care and the first Head Start program. Using the majorities on many location federation social issues committees (see table 5-3) and on the CJF Community Planning Committee, women accomplished rapid changes in the 1980s.

In April 1983, the Task Force on Jewish Child Care was established by a subcommittee of the CJF Community Planning Committee. In November 1984, they published a report on their survey of existing programs, planning issues, and obstacles (Fuld 1984). This suggested that negative community attitudes toward day care were fast disappearing and no longer were a major obstacle. Day care under Jewish auspices was increasingly acknowledged as a useful recruiter and point of attachment to the organized Jewish community for young families. Moreover, the service offered important opportunities for socialization of young Jews and for Jewish life education. At the 1985 CJF General Assembly a resolution was passed calling for expansion of child care not only by means of federation allocations but also by the governments of the United States and Canada through subsidies and tax breaks. In January 1986, the CJF Special Task Force on Jewish Child Care, chaired by Miriam Schneirov of Philadelphia, issued a strong statement and recommendations that said that this service should be a "high priority agenda item for Jewish federations" and called for schemes to be initiated and expanded.

By this time forty-nine federations, as far apart geographically and socially as Kansas City and Boston, had put considerable energy and resources into all-day care for six thousand children. The leading federation in this area has been Philadelphia, which supports a separate Jewish Child Day Care Services agency on a network of eight day care centers, providing for around eight hundred infants to preschoolers.

Now that women are beginning to taste the fruits of power in federations, what are the real issues?[2] First, the federations have still not incorporated the baby boom generation into their system. This is, obviously, a rather large cohort of women. Furthermore, they are more likely to be single or divorced and in the work force than the older women and women of independent means, on whom the federations still concentrate. Moreover, the young women volunteers who enter federations are still uncomfortable with some aspects of the style of the women's divisions. These younger women also want more power than the older women, and the men, think they deserve.

The male leadership and staff often fear that the women will take over. They perceive the women as having more time, more commitment, and more focus than the traditional male leader. They challenge the tradition whereby the term "leader" is used in such circles as a synonym for large donor. Certainly on average, women leaders take their roles more seriously, asking more questions, and "hanging around" the office much more. They are less willing to be the passive "front men," reading someone else's speeches, often favored by many federation executives. Perhaps this is because they failed to be socialized fully into the "big giver equals leader" model. Instead, they see their roles as active participants in the federation decision-making process.

However, some executives have a real fear that as the women take over the turf and an "old girls" network forms, the men will withdraw along with their greater economic resources. This is a danger that has to be reconsidered. In part such fears would be reduced if there were more young men attracted simultaneously with the entry of women. Some of the anxiety also could be reduced if there were more women executive directors. At present there are only twenty or so, mainly in small federations. An additional result of the women's greater success on the voluntary rather than the professional side is that it has produced a potential gender and class conflict between upper-class female volunteers and middle-class male executives.

The political conclusions from this analysis would seem to suggest that feminist calls for "a completely different system—egalitarian, democratic, open to people and ideas" (Cantor 1985, 13), though fine rhetoric probably will not serve to enhance the position of women. Paradoxically weak political systems with questionable legitimacy are easier for minorities to access than coherent democracies guarded by effective bureaucratic gate keepers. (See, e.g., Kosmin 1982 for an example involving the English working class; Ritterband 1983 as applied to Black Americans.) For example, we saw that the Women's Division in Detroit is the most successful philanthropically, yet it operates within a very effective fund raising federation. Hence, women in Detroit have failed, relative to most other federations, in gaining entry into the power elite. Women comprise only 14 percent of Detroit's officers and board members compared with 25 percent in all large cities. They have zero membership on the Finance Committee and hold only 1 percent of committee chairs compared with 43 percent of federation committees nationally (Passon 1987).

The moral to be learned perhaps is to seek Bastilles to storm—empty symbolic shells—rather than well fortified strongholds of male supremacy. Feminists could then use the federation structure for their own ends. Once inside they could gain insights into the whole nature of voluntarism in general and its dependence on the unpaid labor of women like themselves. In addition, they could redefine the general federation agenda once they had entered the mainstream so that they could lead the Jewish community—rather than tail it—on crucial social issues.

Yet, if we move beyond Jewish federations to American philanthropy in general, we can typify it as having a rather confused ideology, idiosyncratic structures, and an archaic agenda. Even more, we could suggest that the voluntary sector as a whole evidences a lack of cohesion when compared with the public and private sectors. This, in turn, makes it vulnerable and so easier a target for those seeking power in order to promote social change.

Notes

1. A May 1987 program from the Federation Endowments Corporation and Women's Leadership Board of the Federation of Jewish Agencies of Greater Philadelphia.
2. We are indebted for many of these insights to Sue Stevens, Director of the CJF Women's Division.

Bibliography

Anderson, Benedict. *Imagined Communities. Reflections on the Origin and Spread of Nationalism.* London and New York: Verso, 1983.

Baskin, Judith. "The Separation of Women in Rabbinic Judaism." In *Women, Religion, and Social Change,* edited by Yvonne Yazbeck Haddad and Ellison Banks Findly, 3–18. Albany, N.Y.: State University of New York, 1985.

Biale, Rachel. *Women and Jewish Law.* New York: Schocken, 1986.

Cantor, Aviva. "Power Plays: Breaking the Male Monopoly of Jewish Community Leadership." *Lilith,* 14 (1985).

Carlebach, Julius. "The Story of a Book for Jewish Women." *L'Eylah,* 23 (1987).

[CJF]. *Fund Raising Survey: Women's Divisions, 1986.* New York: Council of Jewish Federations, September 1986.

Daniels, Arlene Kaplan. *Invisible Careers: Women's Civic Careers from the Volunteer World.* Chicago, Ill.: University of Chicago, 1988.

Falk, Z. W. *Jewish Matrimonial Law in the Middle Ages.* New York: Oxford University, 1966.

Finkelstein, Louis *Jewish Self-Government in the Middle Ages.* Westport, Conn.: Greenwood Press, 1924.

Fishman, Sylvia Barack. "The Changing American Jewish Family in the 80s." *Contemporary Jewry,* 9(2) (Fall 1988): 1–34.

Friedan, Betty N. *The Feminine Mystique.* New York: W. W. Norton, 1963.

Fuld, Joan. *Child Day Care under Jewish Auspices.* New York: Community Planning Department, Council of Jewish Federations, November 1984.

Gold, Doris B. "Women and Voluntarism." In *Women in Sexist Society. Studies in Power and Powerlessness*, edited by Vivian Gornick and Barbara K. Moran, 533–54. New York: Basic Books, 1971.

Ideas Bazaar (Vol. 1–9). New York: Women's Division, Council of Jewish Federations, 1980–89.

Jakobivits, Dr. Sir Immanuel. "Women in Community Service." *L'Eylah* (1987).

[Los Angeles]. *Women in Federation and Agency Leadership.* Los Angeles, Calif.: Jewish Federation Council of Greater Los Angeles, 1983.

Kosmin, Barry A. "Political Identity in Battersea." In *Living in South London*, edited by S. Wallman, 17–50. London: Gower for the London School of Economics, 1982.

———. "The Political Economy of Gender in Jewish Federations." *Contemporary Jewry*, 10(1) (Spring 1989): 17–31.

Kosmin, Barry A., Paul Ritterband, and Jeffrey Scheckner. "Jewish Population in the United States, 1986." In *American Jewish Yearbook 1987* edited by David Singer and Ruth Seldin, 34–56. New York: American Jewish Committee, 1987.

Kosmin, Barry A., and Jeffrey Scheckner. *The Place of Women in Leadership of Federations, 1975–1986.* New York: Council of Jewish Federations, 1986.

MacKenzie, Suzanne. "Women's Responses to Economic Restructuring: Changing Gender, Changing Space." In *The Politics of Diversity: Feminism, Marxism and Nationalism* edited by Roberta Hamilton and Michele Barrett, 80–100. London: Verso, 1986.

Martin, Theodora Penny. "Modest and Muted Managers." Review of *Invisible Careers: Women's Civic Careers from the Volunteer World* by Arlene Kaplan Daniels. *Contemporary Sociology*, 18(6) (November 1989): 870–72.

Passon, M. *The Status of Women in Federation.* Detroit, Mich.: Women's Division, Jewish Welfare Federation of Detroit, 1987.

Ritterband, Paul. "Community Control and the Black Political Agenda." In *Culture, Ethnicity and Identity: Current Issues in Research*, edited by William C. McCready, New York: Academic Press, 1983.

Rosaldo, Michelle Zimbalist. "Women, Culture, and Society: A Theoretical Overview." In *Women, Culture, and Society*, edited by Michelle Zimbalist Rosaldo and Louis Lamphere, 17–42. Stanford, Calif.: Stanford University, 1974.

Roth, Cecil. "Outstanding Jewish Women in Western Europe (15–17 Centuries)." In *The Jewish Library—Third Series*, edited by Rabbi Leo Jung, 247–65. New York: The Jewish Library Publishing Company, 1934.

Schultz, J. P. "The *Ze'nah Ur'enah*: Torah for the Folk." *Judaism*, 141 (Winter 1987): 84–96.

6

Dimensions of Giving: Volunteer Activity and Contributions of the Jewish Women of Rhode Island

Alice Goldstein

The changing demographic and geographic profile of American Jewry has raised many questions about individual involvement in the formal structure of the Jewish community and about giving patterns (Fruehauf in chapter 11; Ritterband and Silberstein 1988). Of particular concern are the effects of an aging population, increasing Americanization, high levels of geographic mobility, and a decline in the proportions self-employed. As part of the increasing assimilation and secularization of American Jewry, greater involvement in the non-Jewish community is also seen as a threat to both Jewish voluntarism and giving to Jewish causes (e.g., Carroll 1988).

Particularly dramatic changes have characterized Jewish women. Like women in the general American population (Bianchi and Spain 1986), they are better educated than ever before, marry at somewhat later ages, have fewer children, and most dramatically, have entered the labor force in increasing numbers (Goldscheider 1986; Goldscheider and Goldstein 1988; Rappeport and Tobin 1987; Tobin 1986). Young women are delaying marriage and childbearing to achieve career goals. Small children at home do not serve as major deterrents to mothers working outside the home.

Recognizing these changes, much of the leadership of the American organizational sector—both Jewish and secular—that relies on voluntarism has expressed concern about the impact of women's changing roles on membership and volunteer activities among women. Women have also often received special attention in fund raising campaigns. Little empirical research has been undertaken to evaluate the impact of these changes or the interrelations between voluntarism and philanthropy. The most notable research for the general American community has been that of Hodgkinson and Weitzman (1988), who found that volunteering had a direct relation to contributions; people who volunteered came from households that on the average made larger contributions than the households of nonvolunteers. Furthermore, the percentage of income contributed rose directly with the number of hours volunteered. Volunteering and contributions were also directly related to religious commitment, measured by Hodgkinson and Weitzman in terms of attendance at religious services.

Since Hodgkinson and Weitzman found such a strong direct relation between volunteering and contributions, the changing characteristics of the population that enhance or diminish voluntarism are also of immediate concern for evaluating giving. The most important relations identified by them were that the level of voluntarism increased with rising years of schooling, and that levels of voluntarism were lower among those who were employed full time. These findings characterized the population as a whole as well as Jews, and the levels of voluntarism for both were quite similar at about 45 percent. However, a smaller percentage (64 percent) of Jewish households contributed than of households for all religions combined (71 percent). In contributing households, over half of the respondents were volunteers; in noncontributing households, only about one-third volunteered. Whether these patterns hold equally for both men and women cannot be determined from the reports of the Hodgkinson and Weitzman study.

Research on voluntarism and philanthropy focusing specifically on Jews is also scarce, especially in terms of how the two aspects of involvement are related. Using pooled data from the North American Jewish Data Bank, Ritterband and Silberstein (1988) found giving to any cause directly related to age and to income. Data for New York City showed, however, that when the amount contributed is considered, the relation to age is less clear and that to income is reversed. Voluntarism is not considered in this study, nor is gender included as a control variable.

Like Ritterband and Silberstein, Cohen (1983) also investigated the relations between giving and a host of characteristics. Based on his analysis of data for Boston in 1975, he has concluded that education and income are directly related to giving to both Jewish and non-Jewish causes, even when age and other background variables are controlled. Family life cycle has a more inverted-U pattern, however, with younger singles and couples and older singles giving less than those who are parents or older couples. Having preschool children also depresses Jewish giving.

The available research thus points to the complexity of the relations among individual characteristics, voluntarism, and philanthropy. This chapter explores these issues for Jewish women living in Rhode Island in 1987. The study uses data from the 1987 survey of the Jewish population. The survey was based on a sample of 1,455 households throughout the state, chosen both from the records of the Jewish Federation of Rhode Island and through random-digit dial screening of eighteen thousand households in the state. In each household, one adult (age twenty-one or older) was randomly chosen as the respondent. Some questions asked of the respondents covered the characteristics of all members of the household; others pertained specifically to the attitudes and practices of the respondent only. Interviews were completed for 1,129 households. The resulting data for households and individuals were weighted to approximate the total Jewish population of Rhode Island. It is these weighted data that will be used in the current study, and all numbers in the following discussion will be the weighted numbers. (For a detailed review of the study design and the overall findings, see Goldscheider and Goldstein 1988.)

The Rhode Island Jewish community is among the oldest established Jewish communities in the United States and is characterized by considerable variation among areas within the state. Nonetheless, comparison of data on the socio-demographic characteristics of Rhode Island Jewry and of several indicators of Jewishness and identification with the organized Jewish community with those obtained from Jewish communities across the United States indicates general similarities (Goldscheider and Goldstein 1988, 399–412). Differences are due in part to the timing of the various studies and to the fact that the Rhode Island population is somewhat older than most, reflecting the considerable net out-migration from the state. On the whole, therefore, patterns identified for Rhode Island Jewry are likely to be quite typical for other communities as well. This may, in fact, become increasingly true as the populations of other communities come to contain increasingly higher proportions of older persons.

This chapter uses the information obtained from the women respondents. The survey asked about a wide array of their characteristics and attitudes. It also ascertained whether they had engaged in volunteer activity during the year preceding the survey, and how many hours per month such activity involved. In addition, a series of questions was asked about household giving patterns and household income. These questions refer to total amount contributed by all household members and, unlike characteristics, are therefore not directly attributable to the respondents. They can, however, provide a rough indication of the relationships among the individual characteristics and voluntary activities on the one hand and household giving and income on the other.

The information obtained from these questions will be the focus of this analysis. Background variables used to help explain variations in degree of involvement and giving will include age, marital status, secular education, number of young children at home, and labor force status. Number of children under age six and age six to seventeen are included among the background variables because the presence of young children may be a constraint both on the amount of time a woman has available for volunteer activity and on the amount of discretionary funds available for charitable giving. Additionally, several indicators of specifically Jewish background will also be used: years of Jewish education, an index of ritual practices,[1] and frequency of attendance at religious services.[2] The analysis will give attention to voluntarism and contributions for both Jewish and non-Jewish activities.

Attention will turn first to patterns of voluntarism, using both rates of voluntarism (whether a respondent had volunteered at all) and intensity of volunteering (number of hours each month). A similar analysis will then be made for contributions. Finally, the interrelations between voluntarism and contributions will be explored.

Volunteer Activity[3]

The Rhode Island survey asked respondents whether they participated in Jewish and non-Jewish volunteer activities, and how many hours each month they devoted to them. The analysis that follows will use the information obtained from this set of questions and information on age, education, marital status, labor force status, number of children at home, and the three indicators of religious identification to assess the factors determining whether or not women are involved with the organized Jewish and non-Jewish voluntary sector. Number of hours volunteered will then be assessed through regression analysis.

Rates of Voluntarism

Among all women respondents, only 34 percent indicated that they participated in Jewish voluntary activities and even fewer—25 percent—did so in non-Jewish ones (see table 6-1). The percentage of women who volunteered varied directly by age for Jewish activities, rising from a low of 18 percent of the 18–24-year-old women to 45 percent of those age 55–64; it dropped to 24 percent for the oldest group. The variation was much less pronounced for non-Jewish activities, and it peaked much earlier. It rises from 26 percent of the youngest group to 32 percent of those age 35–44, and then declines continuously to 22 percent for the aged.

In general being married is associated with the highest rate of volunteering in Jewish activities (see table 6-2). For non-Jewish volunteer activity, however, the never-married had the highest rate of voluntarism. This differential suggests that Jewish activities are somewhat more geared to married women, and that non-Jewish activities meet the needs of singles more than Jewish ones do. Rates of volunteer activity also show only a weak relation to number of preschool and school-age children (see table 6-3). Nonetheless, rates of voluntarism are generally somewhat higher for women who have children at home than for those who do not.

Rates of voluntarism are consistently higher among the more edu-

Table 6-1. *Percentage of Women Volunteering and Making Contributions by Jewish and Non-Jewish Activities, by Age*

Age	Volunteer Activities		Contributions	
	Jewish	Non-Jewish	Jewish	Non-Jewish
18–24	18.3	26.4	71.2	61.0
25–34	29.4	28.6	82.4	94.8
35–44	35.1	32.1	96.9	90.2
45–54	35.6	25.6	94.4	97.8
55–64	45.2	22.4	100.0	96.3
65 and over	28.1	21.9	96.1	88.9
All ages	33.8	25.3	94.7	92.2

Table 6-2. *Percentage of Women Volunteering and Making Contributions, by Jewish and Non-Jewish Activities, by Marital Status*

	Never Married	Married	Divorced	Widowed
Voluntering in:				
Jewish Activities	23.2	39.0	22.7	25.5
Non-Jewish Activities	32.5	23.9	24.6	23.8
Contributing to:				
Jewish Causes	84.5	95.5	87.9	97.9
Non-Jewish Causes	85.8	93.9	88.1	90.7

Note: In this and most of the subsequent tables, data are presented only for all age groups combined. The age–specific data are available on request.

cated than for those with only high school education, both for Jewish and non-Jewish activities (see table 6-4). The exception is among women with postgraduate education compared to those with a college degree only. These highly educated women may be more concentrated in professional careers that place constraints on the amount of time available for volunteer activity. In fact, although labor force participation in general may be thought to restrict volunteer activity, this is not entirely the case. Part-time workers overall have the highest rates of voluntarism (see table 6-5), and among younger women, full-time workers also volunteer more than those not in the labor force (data not shown in table 6-5). The higher education that women have received in recent decades and their greater participation in employment outside the home therefore does not, in general, seem to have any strong effect on rates of voluntarism.

Other studies (Cohen 1983; Hodgkinson and Weitzman 1988) found that strength of religious identification was directly related to membership in Jewish organizations. A similar pattern appears for volunteering in Jewish activities. For each of the three indicators used here—years of Jewish education (see table 6-6), ritual observance index (see table 6-7), and attendance at religious services (see table 6-8)—high levels of religious identification are strongly associated with higher levels of voluntarism in Jewish activities. These patterns do not characterize non-Jewish activities for which the reverse association is generally the case.

On the whole, rates of volunteer membership are therefore sensitive to a number of sociodemographic and religious characteristics of women, but not always in the hypothesized direction. Number of

Table 6-3. *Percentage of Women Volunteering and Making Contributions, by Jewish and Non-Jewish Activities, by Age and Number of Children under Age 6 and 6–17*

Volunteer Activities

Age and Age of Children	Number of Children (Jewish Volunteer Activities)				Number of Children (Non-Jewish Volunteer Activities)			
	0	1	2	3 or More	0	1	2	3 or More
Children Under 6								
25–34	16.0	31.4	59.1	—	27.6	21.1	36.9	—
35–44	35.6	42.0	11.4	—	31.6	42.4	11.4	—
Children 6–17								
25–34	29.8	37.7	0.0	—	29.2	29.7	15.4	—
35–44	26.1	38.5	36.5	57.8	25.0	43.8	28.9	35.0
45–54	35.2	37.6	16.8	*	23.9	26.1	35.0	*

Contributions

Age and Age of Children	Contribute to Jewish Causes				Contribute to Non-Jewish Causes			
	0	1	2	3 or More	0	1	2	3 or More
Children Under 6								
25–34	71.0	90.2	100.0	—	92.5	95.5	100.0	—
35–44	97.0	94.9	100.0	—	86.9	100.0	100.0	—
Children 6–17								
25–34	81.3	89.6	84.5	—	95.6	87.1	100.0	—
35–44	95.9	96.4	97.8	100.0	97.5	90.8	78.2	100.0
45–54	94.3	91.1	100.0	*	100.0	100.0	57.5	*

*Fewer than 20 cases.

Table 6-4. *Percentage of Women Volunteering and Making Contributions, by Jewish and Non-Jewish Activities, by Education*

	High School	Some College	College	Post-graduate
Voluntering in:				
Jewish Activities	19.3	32.6	43.1	36.4
Non-Jewish Activities	12.5	26.1	29.4	31.7
Contributing to:				
Jewish Causes	94.6	93.8	96.9	93.9
Non-Jewish Causes	90.3	83.7	96.0	96.5

Table 6-5. *Percentage of Women Volunteering and Making Contributions, by Jewish and Non-Jewish Activities, by Labor Force Status*

Labor Force Status	Volunteer Activities		Contributions	
	Jewish	Non-Jewish	Jewish	Non-Jewish
Working full-time	31.3	26.6	91.8	95.4
Working part-time	44.5	26.6	97.5	95.2
Not in labor force	30.8	22.2	95.5	88.6

Table 6-6. *Percentage of Women Volunteering and Making Contributions, by Jewish and Non-Jewish Activities, by Years of Jewish Education*

	Years of Jewish Education				
	None	1–3	4–6	7–9	10 or more
Volunteering in:					
Jewish Activities	25.3	29.1	38.8	35.6	42.2
Non-Jewish Activities	18.3	26.8	19.6	24.5	32.1
Contributing to:					
Jewish Causes	87.6	94.9	97.3	97.9	99.2
Non-Jewish Causes	84.9	93.3	96.7	91.6	96.0

children at home seems to have little direct effect on volunteering, while labor force participation enhances voluntarism, especially for those who work part time. The data also clearly show that the factors affecting patterns of volunteering are different for Jewish and non-Jewish activities.

Table 6-7. *Percentage of Women Volunteering and Making Contributions, by Jewish and Non-Jewish Activities, by Ritual Observance Index*

Level of Ritual Observance	*Volunteer Activities*		*Contributions*	
	Jewish	*Non-Jewish*	*Jewish*	*Non-Jewish*
High	47.3	20.4	98.9	95.6
Medium	37.9	24.1	98.0	91.2
Low	19.9	25.3	88.9	91.2

Table 6-8. *Percentage of Women Volunteering and Making Contributions, by Jewish and Non-Jewish Activities, by Attendance at Religious Services*

Level of Attendance	*Volunteer Activities*		*Contributions*	
	Jewish	*Non-Jewish*	*Jewish*	*Non-Jewish*
Often	62.6	27.6	82.3	96.3
Sometimes	39.0	25.8	75.5	93.5
Seldom	19.7	22.2	88.7	89.2

Intensity of Volunteer Activity

Although analysis of the rate of volunteer activity can suggest a number of factors that affect whether women volunteer, a better measure of the intensity of involvement with the Jewish and non-Jewish community is number of hours volunteered. Respondents were asked how many hours each month they devoted to volunteering. They indicated an average of thirteen hours a month in Jewish activities and ten hours in non-Jewish ones. Half of the women who volunteered in Jewish activities did so for at least ten hours each month; 40 percent spent such amounts of time in non-Jewish activities. To obtain a fuller assessment of the factors affecting the amount of time spent in volunteer work, a regression model is used, using the same independent variables as were discussed above (see table 6-9).

When hours devoted to Jewish volunteer activities are considered, both age and education have a positive, significant impact. This finding is consistent with the earlier findings on rates of voluntarism. By contrast, being in a "not married" category lowers the number of hours volunteered compared to those who are married. Having young children at home has no significant impact on hours volunteered, suggesting that the time constraints involved in caring for children do not affect voluntarism. Nor does working full time have any significant impact. On the other hand, part-time workers volunteer more hours than those not in the labor force.

Table 6-9. *Regression on Number of Hours Devoted to Jewish and Non-Jewish Volunteer Activities (Standardized Beta Coefficients)*

	Jewish	Non-Jewish
Age	0.076*	−0.072*
Education	0.057*	0.051
Marital status[a]		
Never Married	−0.028	0.059*
Divorced	−0.052*	0.004
Widowed	−0.041*	0.119*
Children under 6	0.007	0.005
Children 6–17	0.005	0.035*
Labor Force Status[b]		
Working full-time	−0.028	−0.061*
Working part-time	0.061*	−0.080*
Years of Jewish Education[c]		
1–3 years	−0.058*	0.044*
4–6 years	0.094*	−0.010
7–9 years	0.039*	0.069*
10 or more years	0.056*	0.038*
Ritual Observance Index[d]		
High	0.077*	−0.073*
Medium	0.051*	−0.066*
Attendance at Religious Services[e]		
Often	0.030	−0.032
Sometimes	0.152*	0.030
Number of Non-Jewish Volunteer Hours	0.218*	–
R^2	.130	.033

*Significant at $p<.01$.
[a]Reference group is Married.
[b]Reference group is Not in the Labor Force.
[c]Reference group is None.
[d]Reference group is Low.
[e]Reference group is Seldom.

Almost every dimension of the Jewish identificational variables has a significant, positive impact on hours volunteered.[4] The major exception is one to three years of Jewish education compared to none, where the effect is negative. Cohen's (1983) observation that religious commitment is associated with levels of affiliation also holds for amount of time devoted to Jewish volunteer activities.

Number of hours volunteered in non-Jewish activities was also entered into the equation. Number of hours in Jewish and non-Jewish activities are strongly and positively related. The active involvement of women in non-Jewish volunteer activities does not detract from the hours they devote to Jewish voluntarism.

When non-Jewish volunteer hours are examined, a somewhat different pattern emerges than characterized Jewish volunteer activities. Among the sociodemographic characteristics being considered, only having children under age six, and being never married or widowed compared to being married have a significant positive effect on hours volunteered. Most other characteristics have a weak, generally negative impact, although both full-time and part-time work has a significant negative effect on voluntarism compared to not being in the labor force.

The Jewish identificational variables show a much less consistent pattern than for Jewish volunteer hours. Jewish education most often has a positive relation to non-Jewish voluntarism, while medium or high score on the ritual observance index shows a strong negative effect, as does often attending religious services.

Contributions to Jewish and Non-Jewish Causes

Voluntary activity can be seen as one aspect of showing commitment to a community through the giving of time; another form of involvement is the giving of money. In assessing factors affecting contributions using the Rhode Island data, it must be remembered that questions on household contributions cannot be as directly related to respondent characteristics as volunteering can. This is especially true when the respondents under consideration are women, because in couple households much of household giving is still determined by the husband's status. Nonetheless, insofar as making contributions is a general indicator of commitment to a community and its institutions that is likely to reflect the attitudes of most adults in the household, an assessment of the relation between household giving and individual characteristics can provide valuable insights. Furthermore, women have often been singled out in fund raising campaigns because of their growing numbers in the labor force and their subsequent independent sources of income. A focus on women and giving may thus be particularly relevant in any overall evaluation of the commitment of Jews to their community despite the data constraints.

The rate of giving among Rhode Island Jews is very high: 95 percent

of the women reported that their household had made a contribution
to Jewish causes within one year of the interview, and 92 percent
reported contributions to non-Jewish causes (see table 6-1). These
figures are higher than the 71 percent reported by Hodgkinson and
Weitzman (1988) for the general population, and the 64 percent they
report for Jews. The high rate of giving to Jewish causes characterizes
all age groups from 35–44 and over, but is slightly lower for the 25–34
age group, and lower still among women age 18–24. For contributions
to non-Jewish causes, both the youngest and the oldest age groups
have lower rates, but especially the youngest.

Rates of Contributing

The amount contributed also varies by age and between Jewish and
non-Jewish causes, with the median amount being higher for Jewish
causes in each age category (see table 6-10). For all women, a median
of $293 is given to Jewish causes, ranging from a low of $55 among
those age 18–24 to a high of $447 among the 55–64 year group. The
level drops to $270 among the oldest. By comparison, the median
contribution to non-Jewish causes is only $97 overall, with a low of $26
for the youngest women and a high of $196 for those age 35–44. The
amount of non-Jewish giving declines regularly thereafter, with rising
age.

To explore the factors involved in determining the differing patterns
for contributions to Jewish and non-Jewish causes, attention will turn
first to characteristics affecting rates of giving. In doing so, data are
generally presented for all age groups combined. When exceptional
patterns by age appear, they are discussed in the text even though the
age-specific data are not presented in the tables. Following the discus-

Table 6-10. *Median Amount of Contributions to Jewish and Non-Jewish Causes, by Age*

Age	Jewish	Non-Jewish
18–24	$ 55	$ 26
25–34	105	90
35–44	268	196
45–54	302	151
55–64	447	146
65 and over	270	81
All ages	$293	$ 97

sion of rates, a multivariate approach is used to analyze levels of giving.

Just as voluntary activity was highest among married women, so the rate of giving to Jewish causes is also higher among married women than among those who are never married or divorced (see table 6-2). It is just as high among the widowed, who apparently maintain the rate of giving established while they were married. Giving to non-Jewish causes follows a similar pattern. Interestingly, however, while the percentage giving among the married and widowed is somewhat lower to non-Jewish than to Jewish causes, this differential does not hold for those women who were never married or divorced.

It might be assumed that having young children places some constraints on household income so that charitable giving may be reduced. This does not appear to be the case for either Jewish or non-Jewish causes for those women who have children under eighteen years of age (see table 6-3). In fact, the reverse pattern is generally true. Only for those with children age six to seventeen is there some suggestion of lower percentages giving to non-Jewish causes as the number of children rises, but the pattern is not regular.

Education has only a slight impact on rates of giving to Jewish causes, being somewhat higher among the college educated (see table 6-4). Greater variation characterizes non-Jewish contributions for which education is more directly related to giving. Labor force status, too, shows little variation, although women who work full time are generally less likely to give to Jewish causes than those who work part time (see table 6-5). Especially noteworthy is the very low rate of giving of the youngest women who work full time: only 74 percent report that their households contribute to Jewish causes, compared to 92 percent of all full-time working women. This finding is contrary to what was expected, and suggests that some women who work full time may be doing so because they consider the additional income necessary to meet basic needs.

The patterns are different for contributions to non-Jewish causes, with working women generally having higher rates and those not in the labor force having the lower rates. These differentials are not surprising since women who are employed outside the home are more likely to come into contact with solicitations for funds from the general community. They may also consider giving to non-Jewish causes a necessary part of their career activities. Taken together with the low rate of giving to Jewish causes among the youngest group of women, the data suggest that these young women are more likely to give limited funds to non-Jewish than to Jewish causes.

As was true of the relation between rates of volunteering and the Jewish identification variables, contributions to Jewish causes are also strongly related to years of Jewish education and level of ritual observance. Years of Jewish education and rates of giving are very directly related, rising from 88 percent of those with no Jewish education to 99 percent of those with ten or more years (see table 6-6). The relationship is almost as regular for the rate of giving to non-Jewish causes, except for the decrease among women with seven to nine years of Jewish education. When ritual observance is considered, only having a low level of observance lowers the rate of giving overall (see table 6-7). The rate of non-Jewish contributions also shows a mixed pattern, but with those scoring high on the ritual observance index generally having a higher rate of giving.

Attendance at religious services shows a much more mixed relation to rates of giving, with those who report that they seldom attend having the highest rate of giving to Jewish causes (see table 6-8). Women who report that they sometimes attend services are the most likely to have the lowest rate of giving to Jewish causes. For rates of giving to non-Jewish causes the overall pattern is regular and in the expected direction: women who attend services often have higher rates of giving than those who attend only sometimes or seldom. Apparently, unlike volunteer activity, giving to Jewish causes does not appear to be related to attendance at religious services. This negative relation is surprising since attendance at religious services also suggests contact with institutions that have various fund raising campaigns and therefore provides greater exposure to the possibility of being asked to contribute. A clear explanation is not forthcoming, in part because the information on contributions refers to household rather than individual giving.

Because contributions are obviously influenced by household income, attention turns next to the relation between rate of giving and income (see table 6-11). With the exception of women who report household income under $15,000 and income between $75,000 and $100,000, little variation exists in rate of giving to Jewish causes. The lower percentage giving in the lowest income group is quite understandable, the exception among the higher income group is not easily explained. A similar pattern characterizes giving to non-Jewish causes, but the $75,000 to $100,000 group is no longer an exception. Families in this income category may be allocating more of their resources to non-Jewish causes at the expense of giving to Jewish ones. This possibility may also explain the higher rate of giving to non-Jewish causes for those in the 25–34 age group in every income category. Level of income does not, on the whole, appear to affect the rate of giving to either Jewish or non-Jewish causes.

Another variable affecting the rate of giving is involvement in the voluntary sector. Hodgkinson and Weitzman (1988) found a direct relation between the two: those who volunteer are more likely to give than those who do not volunteer. Others have suggested that a trade-off may exist between giving time and giving money. When the rate of giving is examined by whether women volunteer, some very limited support is given to this latter suggestion (see table 6-12). Women who are engaged in Jewish voluntary activities are somewhat less likely to give to Jewish causes than are those who do not volunteer. Of the volunteers, 82 percent make contributions, compared to 92 percent of the nonvolunteers. The opposite pattern holds for contributions to non-Jewish causes. Women who volunteer are more likely to give than those who do not.

The possibility of a substitution effect suggested by the Jewish giving patterns can be explored further by examination of the actual amount contributed by the number of hours volunteered. If a substitution is occurring, then women who volunteer more hours would contribute less in funds. The data on giving to Jewish causes and volunteering in Jewish activities do not support this possibility (see table 6-13). In fact, no clear relation emerges between giving hours and giving funds; if

Table 6-11. *Percentage of Women Contributing to Jewish and Non-Jewish Causes, by Income*

	Under $15,000	$15,000–24,999	$25,000–39,999	$40,000–54,999	$55,000–74,999	$75,000–99,999	$100,000 and over
Contributing to:							
Jewish Causes	89.6	97.0	92.8	94.9	92.5	74.2	97.9
Non-Jewish Causes	74.0	94.2	93.5	91.5	95.9	100.0	100.0

Table 6-12. *Percentage of Women Contributing to Jewish and Non-Jewish Causes, by Whether They Volunteer in Jewish Activities*

	Volunteers	Does Not Volunteer
Jewish Causes	82.4	92.1
Non-Jewish Causes	96.7	90.1

anything, those who give more in one dimension also contribute more in the other.

Level of Contributions

In order to explore this relation further as well as to obtain insights into the effect of all the characteristics discussed above on the amount of money contributed, a regression model is used. In doing so, amount contributed will be treated as a continuous dependent variable even though the data are available only in categorical form, since the categories do form a continuum. The same procedure is followed for income. Other variables entered into the model are similar to those used for the regression on number of hours volunteered. In addition, number of hours volunteered and contributing to non-Jewish causes are included.

The amount contributed to Jewish causes is significantly affected by most of the women's characteristics under examination (see table 6-14). Age, education, and income all have positive effects on contributions, while being divorced has a negative effect. Economic hardships and some degree of disaffection with the organized Jewish community may very well account for some of this latter difference. Having children age 6–17 also enhances level of giving, whereas having children under age six has no significant effect. Quite likely, having children of school age provides more occasions at which households may be solicited for contributions (as, for example, in connection with religious schooling) than is true of women who have only preschool or older children. Surprisingly, working either full time or part time is not significantly related to the amount contributed to Jewish causes when compared with not working at all.

As anticipated, most of the Jewish identification variables have a

Table 6-13. *Distribution of Level of Contributions by Hours Volunteered, Jewish Activities*

Hours Volunteered in Jewish Activities	Level of Contributions of Jewish Causes						
	None	Under $100	$100–499	$500–999	$1,000–4,999	$5,000 or more	Total Percent
None	6.8	31.6	35.0	13.5	10.9	2.3	100.0
1–4	–	19.1	27.0	12.4	29.6	11.9	100.0
5–9	–	10.4	41.0	13.3	25.5	9.8	100.0
10 or more	–	18.7	29.0	10.6	23.4	18.3	100.0

Table 6-14. *Regression on Amount Contributed to Jewish and Non-Jewish Causes (Standardized Beta Coefficients)*

	Jewish	Non-Jewish
Age	0.009*	0.010*
Education	0.018*	0.080*
Income	0.056*	0.129*
Marital Status[a]		
Never Married	0.001	−0.353*
Divorced	−0.447*	−0.566*
Widowed	0.003	−0.429*
Children under 6	0.022	−0.019
Children age 6–14	0.151*	0.021
Labor Force Status[b]		
Working full-time	−0.007	0.216*
Working part-time	0.002	0.175*
Years of Jewish Education[c]		
1–3 years	0.140*	0.010
4–6 years	0.355*	0.204*
7–9 years	0.285*	0.219*
10 or more years	0.581*	0.380*
Ritual Observance Index[d]		
High	0.204*	−0.035
Medium	−0.019	−0.135*
Attendance at Religious Services[e]		
Often	0.472*	0.004
Sometimes	0.239*	0.223*
Number of Hours Volunteered	0.010*	0.016*
Non-Jewish Contributions	0.591*	−
R^2	.549	.269

*Significant at $p<.01$.
[a]Reference group is Married.
[b]Reference group is Not in the Labor Force.
[c]Reference group is None.
[d]Reference group is Low.
[e]Reference group is Seldom.

strong positive effect on level of giving to Jewish causes. The notable exception is medium score on the ritual observance index, which seems to have a weak negative effect. Volunteering in Jewish activities has a significant positive effect, confirming the pattern noted in the bivariate analysis. Finally, contributing to non-Jewish causes has a strong positive effect, even with all other variables controlled.

When contributions to non-Jewish causes are considered, the relations for most of the characteristics are similar to those for contributing to Jewish causes, although some differences appear. The most notable difference is the significant positive impact that being in the labor force either full time or part time has on level of contributions. Such activity clearly exposes women to many occasions on which funds for non-Jewish causes are solicited. Being widowed, on the other hand, depresses such contributions compared to those made by married women. This pattern suggests that if elderly, widowed women are forced to make decisions about contributions in the face of economic difficulties, they are likely to maintain their giving to Jewish causes at the expense of non-Jewish ones. Of the Jewish identificational variables, years of Jewish education and attendance at religious services continue to be positively related to level of giving, but both high and medium scores on the ritual observance index have a negative effect on giving compared to having a low score. Greater secularization, as measured by this index, is here associated with higher levels of giving to non-Jewish causes.

The Dimensions of Giving among Women

Since the early 1970s, American Jewish women have participated in the dramatic changes characterizing American women in general, and have often been in the forefront of those changes. Jewish women have, for example, been among the leaders of the feminist movement in the United States. They have been among the first to lower their fertility, and they have participated equally with their non-Jewish sisters in entering the labor force. They have attained exceptionally high levels of education. Finally, many are spending more time in their life in an unmarried state—single for longer periods while young, divorced at middle age, and widowed when elderly.

These developments have important significance for the organized Jewish community. Many of the activities traditionally associated with voluntarism may no longer hold much appeal for the more educated

Jewish women. At the same time, even though women now spend less time in child care because of smaller family size, their time available for volunteer activity has been considerably constrained by their entry into the labor force. Concurrently, their changing career aspirations may also make the non-Jewish voluntary sector more attractive than the Jewish one since it may be seen as providing important work-related networks. In addition, the aging of the Jewish population means that many more women are now in those age groups in which income is reduced. Older women may also be more reluctant or physically less able to engage in voluntary activities outside the home. Taken together, these changes can be seen as being inimical to women's strong support of Jewish institutions, either through volunteering time or contributing funds.

Yet some of these changes also argue for increased support by women. Their high rates of employment provide many with discretionary funds that can be channeled into charitable giving. Their smaller family size and the fact that many live alone means that they have fewer family obligations constraining their time so that more is available for voluntarism. In addition, increasing feminism may make it desirable for them to participate actively in organizations and institutions that allow them to share in the community power structure (Kosmin 1989).

Several questions are raised by these issues. On the one hand, do women's changing characteristics and aspirations impel them to meet their needs for community involvement more in the non-Jewish sector than in the Jewish one? Second, because of the many demands that work and family life place on their time, will they substitute making contributions for volunteering time, or conversely, will women consider that their time is money and give less if they volunteer more? Finally, does the increasing secularization of American Jewry as a whole have an overall affect on the giving of time and money by Jewish women?

This chapter has begun to answer some of these questions with data about Jewish women in Rhode Island. In doing so, it is important to remember that some of the variables used in the analysis refer not to the characteristics of the individual respondents, but rather to their households as a whole. These include income and contributions as well as the ritual observance index. Women's own contributions cannot, therefore, be isolated and considered alone. Nonetheless, household contributions indicate an overall commitment to the community that encompasses the attitudes of most if not all of the adults in the

household. Similarly, the ritual observance index reflects a general
level of religious identification that affects all household members, just
as household income can affect the level of giving of all household
members regardless of whether the income was earned by one or
another of its members.

The findings indicate the complexity of the relations among women's
characteristics, voluntarism, and contributions of funds, and that these
relations differ for Jewish and non-Jewish activities. The presence of
children makes no clear difference to women's ability to volunteer or
in household level of giving. Yet being married clearly enhances the
rate of voluntarism for Jewish activities but not for non-Jewish ones,
and marriage is related to higher rates and levels of contributions to
both Jewish and non-Jewish causes. Being in the labor force generally
has little impact on voluntarism, but working part time tends to
enhance activity in the Jewish sector. Working also enhances the rate
and level of non-Jewish contributions but not of Jewish ones. As
anticipated on the basis of a number of previous studies, the Jewish
identificational variables are strongly related to volunteering in and
contributing to Jewish activities. They do not have the same effect for
non-Jewish activities; the ritual behavior index in particular is negatively related to non-Jewish volunteering and giving.

The data also suggest that being active in non-Jewish activities is
strongly related to being active in Jewish ones as well. Similarly, level
of giving to non-Jewish causes is strongly related to giving to Jewish
causes. The two spheres of activity seem to reinforce each other.
Despite these strong relations, it is also true that Jewish women are
more involved in the Jewish community at every level than they are in
the non-Jewish one, and their households give considerably more to
Jewish causes than to non-Jewish ones. In response to questions about
the relative importance of Jewish versus non-Jewish activities, about
half of the women indicated that they considered their Jewish activities
more important than their non-Jewish ones (Goldscheider and Goldstein 1988, 289, 301). Within this overall pattern, however, it is important to recognize that younger women are more likely to consider
Jewish and non-Jewish activities of equal importance and that 10
percent think their non-Jewish ones more important. These attitudes
are clearly reflected in lower levels of voluntarism and contributions.

These judgments may be closely tied to those factors that seem to
have the greatest impact on degree of involvement—measures of
religious identification. Strong identification, whether measured by
years of Jewish education, levels of ritual observance, or frequency of

attendance at religious services, was positively and strongly related to the giving of time and funds. Since high level of identification is more characteristic of older women than it is of younger ones, this helps to explain some of the observed differentials by age. Religious identification is apparently associated with values of community service and concern for the general welfare of both the Jewish and non-Jewish segments of the community. This is manifested in more hours of volunteer service and in higher contributions.

These data suggest, therefore, that the changing sociodemographic characteristics of Jewish women do not of themselves generally lead to lower involvement in the community at the voluntary level or in household giving. At the same time, women's changing characteristics do suggest that appeals for their time and money will have to provide stimulation and opportunities for self-expression to make such causes attractive to them. The relatively high levels of voluntarism of younger women in non-Jewish activities suggest that women may increasingly turn to the non-Jewish sector as their contacts with non-Jews increases (as it does in the work place) and if their needs are not met within the Jewish community. In this respect, volunteer activities may be sensitive indicators of increasing assimilation that have not yet appeared in terms of contributions to non-Jewish, as opposed to Jewish, causes.

The strongest factor enhancing community involvement suggested by the data assessed in this paper and one that would lower assimilation is a high level of identification with the Jewish community (measured here by three religious identification variables). Efforts to foster such identification, coupled with a sensitivity to the changing interests and goals of Jewish women, should help enhance the amount of time and funds they give to the Jewish community. The complex relations among changing characteristics, voluntarism, and giving therefore require careful monitoring in order to allow the Jewish community to understand more fully the dynamics underlying support from its constituents.

Notes

1. The index was based on responses to questions on lighting Sabbath candles, buying kosher meat, using separate dishes for meat and dairy, and lighting Hanukkah candles. Responses were categorized as always, usually, sometimes, never, and ranged from 1 for always to 4 for never. The responses on the four variables were summed and respondents were scored high for

scores of four through seven, medium for eight through twelve and low for thirteen through sixteen.

2. Attendance has been collapsed into three categories: Seldom (special occasions or less), Sometimes (few times a year or once a month), and Often (several times a month or more).

3. This section of the chapter draws heavily on A. Goldstein (1990).

4. Judging by the low correlations among these three variables, they measure quite different aspects of Jewish identification. All three are therefore included in the same regression equation.

Bibliography

Bianchi, Suzanne M., and Daphne Spain. *American Women in Transition.* New York: Russell Sage Foundation, 1986.

Carroll, Andrew Silow. "The Big Givers Are Still Jewish but Their Big Gifts May Not Be." New York: Jewish Telegraphic Agency News Release, 18 June 1988.

Cohen, Steven M. *American Modernity and Jewish Identity.* New York: Tavistock Publications, 1983.

Fruehauf, Norbert. "The Bottom Line: Major Gifts to Federation Campaigns." In *Contemporary Jewish Philanthropy in America*, edited by Barry A. Kosmin and Paul Ritterband, 173–85. Savage, Md.: Rowman & Littlefield, 1991.

Goldscheider, Calvin. *Jewish Continuity and Change.* Bloomington: Indiana University Press, 1986.

Goldscheider, Calvin, and Sidney Goldstein. *The Jewish Community of Rhode Island: A Social and Demographic Study.* Providence, R.I.: Jewish Federation of Rhode Island, 1988.

Goldstein, Alice. "New Roles, New Commitments? Jewish Women's Involvement in the Community's Organizational Structure." Forthcoming in *Contemporary Jewry*, 1990.

Hodgkinson, Virginia H., and Murray Weitzman. *Giving and Volunteering in the U.S.* (1988 ed.). Washington, D.C.: Independent Sector, 1988.

Kosmin, Barry A. "The Political Economy of Gender in Jewish Federations." *Contemporary Jewry*, 10 (Spring 1989): 17–31.

Rappeport, Michael, and Gary A. Tobin. *A Population Study of the Jewish Community of MetroWest New Jersey.* East Orange, N.J.: United Jewish Federation of MetroWest, 1987.

Ritterband, Paul, and Richard Silberstein. "Generation, Age, and Income Variability." *Jewish Philanthropy in Contemporary America* (pp. 46–63).

(Information Series no. 2). New York: CUNY Graduate Center, North American Jewish Data Bank, 1988.

Tobin, Gary. *A Population Study of the Jewish Community of Greater Baltimore*. Baltimore, Md.: Associated Jewish Charities and Welfare Funds, 1986.

7

Patterns of Giving of Some Jewish Career Women: A Preliminary Investigation

Rela Geffen Monson

"The Ladies Auxiliary of. . . ." "The Sisterhood of Congrega-tion. . . ." "The Women's Division of. . . ." For earlier generations of American-Jewish women, these organizational forms typified the or-ganic link between being a woman and a Jew. Now these are all phrases that echo anachronism: with massive changes in the social role of women, the rise of feminist ideology, and in particular, the Jewish feminist movement, the organic link has been questioned.

This chapter will begin to address the aforementioned issues of role conflict with respect to one area central to Jewish communal concern, that is, philanthropic giving. Do Jewish women still fit into the "tradi-tional" order of large-scale Jewish philanthropy? Have they created alternative modes or have they dropped out of the system?

Using survey data based on questionnaires completed by 944 respon-dents, the philanthropic and volunteer activities of Jewish career women were examined. For the purposes of this study, a *career* is distinguished from a *job* in that it has an intrinsically demanding character. A true professional does not keep defined hours; hence, executives do not get paid extra for overtime hours that cannot be

117

confined to thirty-five or forty hours per week. Furthermore, in many instances, a career woman is pressured to avoid the role of wife and/or mother in favor of a steady climb up the ladder of success (see Monson 1987 for discussion of this role conflict).

Moreover, a career contains a series of work situations that progress over time, such as moving up a career path or changing to positions where one will receive more responsibility and remuneration. Thus, a career has both a demanding and a developmental character (Rapoport and Rapoport 1971, 1976; Rapoport, Rapoport and Bumstead 1978). In contrast, a job may stay the same for many years.

The Jewish identification factors examined in the study were denominational affiliation, Jewish social circles, membership in synagogues or other Jewish organizations, and attitudes about Jewish life in the United States today. Attitudinal variables included questions about Jewish intermarriage, conflicts over family versus career, whether all Jewish children should have Jewish educations, how being Jewish has affected their careers, and how they perceive the Jewish community's attitude toward "having it all," that is, combining a career with marriage and a family.

Little documentation of the career paths and resulting role conflicts of Jewish career women exists. Moreover, there is no systematically gathered survey material reflecting the attitude of these women toward their identity as Jews and/or toward the organized Jewish community. Furthermore, despite the sheer quantity of studies on women's success routes in business and in the professions (see, for example, Basow 1986; England and Farkas 1986; Gallese 1985; Harris 1978; Kaufman and Richardson 1982; Oppenheimer 1970; *Wall Street Journal* 1986; *Working Woman* and Bryant 1984), there is a dearth of information on if—and how—Jewish women "on the way up" differ from other women, how their aspirations or work-related conflicts might be unique, or how their childhood socialization has been related to their perceptions of Judaism and the Jewish community as a source of support or stress.

By the 1970s the proportion of Jewish men and women who had completed college was about equal (Koltun 1977; Monson 1984). In the decade that followed, Jewish women joined Jewish men as the most highly educated of all ethnic and religious groups in the United States (Goldscheider 1986; Zuckerman and Goldscheider 1984). Moreover, the proportion of Jewish male professionals whose children became professionals themselves was about 80 percent for either sex and significantly higher than that for the non-Jewish population (Goldscheider 1986).

Some earlier studies on the upward mobility of American professional and managerial women were not optimistic. Henning and Jardim's (1977) study noted that despite affirmative action programs, men held 95 percent of the jobs in the census category of "Officials, Managers and Proprietors," even though they were then 61 percent of the labor force. Moreover, in 1977, only 2.3 percent of those earning over $25,000 were women. They also found that women were excluded from the informal networks crucial to successful entree into the halls of power in the business world. Women below the age of thirty-five often had to "mortgage" their personal lives in order to pay for their careers, that is, postpone marriage and beginning a family.

These findings were later corroborated by Harlan and Weiss (1981) and Korn/Ferry (1982): that career women, at least at the professional and managerial levels, face very difficult choices as their careers progress.

When these women do marry, they transfer some of the responsibility for the maintenance of the marital relationship, the child-rearing, and housekeeping to their husbands, often with the support of hired help. Nevertheless, even these dual-career families still have to contend with the stereotyped role definitions espoused by their families, friends, co-workers, and the media (Bird 1977; Hall and Hall 1979; Rapoport and Rapoport 1971, 1976; Rapoport, Rapoport, and Bumstead 1978; Voydanoff 1984).

Although these earlier studies on career women examined these dilemmas vis-à-vis their personal lives, there were few explicit considerations of the impact of religious identity on career paths. In addition, the relationship between these two variables and the combination of religious ideology or ethnic patterns and customs on voluntarism and philanthropy remained largely unknown. The purpose of this study, then, was to begin to fill in this gap.

Method

A total of 944 women completed a questionnaire that included background information such as a set of multidimensional measures of the involvement of respondents' parents in Jewish life while they were growing up. Questions probed parents' formal ties to the organized Jewish community, as well as home ritual practices and respondents' own formal and informal educational experiences. Respondents were also asked about their involvement in Jewish life while in college, their current age, marital status, and background information on their spouses as well as the extent of their current involvement in Jewish communal and religious life and participation in Jewish friendship circles.

Several questions dealt directly with religious and philanthropic activities of the respondents since 1980 and those of their parents. These women were also asked if they donated either time or money to general women's causes such as the National Organization for Women (NOW) or the League of Women Voters. Moreover, respondents were probed for participation in professional organizations, community voluntary organizations, feminist groups, and social or business clubs.

The hypothesis of the study was that positive responses to these items would be associated with certain occupations, levels of individual and household income, exposure to Jewish experiences while growing up, various measures of connectedness to the Jewish community, denominational affiliation, moving in Jewish friendship networks, and attitudes toward various general and Jewish issues of social policy.

The concern here is the relationship between the kinds of organizations Jewish career women give to and how they spend their free time. Table 7-1 shows how philanthropic giving to each of four types of organizations is related to volunteer activity.

Women involved in communal voluntary organizations and social or business clubs are more likely to give to United Way and local federations. However, the most significant relationship is between those involved in feminist groups and philanthropy toward general women's causes (91 percent). Feminist activists are also less likely to give to local Jewish federations (72 percent) than women active in

Table 7–1. *Relationship Between Voluntary Activity and Philanthropy to Four Types of Organizations in Own Name in the Last Two Years (in percentages)*

Voluntary Activity	United Way	Women's Causes	Local Federation	Other Jewish Organizations
Professional organizations (n = 520)	53	70	81	80
Community voluntary organizations (n = 445)	58	70	84	87
Feminist groups (n = 262)	52	91	72	83
Social or business clubs (n = 170)	58	69	85	81

professional organizations (81 percent), community volunteer organizations (84 percent), or social or business clubs (85 percent). This pattern suggests that giving time and money complement rather than substitute for one another.

Nevertheless, the overall trend is that those who participate as volunteers also give more money. For instance, 84 percent of those who are involved in community voluntary organizations give to local federations, compared to 66 percent of those who don't participate in such organizations ($X^2 = 23.4$, 1 d.f. $p < 0.0001$). Similarly, while 70 percent of those who work for communal voluntary organizations give to general women's causes, just 53 percent of those who do not participate give to them ($X^2 = 14.9$, 1 d.f., $p < 0.0001$).

Jewish background factors such as denominational affiliation, synagogue membership, and Jewish friendship circles relate significantly to giving patterns as demonstrated in table 7-2.

Although denominational affiliation is not related to contributions to United Way, it is significantly related to other giving. Self-defined secular respondents are the least likely to give to every cause except women's organizations. This is particularly noticeable in the case of local Jewish federations, to which only 56 percent of secular women give.

Synagogue membership yields a positive impact on giving to both the Jewish federation and other Jewish causes but no real difference to United Way or women's organizations.

The existence of Jewish social circles also correlates with giving to Jewish causes. The higher the proportion of Jews among the respondent's close friends, the more likely she is to give to Jewish causes. However, no such relationship exists for universalist philanthropies such as the United Way or women's organizations. Indeed, totally particularist friendship circles maximize Jewish giving and lower the probability of universalist philanthropy. Simultaneously, exposure to more varied social circles raises the probability that the respondent will give to United Way and general women's causes and may lower giving to Jewish causes.

Respondents were also asked an attitudinal battery of questions as described above. More than 80 percent agreed that the Equal Rights Amendment (ERA) should be passed and that the federal government should provide funding for abortions. There was little relationship between these attitudes and giving patterns, however, except that the 20 percent of respondents who opposed ERA and abortion funding were significantly less likely to contribute to women's organizations.

Table 7-2. *Jewish Factors Associated with Philanthropic Giving (in percentages)*

	Gave to in Own Name in Last Two Years			
	United Way	Women's Causes	Local Federation	Other Jewish Organizations
Denominational affiliation:				
Orthodox	44	47	85	94
Conservative	52	66	81	87
Reform	53	69	79	73
Reconstructionist	49	74	80	97
Secular	44	80	56	73
	n.s.	$p<0.014$	$p<0.0000$	$p<0.0000$
Synagogue membership:				
Yes	54	67	83	86
No	48	70	65	70
	$p<0.013$	n.s.	$p<0.0000$	$p<0.0000$
Proportion of close friends: Jewish at this time				
All	41	55	88	86
More than 75%	51	67	81	83
About 50%	56	74	76	81
25–50%	63	73	56	71
Less than 25%	43	68	61	58
	$p<0.002$	$p<0.0007$	$p<0.0000$	$p<0.0000$

Finally, the women were asked about Jewish life in the United States and their roles as career women. Table 7-3 shows their attitudes on intermarriage; the family; Jewish education; Judaism and careers; and the relationship among the Jewish community, "having it all," and philanthropic giving.

Here secularism was not measured by self-definition (as in table 7-2) but by attitudes toward intermarriage. Hence, a woman who does not view intermarriage as a threat to the future of the Jewish community is "secular." Similarly, feminists are defined as those who do not think that having a family is more important than having a career. Consequently, the more secular and/or feminist a woman is, the more likely she is to give to women's causes. Furthermore, women who think the Jewish community does not support their ideal life styles are more likely to give to women's causes. (This attitude was also associated

Table 7-3. *Relationship Between Agreement With Statements about Jewish Life in America and Giving to General and Jewish Philanthropies (in percentages)*

Statements about Jews	Gave to in Own Name in Last Two Years			
	United Way	Women's Causes	Local Federation	Other Jewish Organizations
Intermarriage a threat to survival:				
Agree (n = 593)	50	64	85	84
Undecided (n = 145)	50	66	68	72
Disagree (n = 136)	53	75	58	75
	n.s.	$p<0.06$	$p<0.0000$	$p<0.0007$
For a Jew, family is more important than career:				
Agree (n = 264)	54	59	85	81
Undecided (n = 223)	49	66	72	82
Disagree (n = 322)	48	71	75	77
	n.s.	$p<0.007$	$p<0.0004$	n.s.
Every Jewish child should have a Jewish education:				
Agree (n = 636)	51	66	82	83
Undecided (n = 101)	50	64	64	72
Disagree (n = 98)	48	75	64	68
	n.s.	n.s.	$p<0.0000$	$p<0.0002$
How being Jewish has affected career:				
Positively (n = 271)	49	65	83	86
No effect/neutral (n = 422)	52	68	76	77
Negatively	50	67	71	80
	n.s.	n.s.	$p<0.02$	$p<0.01$
Jewish community's attitude toward women combining marriage, children, and careers:				
Supportive (n = 367)	52	61	80	80
Neutral (n = 129)	52	58	78	81
Unsupportive (n = 285)	49	76	77	82
	n.s.	$p<0.0000$	n.s.	n.s.

with definitely calling oneself a feminist.) However, this factor does not lessen giving to federations or Jewish organizations.

With regard to other attitudinal variables, however, those who had a traditional Jewish stance (i.e., subscribing to the ideas that intermarriage is a threat to survival; for a Jew family is more important than career; every Jewish child should have a Jewish education) were significantly more likely to have given to local federations in their own names than those who were undecided or disagreed.

The findings also indicated that women who thought their Jewishness had played a positive role in career advancement were more likely to give to their local Jewish federations than those who saw no effect or a negative one.

Conclusion

That affiliated Jewish career women are more likely to give to Jewish causes parallels findings about the general Jewish population found in demographic surveys of major communities in the United States (Cohen 1981; Fowler 1977; Silberstein, Rabinowitz, Ritterband, and Kosmin 1987). Jewish identity connected to Judaism as a religion and translation of that into synagogue affiliation have consistently been associated with involvement in and giving to local federations.

An analysis of the findings reveals that Jewish experiences encourage all giving but increase particularist philanthropy and lower the universalist. These relationships should be explored among other samples to see if this is an idiosyncratic finding or one that may be replicated.

Jewish women have, until now, supported the Jewish community, even when they believe that they have little or no support from it. If a woman is positively disposed toward her Jewishness, it will enhance the desire to give. However, anger at the community—at least for these women—does not diminish giving.

In sum, philanthropic activity is based on two kinds of variables—the social affiliation factors tested in table 7-2 and the structural ones tested in table 7-3.

In both cases, giving to the United Way seems to have no relationship to strong Jewish identity. Jewish identity means survivalist and maximalist stances as indicated by both contributions to local federations and other Jewish organizations. Those women whose philanthropic activities are directed toward women's organizations see these organizations as an alternative identity, which neither complements nor supplants their Jewish identity. As table 7-2 indicates, women who describe themselves as secular are more likely to contribute to women's organizations (80 percent) and less to their local federation (56 percent).

Similarly, while one's perceptions of the Jewish community's attitudes toward women who "have it all" does not strongly affect her own philanthropy to local federations (80 percent to 77 percent, see table 7-3), it has a strong correlation with giving to women's organizations, so that 61 percent of those who think the community is supportive are versus 76 percent of those who do not, give to the latter (see table 7-4).

That women will continue to feed the hand that bites them is an assumption that the Jewish community cannot safely make. Currently, a transitional generation still steeped in traditional values and practices is under examination.

Given the flourishing of a particularist Jewish feminism, it is difficult to predict if the primary identity will be "Jewish" or "female" and how that will affect future philanthropic giving. (For an examination of similar trends see Horowitz, chapter 12, on *havurah* Jews.)

Finally, the role of external social, political and economic factors, which have a direct impact on women, must be considered. While American women in general are entering the labor force in record numbers (60 percent in 1980), the data indicate that Jewish women are more likely than their non-Jewish cohorts to be in the labor force because they are more highly educated (which, in turn, means they are motivated to enter the public realm) and have lower fertility rates than non-Jewish women (Chiswick 1988).

Whether one can remain simultaneously "Jewish and feminist" with each role having equal salience depends in large part on how the organized Jewish community responds to the changing role of women. This, in turn, will surely affect patterns of philanthropic giving by women who "have it all." The key question is "will federations and other Jewish organizations continue to receive the support of Jewish career women, if they do not feel themselves a valued part of the Jewish community?"

Appendix: Analysis of the Sample

The questionnaire reached the potential respondents through two primary means:

1. It appeared in the April 1985 issue of *Lilith*, a Jewish feminist magazine. *Lilith* published 4,500 copies of that issue; 441 surveys or 11 percent were returned for analysis.

2. Professionals at Jewish federations in Hartford, Syracuse, Philadelphia, Los Angeles, Chicago, Boston, and Miami distributed a total of 405 questionnaires to members of their business and professional women's groups. American Jewish Committee (AJC) field offices in major metropolitan areas and suburban districts distributed an additional 547 surveys. Finally, another 215 surveys were distributed to Jewish career women through the following channels: Jewish members of the Committee of 200, an elite group of executive women; Orthodox or traditional career-oriented women whom the investigator personally knew; and referrals from earlier respondents. In sum, 1,162 "known" Jewish career women recieved the questionnaire; 503 surveys (or 43 percent) were returned.

Sample Comparison

This was by no means a representative, random sample. *Lilith* readers are by and large committed feminists, who are liberal and young. They are usually on the beginning rungs of the career ladder. Many of their mothers worked outside the home when they were growing up. While all had some ties to the Jewish community, reading the magazine was the sole formal connection to Jewish life for many. In addition, whether one was a career woman was based on self-definition.

The "known" Jewish career women had a greater connection to the Jewish community. They were more middle-aged and further up the career ladder than the *Lilith* sample. This second group was more likely to meet the general criteria for professionals, business people, and managers, due to the general membership rules of federation business and professional groups as well as the status of women known to the leadership of the AJC. Despite their career advances, however, they were less likely to have gone to graduate school than the *Lilith* sample.

Nevertheless, the two groups were remarkably similar in some ways. For example, about the same proportion of each were first-born or only children, currently married, and professionals or managers. In addition, similar proportions had been to Israel, said that at least 75 percent of their dates were with Jewish men if they were single, had a father who completed graduate school, attended three-day-a-week religious school, had a Christmas tree in their homes when they were growing up, and were married to men who were professionals or managers (see Appendix table).

There were, however, four notable variables on which the two samples differed markedly. First, more of the women in the "known" career group considered themselves Reform (44 percent) Jews than in the *Lilith* group (30 percent). This is not surprising since Reform Judaism has traditionally dominated both the Federation and AJC leadership (see Rimor and Tobin, chapter 3). "Known" career women were also more likely to have annual personal salaries surpassing $25,000. This was largely attributed to a differential distribution in occupations: fewer of the respondents from the *Lilith* sample were in

Appendix Table. *Comparative Profiles of Lilith Readers and "Known" Career Women (in percentages)*

Variable	Group I Lilith Sample	Group II "Known" Career Women
Family background:		
First-born or only child	56	57
Attended three-day-a-week religious school	41	38
Had Christmas tree	12	11
Father completed graduate school	27	31
Mother worked outside home	55	43
Adult characteristics:		
Average age (actual age)	40	43
Single, never married	20	17
Married or remarried	66	64
Personal income over $25,000/yr.	45	72
Husband professional or manager	84	87
Completed graduate school	66	54
No children planned	17	15
Professional or manager	87	88
Definitely a feminist	73	40
Jewish commitments:		
Ever been to Israel	69	71
Intermarriage remote or out if single	60	53
Consider self Conservative Jew	37	34
Consider self Reform Jew	30	44
Jewish community is "very" or "somewhat" supportive	40	52

business, banking, management, and law and more of them were in education, social work, Jewish communal service, communications, and the arts.

Third, substantially fewer of the "known" career women (40 percent) defined themselves as feminists than those who read *Lilith* (73 percent). While older women are less likely to unabashedly take on the feminist label, *Lilith* readers subscribe to a declared feminist magazine. Thus we would expect them to identify with that label in a definite way.

Their feminism notwithstanding, *Lilith* readers were more traditional in their Judaism than the career sample. More of them belonged to Jewish youth movements in high school, came from homes where dietary laws were observed, and were involved in Jewish student life during their college years. Where the two subsamples do coincide, however, is that at least half of the women in each do not feel that the Jewish community is even somewhat supportive of them as career women.

Review of the data contained in the Appendix table led to the conclusion that the similarities between the two groups outweighed the differences. Consequently, the two subsamples were merged for the purpose of analysis.

Education and Occupation

General demographic data revealed that the respondents had a very high level of secular education: 90 percent acquired some college education and 60 percent completed graduate programs.

A vast majority (93 percent) are currently employed, with the rest still in school or on child-care leave. Of those who are employed, 60 percent are professionals, 24 percent are in managerial positions, and an additional 4 percent are simultaneously in professional and managerial positions, i.e., a professor who is now president of a college. Five percent are in technical or semiprofessional occupations, leaving 7 percent in other service and sales fields.

Volunteer and Philanthropic Activities

Table 7-2 shows the extent of philanthropic and volunteer activities among the respondents. About three-fifths (61 percent) reported that they participated in a professional organization. A little more than half worked for community voluntary organizations (52 percent) such as the United Way. One in five belonged to social or business clubs and slightly less than one-half participate in feminist groups. More than one-third (38 percent) of the respondents have received some community recognition in the form of awards or media attention since 1980.

As for philanthropic activities, several general factors may influence giving. These include region of residence, current marital status, occupation, income, and voluntary participation in the general community. In addition, particularist and Jewish factors such as denominational affiliation, synagogue membership, having been on a trip to Israel, and activity in Jewish friendship networks also related to Jewish and general giving.

Furthermore, both factors—general and particularist—individually reflect an entire subset of attitudes. For example, the general factors affect individual stances on the women's movement in general, the Equal Rights Amendment (ERA), abortion rights, affirmative action programs, and the use of quotas as well as the effect of being a woman on career advancement.

The particularist concerns measure attitudes related to Jews in American society. These include the position of the Jewish community toward women who "have it all," i.e., combine family and career, views on intermarriage, the role of the family, the importance of a formal Jewish education for every Jewish child, perceptions of anti-Semitism in the United States, whether all careers are open to Jews, and the impact of being Jewish on career development.

Bibliography

Bird, Caroline *The Two-Paycheck Marriage*. New York: Pocket, 1979.

Basow, Susan A. *Gender Stereotypes—Traditions and Alternatives* (2nd ed.). Monterey, Calif.: Brooks/Cole, 1986.

Chiswick, Barry. "Labor Supply and Investment in Child Quality. A Study of Jewish and Non-Jewish Women." *Contemporary Jewry*, 9(2) (Fall 1988): 35–62.

Cohen, Steven M. "Trends in Jewish Philanthropy." *American Jewish Yearbook, 1980* (pp. 29–51). New York: American Jewish Committee and Jewish Publication Society, 1981.

England, Paula and George Farkas. *Households, Employment and Gender: A Social, Economic and Demographic View*. New York: Aldine, 1986.

Fowler, Floyd. *1975 Community Survey: A Study of the Jewish Population of Greater Boston*. Boston: Combined Jewish Philanthropies, 1977.

Gallese, Liz Rowman. "Women like Us." *Working Women*, (February 1985): 113.

Goldscheider, Calvin. *Jewish Continuity and Change*. Bloomington: Indiana University, 1986.

Hall, Francine S. and Douglas T. Hall. *The Two-Career Couple*. Reading, Mass.: Addison-Wesley, 1979.

Harlan, Anne and Carol Weiss. *Moving Up: Women in Managerial Careers*. (Working Paper no. 86). Boston, Mass.: Wellesley College, Center for Research on Women, September 1981.

Harris, Barbara J. *Beyond Her Sphere: Women and the Professions in American History*. Westport, Conn.: Greenwood, 1978.

Hennig, Margaret and Anne Jardim. *The Managerial Woman*. New York: Pocket Books, 1977.

Horowitz, Bethamie. "Havurah Jews and Where They Give." In *Contemporary Jewish Philanthropy in America*, edited by Barry A. Kosmin and Paul Ritterband, 187–204. Savage, Md.: Rowman & Littlefield, 1991.

Kaufman, Debra R. and Barbara L. Richardson. *Achievement and Women: Challenging the Assumptions*. New York: Free Press, 1982.

Koltun, Elizabeth, (ed.). *The Jewish Woman: New Perspectives*. New York: Schocken, 1977.

Korn/Ferry International's Profile of Senior Women Executives. New York: Korn/Ferry International, November 1982.

Monson, Rela Geffen. *Jewish Campus Life*. New York: American Jewish Committee, 1984.

———. *Jewish Women on the Way Up. The Challenge of Family, Career and Community*. New York: American Jewish Committee, 1987.

Oppenheimer, Valerie Kincade. *The Female Labor Force in the United States*. Westport, Conn.: Greenwood, 1970.

Rapoport, Rhona and Robert Rapoport. *Dual-Career Families*. Harmondsworth, Middlesex: Penguin, 1971.

———. *Dual-Career Families Re-examined: New Integrations of Work and Family*. New York: Harper Colophon, 1976.

Rapoport, Rhona, Robert Rapoport, and Janice Bumstead. (eds.). *Working Couples*. New York: Harper Colophone, 1978.

Rimor, Mordechai and Gary Tobin. "The Relationship Between Jewish Identity and Philanthropy." In *Contemporary Jewish Philanthropy in America*, edited by Barry A. Kosmin and Paul Ritterband, 33–56. Savage, Md.: Rowman & Littlefield, 1991.

Silberstein, Richard, Jonathan Rabinowitz, Paul Ritterband, and Barry A. Kosmin. *Giving to Jewish Philanthropic Causes: A Preliminary Reconnais-*

sance. (Reprint Series no. 2). New York: CUNY Graduate Center, North American Jewish Data Bank, 1987. (Originally published in *1987 Spring Research Forum: Working Papers.*)

"The Corporate Woman, a Special Report." *The Wall Street Journal*, Section 4, 24 March 1986.

Working Women Editors and Gay Bryant. *The Working Woman Report— Succeeding in Business in the 80's*. New York: Simon & Schuster, 1984.

Zuckerman, Alan and Calvin Goldscheider. *The Transformation of the Jews*. Chicago and London: University of Chicago, 1984.

8

Tzedakah: Orthodox Jews and Charitable Giving

Samuel C. Heilman

In 1975, when I first published a paper about Orthodox Jews and charity, I explored the particular bond between donor and recipient that was established and reflected in face-to-face almsgiving. In this chapter, I would like to consider the phenomenon more generally. As in the 1975 paper, I shall try to suggest that there is more to charitable giving than simply providing for the needy. In fact, charitable giving also fulfills a number of indirect functions and offers ancillary advantages to the contributor and to the community that supports it. These uses and benefits—as well as illustrative examples of them in Orthodox Jewish life—comprise the sociology of Orthodox *tzedakah* (charity) upon which I shall focus.

To begin with, however, a definition of Orthodox Jews is in order. Although no universally agreed upon designation of precisely who the Orthodox are can be provided in a few words—Orthodoxy is after all a syndrome of qualities including practices, beliefs, affiliations, and ethos—a good place to begin is by proposing that they are Jews who generally attach themselves, at least in principle, to the *halakha*, codified Jewish law. Indeed, in a recent survey of approximately one thousand American modern Orthodox Jews, respondents overwhelmingly associated themselves with an attachment to *halakha* and the

Torah. They agreed that *halakha* must not be ignored even in the face of the exigencies of modern life and that the Torah could indeed rule conduct even in the face of the complexities inherent in the modern world. Throughout the spectrum of Orthodoxy from the most traditionalist to the least, between 55 percent and 96 percent generally did not think *halakha* should be ignored in the modern world and between a third and two-thirds thought the Torah should even be followed in blind faith (Heilman & Cohen 1989, table 3–3).

Given such devotion, one might reasonably expect that Orthodox Jews would be committed to giving charity because "the Torah commands it." Or, as I put it earlier: "The giving of charity is and always has been an integral part of the religious life of Orthodox Jews. To give of one's wealth to another Jew in need is an imperative, commanded both by the laws and by the traditions of Jewry, and no man may consider his religious obligations completely fulfilled without his having engaged in charity-giving" (Heilman 1975, 371). See also Maimonides, *Mishna Torah*, Hilchot Matanot 7:1, in which the commandment to give and precisely how to give is fully elaborated. In fact, this is the case. In our survey, when Cohen and I asked the Orthodox respondents to agree or disagree with the statement that "one should give alms because the Torah commands or because it's the kind thing to do," while only between one-quarter and one-half of our respondents (the latter proportion characterizing the most and the former the least traditionalist in our sample) answered that the Torah's commandments alone were sufficient reason for giving, most respondents (between 80 percent to 98 percent), included the Torah's injunction as a reason to give alms. As one Orthodox Jew, explaining why he gave *tzedakah*, remarked: "I give *tzedakah* for lots of reasons but foremost because it is a *mitzvah* that the Torah commanded me to do and by doing so I am fulfilling my obligation to be a good Jew." And then he added, as if to affirm his faith in the righteousness of this commandment: "I'm sure that if I give, *Hashem* [the Almighty] will more than pay me back."

As these remarks make clear, persons can give charity out of an attachment to religious belief, affirming thereby that they have abided by the doctrines and commandments they believe to be sacred. When they do so, they share in the advantages that Emile Durkheim argued are the rewards of true belief. These include a feeling of being "stronger" than the unbeliever, a sense of greater moral rectitude, and the consequent well-being it provides (Durkheim 1915). These feelings are enhanced when believers have performed their morally righteous and religiously significant acts publicly and conspicuously among their peers, with subsequent public acclamation and approval. In such cases, believers reinforce a sense of religious well-being with a social one: they are righteous in the eyes of God and their fellows.

While there are many such public displays of religious righteousness that Orthodox Jews can carry out—from praying in the synagogue to performing certain public acts of piety such as letting a beard grow during the seven weeks of the Omer between Passover and Shavuot—the giving of charity in the presence of others is a relatively simple and unmistakable one. (For a fuller discussion of how Orthodox Jews display their religiosity, see Heilman 1982.) Specifically, giving charity to some needy or worthy cause in the context of other manifestly religious behavior and in the presence of coreligionists has the potential for making the giver feel even more emphatically that he is engaged in a sacred activity, and hence yields feelings of moral and social well-being. Orthodox Jews often find themselves in precisely this situation. They regularly give charity in the context of other public religious activities, most notably, but not exclusively, during the sacred synagogue service.

During daily public prayer services, a *pushke* or charity box is commonly passed around in the course of the proceedings. Although this kind of collection normally focuses on small change and minor amounts of money, its regular and institutionalized character leaves the unmistakable impression that charity and prayer go together. As one of these actions improves the moral condition of the performer, so does the other. Indeed, almost no one declines to donate to the *pushke*; the clatter of coins striking the other change in the box or the sound of crumpling paper as bills are shoved through the slot are obvious public testimony to the act of charity. In many Orthodox synagogues, moreover, the *pushke* is placed in a prominent place so that all the other congregants can watch the act of giving, or else a conspicuous display is made of passing the charity box around—as for example when a young child is sent through the congregation, noisily shaking the box as he approaches each worshiper for a donation. Much the same process occurs when alms-collectors, a ubiquitous feature of many Orthodox daily services, come around collecting (see Heilman 1975). One should bear in mind that the alms collectors are more likely to come to Orthodox synagogues because they can be relatively more certain that there will be a daily gathering of people here than they can be at non-Orthodox synagogues that frequently have more difficulty mustering enough regular congregants to hold a daily service.

Not only during daily prayers, but often—particularly in densely populated areas of Orthodox Jewish residence—before and after funerals, a line of mendicants and alms-collectors greet mourners. As people arrive for the funeral, those harvesting the charity frequently remind them of their religious obligations by vocally repeating—almost chanting—the Jewish dictum that *tzedakah tatzil mi movess*, the giving of charity will save the giver from death.

In many Orthodox synagogues, a call to the Torah is followed by an opportunity to publicly pledge some funds, either to the congregational treasury (the charity that begins at home) or some other worthy cause. Although by no means limited to Orthodox synagogues, this practice is particularly elaborated in them. Commonly associated with a prayer of blessing recited on behalf of the donor and his loved ones, the pledge—as inserted in the prayer—becomes the justification for the blessing. The formulaic refrain is "May The Holy One Blessed be He compensate and bless [this man] because he has pledged so and so much to such and such a cause." In some Sephardic congregations, the turns at the Torah (*aliyot*) are actually auctioned off before the reading, with the proceeds going to charity.

Beyond this mechanism is the collection of special funds in the synagogue on particular occasions. Such collections are presented formally as religious obligations. Included here is the money collected in the synagogue on the holiday of Purim. Following the reading of the *Megillah*, the scroll that recounts the events around which the holiday is based and that concludes with the charge to celebrate the day by giving to the needy, plates are often set out on the pulpit and congregants rise to fill them with bills or change.

In many congregations, this giving has come to be associated with the ancient biblical practice of *Machtzit Ha-Shekel*, the Mosaic census by which each Israelite was asked to give an equal amount toward the building of the holy tabernacle and thereby be counted among the assembly. As if to repeat that act of giving so that one is counted among the congregation, Orthodox Jews today continue to give this symbolic shekel. Often, a series of plates containing three silver coins (usually dollar or half-dollar pieces in the United States) are set out. Worshipers approach the plates, deposit some money into them, and then, holding the specifically dedicated coins (tokens of the shekel) in hand, lift and then ritually drop them into the plates—as if symbolically to reenact the ritual of everyone giving exactly the same amount. Here, too, giving is carried on as part of religious ritual activity.

Similar collections are also made around Passover time—the funds this time being called *Ma'ot Chittim*, money for the wheat that the needy are to buy in order to bake the *matzah* they are obligated to eat on the holy day. And on the eves of Rosh Hashanah and Yom Kippur, the days of awe and atonement, similar collections are made—this time in line with the liturgy of the day that proclaims that "repentance, prayer, and charity" will nullify the decrees of punishment that transgression the rest of the year would otherwise occasion.

Finally, the *Yizkor* or memorial prayer recited four times a year—an event that often stimulates even the most reluctant of synagogue worshipers to come to pray—concludes with a pledge of charity. This time the pledge is made on behalf of the soul of the departed who is being memorialized. Providing the timely recipient for the pledge, Orthodox congregations often schedule charitable appeals just before the recitation of the prayer. The juxtaposition reminds the congregants that charity is an indispensable feature of the religious activity in which they are engaged.

And anyone who has on a weekday visited the *Kotel*, the Western Wall of what was the courtyard of the Holy Temple in Jerusalem, a place that has become an outpost in the guardianship of the Orthodox, cannot help but notice the many collectors of funds who weave their ways among the faithful or the numerous slots built into the walls into which charity may be deposited. What these unmistakably communicate is that pilgrimage to one of the holiest Jewish sites on earth is clearly to be accompanied by charitable giving. Indeed, while a number of secularists have sought to end such soliciting of funds at this site that they consider a national rather than a religious shrine, the Orthodox rabbinate and its supporters have successfully pressed for continued, albeit controlled, charitable solicitation and donation.

In short, there is almost no occasion of public gathering for religious or quasi-religious activities that the Orthodox do not accompany with an obbligato of charitable giving. It is very simply a persistent motif of their Jewish religious gatherings. On weekdays, the time that according to Jewish law money may be handled, actual currency may be given; on holy days, when money is off limits, only pledges are made. The net result is the same. Indeed, where only a pledge rather than actual funds are offered, the amounts in question are often higher—as if mere promises require more than actual on-the-spot donations. If by attending and participating in these events and gatherings, Orthodox Jews are made to feel they are better Jews, then clearly the giving of charity becomes for them part of what they must do in order to feel they have acted according to the highest moral standards.

But there is more at stake here than religious performance or feelings of moral well-being. There is also something far more eminently social. For the giving of all these charitable donations—particularly the more substantial ones that are made during appeals—are acts carried before an audience. As such, they are governed by the dynamics and requirements of public behavior and become matters of display and impression management.

To understand this element of charitable giving among the Orthodox, it is worthwhile reviewing briefly certain basic features of Orthodox Jewish life. Perhaps the first of these is to note that because Orthodox Jews generally abide by the prohibition against any travel other than by foot on Sabbaths and holy days, they accordingly find themselves not only living within walking distance of their synagogues but also necessarily of one another, the congregants who populate those synagogues. Moreover, because synagogue attendance is a common feature of Orthodox life, these people come into continuing and regular contact with one another. For some this is once a week; for others—those who attend daily prayers or a variety of other functions in and around the synagogue—it may be more often.[1] As such, the synagogue is not only a house of worship; it is also a house of assembly, a kind of community center (Heilman 1976). And in areas where the Orthodox constitute a minority in a larger sea of the non-Orthodox or non-Jewish, it has many of the characteristics of a ghetto, an intimate and protected place in which all those assembled share a whole variety of characteristics, ethos and world view in common (Heilman 1976).

As a consequence, for Orthodox congregants, coming to the synagogue enables them to display at least two aspects of themselves. First and most obviously, it provides people with a place and opportunity to carry out religious and ritual activities in public: they can show themselves engaged in prayer, reading or reviewing the Torah, celebrating a variety of customs or rituals, and not least of all giving charity. But, because for the Orthodox the synagogue is also a community center, a place where they meet their neighbors and friends, the people who by virtue of their Orthodoxy share a great deal in common with one another, coming to it serves another function. Every gathering at once demonstrates and reaffirms another aspect of themselves: their belongingness to the community. Indeed, for many who view orthodoxy positively, precisely this capacity of orthodoxy to provide intimacy and a sense of community to its adherents is crucial. For such people, social matters, far more than theological matters, are at the heart of orthodoxy's appeal.

While there are many ways that persons can display their belongingness to the community and symbolize their gathering—among them demonstrating that they know others and are known by them—one of the easiest ways of doing so is through the giving of charity to some community cause. Specifically, by giving such charity, the Orthodox can display their communal alignment and belongingness. Moreover, the more they collect, the more powerful the collectivity. Weak groups can engender only a weak level of participation in giving; robust ones do the opposite. Thus, giving to the synagogue or another cause with which the community has associated itself is a way for the individual giver to demonstrate clearly and unequivocally that he or she is a member of that community. A high level of participation in the giving is a way for the community to evidence its vitality. This is of no small significance to a sector of the Jewish community that understands itself to be a minority, and one often beleaguered by the assimilating and capitulating trends of the majority of other American Jews. After all, the Orthodox are still less than 10 percent of American Jewry, and probably an even smaller proportion of the world Jewish population.

To demonstrate that charitable giving for the Orthodox carries within it reverberations and affirmations of group solidarity, Cohen and I asked respondents in our survey the following two questions: If you had $100 to give to charity, how much would you give to general causes (for example, the cancer society), general Jewish causes (for example, the United Jewish Appeal), or Orthodox Jewish causes (for example, yeshivas or synagogues)? We also asked, in actuality how much did you give last year to each of these causes? The responses to these questions vividly reveal the communal and sectarian character of Orthodox giving. Of their hypothetical $100, most of the Orthodox gave between half and three-quarters of the total to Orthodox Jewish causes and nearly all the rest to general Jewish causes. In their actual giving, the most traditionalist Orthodox among the sample gave 83 percent of their charitable donations to Orthodox causes ($1,375 on average) while the largest group of our sample, those more modernist in orientation (as measured by a variety of criteria), people we called the "Centrist Orthodox," donated 63 percent of their dollars ($975) on average to Orthodox causes. While there may be a variety of explanations for this behavior, including commitment to group perpetuation and separationist tendencies, it clearly demonstrates that Orthodox Jews can look upon their giving as a way of declaring and demonstrating their association with one another.

This general pattern is underscored in the giving that goes on regularly in the Orthodox synagogue. Here the very act of publicly giving acts to show that one is identifying with the group of givers, the congregation both as individuals and a whole. Moreover, because of the intimate and familiar character of many Orthodox settings in which such public giving occurs, an even more powerful feeling of coercion is experienced. A person may give money not only because of the religious obligation and not only because he identifies with the cause and the other givers but because those who are soliciting the funds come in contact with him more often than others. The public rewards and pressures to give are thereby multiplied. As one Orthodox Jew explained it, when asked what makes him give charity at a synagogue appeal: "It's social pressure. You hear what everyone else is giving, and it's your friends asking you for the money, and you know you should give like everyone else or maybe even a little more than everyone else—especially because if it's one of your own charities, say the *shul* or some yeshiva—so you give; you have to give. I mean, what are you going to do; you don't want to be the only one left out. If you want to belong, then you've got to give. It's as simple as that."

The matter of giving as a reflection of social position needs to be considered further. Thorstein Veblen (1934) established the principle of conspicuousness and its relationship to social status. He wrote of "conspicuous leisure" and "conspicuous waste" as ways for persons to demonstrate their wealth, the former being the result of having so much time that one could afford to spend it publicly in unproductive leisure activities and the latter being the result of having so many resources that one could afford publicly to waste some. Against the backdrop of a Protestant ethic that inhibited both leisure and waste, these activities undeniably marked one as extravagant and above need (Weber 1958).

In some ways, Orthodox Judaism shares some of the ethos of the Protestant ethic. As Sombart (1951) wrote: "Now if Puritanism has had an economic influence, how much more so has Judaism, seeing that among no other civilized people has religion so impregnated all national life" (192). It, too, emphasizes the serious aspects of life and the need to temper pleasure with hard work, dedication, and thrift. It sees that "riches are a blessing if only their owner walk in God's ways" (Sombart 1951, 220). Among the Orthodox, time and resources to waste are viewed as a mark of excess. "Let not the rich man glory in his wealth," the prophet Jeremiah (9:22) warns. "Who is rich?" the rabbis asked and then answered, "He who rejoices in his portion" (Avot 4:1). And as the great exegete Rashi added, "he who has no urge to pursue greater wealth . . . it will be well with him in the World-to-Come."

One way to offset the implied indulgence of wealth is to give of it to charity. Prosperity must be balanced by philanthropy in order for it to rebound to the possessor's benefit. As the Jewish codes point out, "we are forbidden to reap the whole of the harvest; a remnant in a corner must be left for the poor" (Maimonides 1967, 204). According to the rabbis, depriving the poor of their due brings about severe punishments for all humanity: "he who says 'what is mine is yours and what is yours is yours' is, the rabbis advised, truly pious" (Avot 5:9–10). Thus giving is more than a commandment; it is viewed by those who adhere in principle to the world of Orthodox attachment to the codes and rabbinic dicta as a way of improving their moral condition.

But not only that, it is also a way of establishing an enhanced and positive social position and reputation. In brief, conspicuous waste and leisure among the Orthodox by and large require conspicuous philanthropy.

Giving means living up to communal expectations and obligations. It means affirming or establishing a position as insider and as donor—two identities that become simultaneous and to some extent indistinguishable in the context of much Orthodox giving. Only those who would dare deny these can avoid giving. As Barry Schwartz suggests: "The presentation of self . . . is often made with symbols of one's connections to others. And gifts represent the purest forms of such symbols" (1968, 1). In this case, the "gift" is charity, and the giving is a demonstration of belonging.

To be sure, Orthodox Jews are by no means unique in experiencing these social pressures, nor are they only Jews who use philanthropic giving as a way of symbolically aligning themselves with the community of their co-religionists. However, the intensity of Orthodox Jewish communal life along with the perception of charity as an essential religious obligation serve to intensify the entire process among the Orthodox.

Examining the relationship between Jews and their giving, Cohen (1978) pointed out that there is a relationship between ritual observance and contribution: specifically, he found that the more people observe Jewish ritual, the more they are likely to give to Jewish charities. And yet, the Orthodox seemed to be an exception to this principle; they gave less money to the general Jewish causes that researchers used as the empirical basis for their conclusions. However, when we look at the data on giving more closely, we discover that in fact rather than being an exception to the rule, Orthodox Jews turn out to confirm it. In fact, as a percentage of income, Orthodox Jews do indeed give more money to charity than any other Jews. However, they do not give to *general* Jewish causes; they give to Orthodox Jewish causes.

And why do they not give to the general Jewish but rather to Orthodox Jewish causes? First there are practical reasons: no one else seems to support these latter causes to the same extent. Indeed, of the non-Orthodox Jews surveyed, Heilman and Cohen (1989) found that only 16 percent of their hypothetical $100 would go to Orthodox Jewish causes and only $201 or 19 percent of their giving on average was donated to them. This is considerably below the 44 percent given by even the most marginal of Orthodox Jews to Orthodox causes and the 83 percent given by the most traditionalist of Orthodox Jews to these causes. Orthodox Jews apparently surmise—by and large correctly—that they are primarily accountable for the support of their own charities and act accordingly.

Beyond this instrumental reason for Orthodox Jewish support, there is a symbolic one. Through their increased giving to the Orthodox institutions—institutions that are undeniably "their own"—these Jews bind themselves to the Orthodox community in particular more than to the Jewish community in general. They give to a yeshiva or some Orthodox Jewish charity rather than to the UJA or a Jewish federation campaign because they consider the former causes extensions of their community and share a sense of common destiny and responsibility with them. Moreover, they choose to give to these causes as a symbolic means of distinguishing themselves from those who do not share that same sense of community. As one Orthodox Jew put it: "If we don't support the yeshivas and Orthodox institutions, no one else will."

Indeed, the charitable causes that generally garner the most donations during communal appeals are commonly those that the community perceives to be closest to its own orientation and character—although, to be sure, there may be meaningful and relatively wide variations among different Orthodox Jewish communities as to precisely which cause is in harmony with a particular community. Thus, for example, a traditionalist yeshiva will do better collecting funds from Orthodox Jews who are likely to send their children to it or are themselves its graduates, while Yeshiva University looks for greater support among those who share its more modernist worldview.[2] In short, charitable commitments are entangled "in the web of community bonds, both in a metaphysical as well as a material sense," and governed by a sense of obligation toward the expectations and standards of that community (Liebman 1981, 28).

To sum up, the various functions of charitable giving among the Orthodox may be divided into three categories: the economic, the religious and moral, and the symbolic and social. The first is quite straightforward: Orthodox Jews give to support a variety of causes because those causes are needy; and were it not for the Orthodox no one else would support them. With their own network of charities—from synagogues to yeshivas and *mitzvah* funds—the Orthodox constitute a recognizably separate group of givers.

Second, Orthodox Jews give out of religious inclinations and as part of their observance of ritual. As they are scrupulous in the effort to comply with the demands of all ritual, so are they conscientious in their fulfillment of the obligations of *tzedakah*. This conscientiousness leads to their experiencing a sense of moral improvement and righteousness, an added incentive to their giving.

Third, charitable giving fulfills several social functions. It provides donors with a means for demonstratably enhancing their social position—those who give away a great deal are venerated and acclaimed above those who are closefisted. Giving is a way to conspicuously enhance one's social position and counteract any negative aspects of wealth. It is a response to social pressure and the social expectations of what, in the Orthodox case, is more often than not a local and intimate face-to-face community that is soliciting the funds. Moreover, by giving, individual contributors bond themselves to the community of givers, as well as to the recipients of the charity. And when the recipient is the community, the act of giving is a way of participating in a demonstration of group vitality and strength, being symbolically counted in the congregation—something of special significance to minority groups like the Orthodox. Indeed, from the point of view of the community, giving to Orthodox charities acts as a counterforce and antidote to the situation of minority status. The more money collected, or more precisely, the larger the population of givers, the more the givers and collectors feel they are part of a community. This is, of course, true for Jewish giving in general.

While a number of these functions are not unique to the Orthodox, they are nevertheless particularly accentuated among them. Indeed, looking at charity and the Orthodox, one might paraphrase a well-known comment once made by Eliott Cohen of the American Jewish Committee: Orthodox Jews are like all other Jews, only more so.

Notes

1. To be sure, Orthodox Jews are by no means the only Jews who see one another on a regular basis in the synagogue, but they are certainly the most prominent to do so among American Jews.

2. To be sure, these various institutions need to reach beyond the natural constituencies for financial support if they are to sustain themselves. To do so, they often need to create some sense of affinity and alliance between themselves and potential donors. This they do by focusing on some element of their institution that can be made to appear as in line with the donor's world view. Hence, a traditionalist yeshiva may stress its capacity to prevent assimilation rather than its antimodernism when soliciting funds among the more modernist-inclined but nevertheless committed Jews.

Bibliography

Cohen, Steven M. "Will the Jews Keep Giving? Prospects for the Jewish Charitable Community." *Journal of the Jewish Communal Service,* 55 (Autumn 1978): 59–71.

Durkheim, Emile. *The Elementary Forms of the Religious Life.* London: Allen & Unwin, 1915.

Heilman, Samuel C. "The Gift of Alms: Face-to-Face Almsgiving among Orthodox Jews." *Urban Life and Culture,* 3(4) (January 1975): 371–95.

———. *Synagogue Life.* Chicago, Ill.: University of Chicago, 1976.

———. "Prayer in the Orthodox Synagogue: An Analysis of Ritual Display." *Contemporary Jewry,* 6(1) (1982): 2–17.

Liebman, Charles S. "The Sociology of Religion and the Study of American Jews." *Conservative Judaism,* (May/June 1981): 16–33.

Maimonides. *The Commandments* (vol. II, 210). (C. B. Chavel, trans.). New York: Soncino Press, 1967.

Schwartz, Barry. "The Social Psychology of the Gift." *American Journal of Sociology,* 73 (1968): 1–11.

Sombart, Werner. *The Jews and Modern Capitalism.* (M. Epstein, trans.). Glencoe, Ill.: Free Press, 1951.

Veblen, Thorstein. *The Theory of the Leisure Class.* New York: Modern Library, 1934.

Weber, Max. *The Protestant Ethic and the Spirit of Capitalism.* New York: Scribners, 1959.

9

Intergenerational Philanthropic Slippage: The Case of Children of Major Jewish Philanthropic Families in New York City

Egon Mayer

In Abraham Karp's colorful account of the history of the United Jewish Appeal (UJA), *To Give Life* (1981), he retells the story of how Julius Rosenwald, the ancestor of the Sears-Roebuck fortune and the giant of Jewish philanthropy in his day, gave $1 million to the fledgling efforts of the Joint Distribution Committee in 1916. Rosenwald's gift both set the standard goal for other major Jewish philanthropists and "rescued" the then forming organization.

About thirty years later, William Rosenwald, a son of Julius and chairman of the newly formed UJA, pledged $1 million to its campaign. He thereby helped establish for the first time a campaign goal of $100 million for the emerging agency of organized Jewish fund raising. At the time all of the other major philanthropic actors in the Jewish community believed a $100 million goal was wholly unrealistic.

Karp's history is concerned largely with the pre-1967 evolution of the UJA. Consequently, there is little discussion of the role of some of Julius Rosenwald's grandchildren. Throughout the 1980s, they continued to be pillars of the UJA-Federation system through their own philanthropic activity.

There is no doubt that similar multigenerational philanthropic Jewish families exist in New York and in other cities. Their generosity plays a pivotal role in providing the financial base for the many cultural, social welfare, and educational institutions that come under the umbrella of the UJA-Federation structure.

Studies of the giving patterns in the various "Federated" Jewish communities throughout the United States have shown that between 40 and 60 percent of the total sum of gifts received by their annual campaigns are collected from about 1 percent of the donors (Silberstein et al. 1987). In other words, a relatively small handful of very generous donors contributes the lion's share of the dollars. Anecdotal evidence suggests that that generous and wealthy 1 percent includes a number of families that have a multigenerational history of giving to Jewish causes in general and to the UJA-Federation system in particular.

The mechanisms that secure such a multigenerational pattern—the structure of wills, parental pressure, strong family socialization, exposure of intense solicitation pressure from the community, etc.—have never been explored. However, anecdotal evidence also indicates what might best be described as "intergenerational philanthropic slippage (hereon referred to as IGPS). This concept will be used to describe the phenomenon of Jewish philanthropic discontinuity on the part of children and grandchildren whose parents and grandparents were and/or are major benefactors of the organized Jewish community, but who themselves have chosen not to continue the same pattern of giving to the Jewish community even though they have the financial means to do so.

No systematic information exists on how frequently the children and/or grandchildren of major philanthropic families fail to follow in the steps of their forebears. However, there is considerable evidence from the impressions of the professional fund raising staff of UJA-Federation throughout the United States that this phenomenon does, in fact, occur. Furthermore, it may be occurring at an increasing rate, particularly in large, metropolitan Jewish communities like New York City. Hence, one would look in vain for evidence of IGPS in the broad picture of statistical trends that describe the pattern of giving to UJA-Federation campaigns.

As Fruehauf (see chapter 11) indicates, the total number of gifts exceeding $10,000 has grown by about 42 percent between 1981 and 1987 in the 125 "Federated" Jewish communities. During the same period the total number of gifts to Jewish fund raising campaigns has increased by only about 9 percent. It would seem that large givers abound despite the existence of IGPS. Yet, there is a persistent concern, among those who are faced with the task of raising the Jewish philanthropic dollar, that obtaining the "large gift" may all too often be a single-generation phenomenon. Substantial Jewish family fortunes pass out of the orbit of the organized Jewish community because the inheritors of those fortunes do not inherit the legacy of their parents' and grandparents' Jewish philanthropic impulses. Thus, the cistern of Jewish communal funds needs to be replenished from ever-new sources, rather than being able to depend upon constant well-springs.

Preliminary Research

This chapter is based upon a pilot study sponsored by the Human Resources Committee of the UJA-Federation of New York City. Its purpose is to take a closer look at IGPS.

A small sample of eight individuals were identified by the members of the committee. Four were men, four were women; half were single, the other half married; and five were engaged full-time in family business. The committee estimated that their parents and/or grandparents were "major Jewish philanthropists." However, our sample has thus far not indicated that they would follow in the footsteps of their forebears with respect to giving to UJA-Federation or to Jewish causes in general. Thus, they were judged to be good examples of IGPS.

The interviews revealed that individual philanthropic activities were in areas other than those supported by their parents and/or grandparents. Respondents were probed deeply on their perceptions of and feelings about Jewishness in general and organized Jewish philanthropy in particular. The central goal of the interviews was to try to identify the reasons for IGPS, at least as perceived through the eyes of an exemplary sample of cases.

It should be noted parenthetically that although the individuals in the sample were selected because they did not follow in the Jewish philanthropic footsteps of their parents and/or grandparents, it would be misleading to suggest that these individuals had no philanthropic impulses. Indeed, all eight exhibited what one might call an intergenerational continuity of generosity that is truly exemplary. All were deeply committed to philanthropic endeavors of their own choosing. Their departure from the patterns of their parents or grandparents was only with respect to "traditional Jewish giving" to the UJA-Federation enterprise.

From direct "hands-on" involvement with helping the homeless or with abused women and children, to African famine relief, to local neighborhood improvement and arts projects, the personal generosity of each of the interviewees was far above what one might expect to find among their peers.

Thus, the notion of IGPS refers only to the relative conformity of consecutive generations to the specific Jewish philanthropic commitments of their predecessors.

Reasons Have Reasons

IGPS, as any social phenomenon, can be explained on a number of different levels. The pilot study approached it entirely from the perspective of the individuals who represent what one might call the "slipping generation." One could conceivably approach the same subject from the vantage point of their parents to see how they account for their children's "slipping," or one could approach it from the vantage point of the outsider, the "objective" social scientists.

In this chapter IGPS will be approached primarily from this last perspective; though, to be sure, the analysis makes use of qualitative interview data, which reflect the subjective perceptions of the children and grandchildren of IGPS. In other words, the chapter will attempt to account for IGPS within a broad, interpretive framework that can both render the phenomenon more understandable and at the same time provide some guide to action on the part of those to who it is of some serious programmatic and life concern.

The verbatim details of the interviews that were conducted can be found in Mayer (1988). Without repeating them here, it is possible to highlight the salient themes:

1. The "slipping generation" views their parents' and grandparents' Jewish philanthropic involvements as an expression of their own unique, personal values and commitments possibly rooted in their own life, which were neither communicated nor made particularly accessible, much less compelling, to their children themselves.

The Federation found a way to tap my father's generation because they seemed to need a kind of gentrified Jewishness. Federation gave them a sense of image and power in exchange for hard cash. But, to tell you the truth, every time I see my dad honored at one of those dinners for yet another of his major gifts I feel a little embarrassed that this is the way he seems to be buying honor in the community. I don't want to buy my honor that way. I guess, I really don't need it.

My dad seems to get a kick out of meeting with the Prime Minister of Israel or the ambassador or what have you. If I wanted that kind of access to power, I wouldn't go through UJA or any of the Jewish organizations. I'd become active in the Democratic Party or the Foreign Policy Association. I don't feel I need the Jewish organizations to give me access to power.

2. The "slipping generation" views the Jewish philanthropic involvements of their parents and grandparents as a range of activities and associations that are closely connected to their business and political involvements, and therefore not relevant to, much less incumbent upon the children except insofar as the children may play a role in the family business. In fact, some indicated that if and when they take their appropriate roles in the family business, they'll also continue some of the Jewish philanthropic activities of their parents and grandparents, simply as an adjunct of their business responsibilities.

If you want to do business, if you want to belong, you have to go to the luncheons. Your firm's name has to appear on the roster of sponsors; you have to serve on this board and that committee. It's strictly business. I really want to have nothing to do with these organizations for myself. In fact, sometimes I get so infuriated with these social obligations that I wonder if I want to stay in the family business.

3. The "slipping generation" largely views the Jewish philanthropic activities of their elders as having been highly successful (as the elders themselves) in creating such large and powerful organizations that the children do not see how they can better these structures or have any impact upon them. Therefore, they feel that their own contributions could only be of minor importance.

I think UJA-Federation is highly effective in getting money out of the Jewish business community. What I see in them is a group of organizations with lots of power, sophistication, success and a lot of so-called professionals who are in the business to raise money for the organization. Frankly, I don't see much there that evokes my feelings of sympathy or generosity. There are many things that touch me deeply. But I don't see the UJA-Federation having much to do with those things.

4. The "slipping generation," for the most part, has had a meager exposure to Jewish education or Jewish associations. Their socialization, *as Jews*, has been so minimal that most do not see how they can play an active, much less a "leadership" role in the community that would be commensurate with their financial capability. In most cases they are unfamiliar with and largely uncommitted to the organized Jewish community. They have little familiarity with its history, language, culture, or needs. Yet, they frequently hear senior representatives of the community refer to them as "young leaders" by virtue of their families' reputation, and possibly their own philanthropic potential.

> I am intensely uncomfortable with being labeled a "young Jewish leader" by UJA-Federation. I can barely read Hebrew, for heaven's sake! How am I supposed to be a "Jewish leader"? What am I supposed to be a leader of? I know it's just a phrase the organization uses to designate people like me who have the potential to give a lot of money. But I really don't like it. It's dishonest. I don't see myself as the "young leader" of anything; at least not anything Jewish.

Given the highly subjective nature of such qualitative data, drawn as it is from a very small sample, with unknown selection biases as well as unknown response biases, it is obviously impossible to draw any robust conclusions about the "real reasons" for IGPS. However, such data do trigger questions that point in the direction of both further research as well as theoretical and programmatic development.

Implications for Research

Given the variety of "reasons" offered by the interviewees for their own defection from their parents' and grandparents' Jewish philanthropic commitments, and given the variety of ways in which such defection may be expressed in the course of any particular person's life cycle, it remains an open empirical question as to when and to what degree can it be said that IGPS has, in fact, occurred within the life of a particular family or the community as a whole. Indeed, it remains an open methodological question as to what is the proper conceptual *unit of analysis* within whose life IGPS is a phenomenon to be measured. Is it a particular nuclear family? Is it the extended family? Is it the whole community? Moreover, what is the proper time frame within which such "slippage" can be said to occur?

From the comments of the interviewees, it is clear that they have some strong feelings about their parents' Jewish involvements as well as about their own Jewishness. However, they also have older and younger siblings who were not interviewed. Furthermore, they themselves will pass through an entire life cycle within which the totality of their philanthropic attitudes and involvements will unfold.

In order to properly demonstrate the reality of IGPS, sufficient information is needed on the philanthropic history of all the members of the families under consideration throughout a fairly extensive stretch of their respective life cycles. Only with such detailed data in hand will it be possible to determine the extent to which IGPS occurs within different families and communities. Similarly, that data will enable us to identify the particular psychogenic, sociogenic, and demographic factors, as well as the interactions among them, which would account most systematically for IGPS.

Implications for Theory

However one might come to measure its extent and its precise determinants, it is also clear from the interview data that, at least from the perspective of the subjects who were spoken to, their own philanthropic interests, as well as actual giving patterns, did depart significantly from the Jewish foci of their parents and grandparents. While these discontinuities can be interpreted as reflecting idiosyncratic tendencies on the part of unique individuals, they can also been seen as expressions of wider patterns that have been previously observed by students of American Jewish life and social behavior in general. These patterns include "Hansen's Law," the social-psychological ramifications of ecology, and the social psychology of philanthropy and money.

"Hansen's Law"

One of the key social-psychological processes that have been identified by social scientists to account for changes in the group identification of ethnics in America is the observation made by historian Marcus L. Hansen (1938) that is is "almost a universal phenomenon that what the son wishes to forget the grandson wishes to remember." Hansen observed that among the descendants of Swedish-American immigrants, the American-born children or so-called second-generation was often eager to dissociate themselves from the old country ways of their parents. However, the grandchildren of the immigrants were often more interested in recapturing some of the habits and styles of their forebears.

Hansen's Law, which suggests a strong need on the part of the second-generation to dissociate itself from the ways and values of its parents, has been widely used to account for the social distancing of American Jews in general from the ways and values of their immigrant parents. It has also been used to explain as well as predict a certain amount of "returning" to Jewish traditions on the part of third- and subsequent-generation American Jews.

While Hansen's Law has been widely used to account for generationally linked changes in Jewish identification patterns in general, its application to philanthropy, and Jewish philanthropy in particular, has not been explored. Yet, our interview data indicate that it has considerable relevance. All of our subjects were adult children of parents who had made their wealth within their own lifetime. In all instances the interviewees knew that their own parents did not grow up in the same climate of wealth and well-being as they. Simply stated, the sample was equivalent to second-generation immigrants within their social world. They were conscious that their parents, the source of their own wealth, were quasi-"foreigners" to the social class in which they grew up. In their eyes, their first-generation wealthy parents were analogous to first-generation immigrants, carrying with them the habits of mind and behavior style associated with mobility striving and the passion for *acquisition* of power, status, security, and wealth. In the case of America's Jewish wealthy, they have also borne within themselves a deeply ingrained concern for their less fortunate brethren, both locally and internationally.

In his history of American Jewish philanthropy, Milton Goldin (1976) calls it a "tool for survival." More specifically, he reports that Jewish philanthropists in America (and possibly elsewhere throughout Jewish history) have been animated by the commitment to the *relief, reconstruction,* and *ransom* of their brethren and the Jewish community. Such a commitment, no matter how noble, betrays the humble and insecure origins of the philanthropist. Thus, it would seem that the passion for Jewish philanthropy on the part of first-generation Jewish wealthy may be fueled not only by a sense of noblesse oblige but by a deep psychological attachment to their roots as well as a realistic appreciation of how their own security and well-being continues to be linked to that of their less fortunate brethren.

Like the second-generation children of immigrants who wish to feel at home in their own native world, and therefore feel impelled to dissociate themselves from the "foreign" elements of their parents' lives, the second-generation wealthy children of Jewish philanthropists apparently also feel a need to disassociate themselves from those aspects of their parents' philanthropic tradition that would betoken inappropriate striving for power, status, or security—all of which the second-generation was raised to take for granted.

Since much of the solicitation techniques of the major Jewish organizations are predicated upon such stirrings and strivings, it comes as no surprise that the children of Jewish philanthropists would find continued involvement in the Jewish philanthropic enterprise somewhat alienating. It would also come as no surprise that the newly wealthy in the Jewish community as well as the grandchildren of Jewish philanthropists would be more amenable to sustaining the traditions of Jewish philanthropy.

In point of fact, those one or two respondents who were the grandchildren of Jewish philanthropists expressed more openness to and interest in organized Jewish philanthropy than those who were the children of major Jewish philanthropists. However, in addition to the psychodynamic forces of Hansen's Law, there are other social forces that seem to shape the orientations of the second- and third-generation Jewish wealthy toward organized Jewish philanthropy as indicated below.

Ecology and Identification

It has been a virtual truism of Jewish residential patterns, particularly in large metropolitan areas such as New York City and its suburban environs, that Jews tend to concentrate in neighborhoods with other Jews. The poor and working-class ghettos on the Lower East Side gave way to the gilded ghetto of the middle- and upper middle-class in post-war suburbia (Moore 1981).

This geographically based community has served both as the physical and organizational center for the sense of identification that Jews continue to have with one another, even as they carved their ever-upward individual paths to social mobility within the wider American society.

The children and grandchildren of Jewish philanthropists, who were the subjects of the pilot study reported above, were generally raised in much less densely Jewish environments and educated to maturity with far less geographic grounding in a concrete Jewish community. As Robert Coles (1977) states, these are children who live comfortable lives in comfortable places—in large homes, on many acres, in opulent places, often in several homes (see also Kirstein 1968; Wixen 1973). Travel, tennis, private schools, lavish entertainment, and limitless consumption punctuate their lives as well as that of their parents and peers:

> These children learn to live with *choices*: more clothes, a wider range of food, a greater number of games and toys, than other boys and girls may ever be able to imagine. . . . They learn to take for granted enormous playrooms, filled to the brim. . . . They learn to assume instruction—not only at school, but at home—for tennis, for swimming, for dancing, for horse riding. And they learn often enough to feel competent at those sports, in control of themselves while playing them, and, not least, able to move smoothly from one to the other, rather than driven to excel. . . .
>
> Something else many of these children learn: . . . that the "news," that events, may well be affected, if not crucially molded, by their parents as individuals or by their parents as members of a particular segment of society. . . . (Coles 1977, 26–27)

The ecology of wealth and the reference groups it provides in the contexts of private schools, second and third homes, and seasonal leisure-time activities are, thus, likely to be much more formative influences upon the identity formation of the children of Jewish philanthropists than structures and ambience of the organized Jewish community. It is the former that represents "familiar turf" and the sphere of personal competence; the latter represents a zone of unfamiliarity, exuding vague claims on the individual's loyalties, which he or she neither fully understands nor feels competent in meeting. Therefore, they tend to shy away from if not altogether reject those claims.

The segregation that wealth affords, perhaps even compels, results in the isolation of the children of Jewish philanthropists from the common experiences of the wider Jewish community. At the same time, their wealth makes it even easier and more desirable to blend into the social world of their class equals.

In other words, their social class socialization both precedes and supercedes their ethnic-religious socialization as Jews. Coupling that reality with the pressures of second-generation status, as described above, results in a convergence of psychosocial influences drawing the children of Jewish philanthropists away from the Jewish communal commitments of their elders.

Thus far the line of analysis presented here has focused on those general social-psychological forces that may have shaped the Jewish commitments of the children of Jewish philanthropists. In the following section attention is turned to their orientations to philanthropy as such, which may help shed additional light on the reasons they might have for turning away from organized Jewish philanthropy.

Philanthropy as Production

In the lexicon of the organized Jewish community, roles are divided between "professionals" and "lay people." Those who give money, no matter how large their gifts might be, are regarded, both by others and by themselves, as the "lay people," that is, mere enablers, whose largess makes it possible for "professionals" to provide services to a clientele with specific needs. Their acts of philanthropy are legitimate only insofar as those acts are geared to meeting the needs of others. Neither the language of philanthropic organization nor the ideology of service and social problem solving, which legitimate the entire structure of Jewish communal organization, allow for the expression of the needs of benefactors or for the expression of their creative, generative, or other productive propensities.

Yet, both the aforementioned interviews and a much larger study of philanthropists, by Schervish and Herman (1987) suggest that personal needs and a vision of philanthropic activity as "productive activity" play an important role in the motivational calculus of individuals when they engage in philanthropy:

> Although not directed toward the accumulation of financial profits, philanthropy as a production process does strive to maximize the accomplishment of specific goals by the application of accumulated resources.

Particularly among those who are both accustomed to and who also want to change various aspects of their world by the manipulation of wealth and its symbols, it comes as a matter of surprise, and no small frustration, that their acts of philanthropy are received as acts of generosity—no matter how noble—enabling others, such as professionals, to play the serious role of effecting change in the world.

Since the organized Jewish community also tends to be highly bureaucratized at the present stage of its development, the opportunity afforded most philanthropists to see how they themselves have had any concrete impact on the attainment of some specific goal or social good is remote indeed. The lack of opportunity *to see* the impact of one's philanthropic acts, much less *to actually participate* in the material activities that are involved in solving human and social problems (e.g., preparing meals for the homeless, driving the frail elderly to a doctor, tutoring the illiterate, etc.) appears to be particularly dispiriting to the younger generation. The post-war, baby-boom generation, coming of age in the 1970s, seems to exhibit a greater need for direct experience and a hands-on sense of effectiveness than their elders.

Thus, two key points emerge from an analysis of philanthropic motivation. One is that, from the vantage points of philanthropists, philanthropic activity is intended as productive activity, a form of production, and not simply as facilitative or enabling activity. The second point, of particular relevance to understanding the philanthropic behavior of people entering adulthood in the 1970s, is that philanthropic activity must engage the hearts, minds, and hands of the individuals. The desire for direct experience on the part of this generation makes the vicarious social problem solving, which characterizes large-scale organized Jewish philanthropy, emotionally unappealing.

Money and Identity

In a legendary exchange of observational prowess, F. Scott Fitzgerald is said to have noted, "The rich are different than you and me." To which Ernest Hemingway is said to have retorted, "Yes. They have more money."

Just how different the psychological formation of the wealthy is from that of others remains a matter of debate among psychologists. It is not the aim of this chapter to review or resolve that debate. For the purposes at hand, however, it is important to note some of the psychological consequences of growing up wealthy, which seem to have relevance to our understanding of IGPS.

While these impacts may not apply universally to all who grow up in wealthy families, they seem to be characteristic of a large number of people in such circumstances. Therefore, they warrant attention here. These psychological consequences of growing up wealthy include (1) guilt about having when others have not; (2) the ready transmutability of money into things, services, and people; (3) fear of being valued only for what one *has* and can spend, rather than for what one *is*; and (4) the need to feel "normal" in the face of being made to feel singularly different by virtue of one's family's wealth. How the solicitation techniques and human relations strategies of the organized Jewish community vis-a-vis the children and grandchildren of major philanthropists intersect with the unique psychological dispositions of those adult children of wealth may determine to a large degree the probability of IGPS.

To be more specific, one of the significant determinants of IGPS may be the ways in which Jewish communal organizations perceive and relate to the children and grandchildren of their major benefactors with but little regard to those psychological dispositions that characterize those who are born and raised in wealth.

Since there are no "services" that the organized Jewish community can provide to the wealthy as such, the primary contact of the wealthy and their children is more likely to be the fund raisers of the community rather than its service providers. Moreover, the principal objective of those contacts—at least from the vantage point of the representative of the Jewish community—is likely to be the solicitation of funds from the philanthropist. Thus, the relationship between the philanthropist and his children, on the one hand, and the representatives of the organized Jewish community on the other, is apt to be shaded by the extrinsic motive of obtaining money by the latter. In return for the money, the philanthropist receives honors and titles, usually bestowed upon him via the self-same representatives of the Jewish community, at ceremonial occasions that are attended by both the family and some of the wealthy social peers of the philanthropist.

To be sure, the Jewish philanthropists, who are generally familiar with and are also deeply committed to ideological goals and the social programs pursued by the Jewish organizations to which they contribute, also receive the intrinsic satisfaction of knowing that their gifts are helping to fulfill their own deeply held commitments. Perhaps as a result of those deeply held commitments, they are also more willing to share in the extrinsic rewards and motivations surrounding their philanthropy. Undoubtedly, many are also quite satisfied, perhaps even enamored with those extrinsic rewards. Those whose wealth is relatively newly acquired welcome the honors and titles bestowed upon them by their erstwhile peers.

The children and grandchildren of philanthropists, who grow up in wealth, however, will generally find both the relationship with the fund raisers of the organized Jewish community, as well as the extrinsic motivations and rewards that surround the fund raising enterprise, to be offensive if not psychologically threatening. At the same time, they are likely to perceive the rewards (viz. honors, titles, ceremonial occasions) as of little value within their own psychic economy. Moreover, because of their general lack of familiarity with and lack of commitment to the ideological goals and social programs of the organizations that seek their largess, they are also not likely to derive the intrinsic satisfaction that their elders did from the knowledge that their money is helping the organizations accomplish those goals and programs.

The fact that they are, more often than not, looked to only for money (or so they believe), and particularly the manner in which money is most often solicited in the Jewish community (in public gatherings and display of comparative largess), communicates to the innermost fears of individuals who grew up in wealth; that is, they are principally valued for what they *have* and can *give* rather than for what they *are*; that those currying favor with them do not regard them as "normal" members of the community; and, that they "owe" something more to the organized Jewish community than others of lesser means and should "feel guilty" for having more unless they also give more.

It should come as little surprise that a form of communal organization and a method of fund raising that would so thoroughly ignore, if not transgress, the psychological sensibilities of the children of its wealthiest philanthropists, might well experience a significant amount of IGPS.

It remains only to be added that both more empirical and theoretical work needs to be done to describe and explain IGPS within the Jewish community. Finally, even more work is required to determine how the phenomenon might manifest itself and be explained in philanthropy in general.

Note

The author acknowledges with appreciation the support of the UJA-Federation of Jewish Philanthropies of New York, and its Human Resources Committee in particular, in carrying out the research in preparation of this chapter.

Bibliography

Coles, Robert. *Privileged Ones: The Well-Off and the Rich in America*, Volume V of *Children of Crisis*. Boston: Little, Brown and Co., 1977.

Fruehauf, Norbert. "The Bottom Line: Major Gifts to Federation Campaigns." In *Contemporary Jewish Philanthropy in America*, edited by Barry A. Kosmin & Paul Ritterband, pp. 173–85. Savage, Md.: Rowman & Littlefield, 1991.

Goldin, Milton. *Why They Give: American Jews and Their Philanthropies*. New York: Macmillan, 1976.

Hansen, Marcus L. *The Problem of the Third Generation Immigrant*. Rock Island, Ill.: Augustana Historical Society, 1938.

Karp, Abraham. *To Give Life: The UJA in the Shaping of the American Jewish Community*. New York: Schocken, 1981.

Kirstein, George. *The Rich: Are They Different?* New York: Houghton Mifflin, 1968.

Mayer, Egon. "Discomforts with Jewish Philanthropy. Some Perspectives of the Children of Philanthropists." *Journal of Jewish Communal Service,* 64(3) (Spring 1988): 223–33.

Moore, Deborah Dash. *At Home in America: Second Generation Jews in America*. New York: Columbia University Press, 1981.

Schervish, Paul G., and Andrew Herman. "Varieties of Philanthropic Logic among the Wealthy." In *Spring Research Forum: Working Papers*, 215–35. Washington, D.C.: Independent Sector and United Way Institute, 1987.

Silberstein, Richard, Paul Ritterband, Jonathan Rabinowitz, and Barry A. Kosmin. *Giving to Jewish Philanthropic Causes: A Preliminary Reconnaissance*. (Reprint Series no. 2). New York: CUNY Graduate Center, North American Jewish Data Bank, November 1987. (Originally published in *Spring Research Forum: Working Papers*, 265–74. Washington, D.C.: Independent Sector and United Way Institute.)

Wixen, Burton. *Children of the Rich*. New York: Crown, 1973.

10

Generous Fathers, Ungenerous Children: A Small City Perspective

Arthur S. Goldberg

My father thought of himself as a member of the Jewish Community of Rochester. I think of myself as a Jewish member of the Rochester community.

—45-year-old respondent

This chapter is based on a study conducted for the Jewish Community Federation of Rochester, New York in August–September 1982. The Greater Rochester Standard Metropolitan Statistical Area (SMSA) has a population of 960,000, and in a recent study (Tobin and Fishman 1987), the Jewish population of that SMSA was estimated at 25,000. The respondents in this study were drawn from a list provided by the federation. They were promised anonymity in return for candor.

Goal

The central purpose of this study was to provide the Rochester federation with increased insight into what factor or factors inhibit some members of the Jewish community from greater participation in the federation. Specifically, we focused our attention on the federation,

161

and we focused our attention on those who seemed to have the potential to increase their financial contributions and time commitments to the federation from their then-current level.

Sample

A series of fifteen one-to-one open-ended interviews were conducted. A cross-section attitude study seemed inappropriate since its cost would have been too great. In-depth probing was considered impractical as well and somewhat redundant in light of other federation studies. Similarly, the use of focus groups was eliminated since early investigation indicated that desired respondents were more likely to be candid with a reputable researcher on a one-to-one basis but would not provide that level of candor in front of other people.

All potential respondents were "undergivers," that is, their current level of involvement and/or financial contribution was less than what the federation estimated to be their potential. The federation list was divided into three categories: (1) "Young" professionals and business persons with potentially—although not necessarily currently—large resources; (2) persons with substantial resources who were not currently at the top of the resource group; and (3) those in the highest resource category.

The list contained more names in each category than were needed to draw a sample, which, therefore, ensured both a representative sample from each category and anonymity of the respondents. Persons in whom the federation expressed extra special interest were singled out in each category. For the most part, these were either (1) individuals judged capable of giving large amounts of money who had not as yet done so, or (2) individuals who had once been large contributors but who had reduced their contributions. The majority of respondents in each category (three out of five) met one of these two criteria.

The respondent profile in each category was as follows:

	Group I	Group II	Group III
Number Interviewed	5	5	5
Number of Extra Special Interest	3	3	3
Age Range	40s	Late 40s to early 60s	Late 50s to late 70s

A Note on the Sample Size

While a sample size of fifteen may not be regarded as representative of any substantial population of respondents, this was not a simple random sample of the whole Jewish population. Rather, the Rochester sample reflected a very special part of that population; namely, individuals known by the federation leadership and considered "undergivers."

The fifteen respondents were selected from a list containing several hundred "undergivers." While such a small study would have been worthless if the respondents' views of the federation were markedly different from one another, strong recurrent themes surfaced—some more and some less—in almost all of the interviews. That such themes should recur *independently*—without the mutual stimulation and reinforcement present in a focus group—offers some reason to believe that the results are *at least suggestive* of the attitudes and perceptions of "undergivers." Nevertheless, it should be borne in mind that the sample size was only fifteen; therefore, the results should be evaluated in the context of the other chapters in this volume.

A Note on the Jewishness of the Sample

Before proceeding with a description of the attitudes and perceptions of these respondents, we had to ascertain if their current levels of giving to the federation reflected an apathy about Jewish affairs. In order to address this problem, we asked respondents to indicate how much personal satisfaction they received from giving to each of a variety of special causes. They were asked then to concentrate on the amount of satisfaction they derived rather than the amount they gave, in recognition of the possibility that some large donations might reflect pressure rather than satisfaction. The results are presented in table 10-1.

In examining table 10-1, it may be useful to take two non-Jewish items as base points: cancer research and the Community Chest (United Way). We recommended the former because it is so emotionally loaded and the latter because it is nearly universal.

Note that on a scale of 1–10, where ten represents a maximum, the mean score given by the respondents to the satisfaction derived from providing financial support for cancer research was 5.67 and that the counterpart for contributions to the Community Chest (United Way) was 5.25. By contrast, the mean score given to satisfaction derived

Table 10-1. *Levels of Satisfaction from Giving*

Assigning	Mean Satisfaction Score (n = 12)	No. Assigning 7 or greater	No. Assigning 8 or greater
Program			
Strengthening the Jewish family	7.67	8	7
Support for Israel	7.58	8	6
Combatting anti-Semitism	7.17	7	7
Support for synagogue or temple	6.83	7	5
Care of elderly in a Jewish environment	6.08	6	6
Jewish education in Rochester	5.67	4	4
Cancer research	5.67	3	3
Social, athletic, and leisure time to develop and main Jewish identity	5.42	2	2
Community Chest (United Way)	5.25	3	2
Support for Hillel college campus programs	3.75	2	1
Civil rights	3.17	2	2
College alumni fund	1.97	0	0

Note: Only twelve of the fifteen respondents completed the form. The other three were overwhelmingly involved with things Jewish, and so intensely caught up in their own narratives as to have made the introduction of the form inappropriate. The possible mean scores can vary from one to ten with ten indicating the greatest satisfaction and one the least.

from providing financial support for "Strengthening the Jewish family" was 7.67; for providing financial support for Israel, the mean score was 7.58; and for providing such support for "Combatting anti-Semitism," the mean score was 7.17.

One may examine table 10-1 in any number of ways—the rank order of item scores, the relative mean scores, the assigning a particular score or higher, etc. No matter how one looks at the data in that table, one has to conclude that respondents were people who (1) cared about Jews, and (2) derived high levels of satisfaction from providing financial support to core Jewish concerns.

Therefore, if these people were giving less than they might to the federation, it was *not* because of indifference.

Basic Findings

The basic findings reported below are quite pervasive in this sample and are manifest in each of the groups of the sample (I, II, III), albeit to a somewhat lesser extent in Group III. (The difference, such as it is, in Group III seems to reflect the age of the respondents more than anything else.)

Respondents and Identity: Jewish and Rochesterian

All of the respondents had strong identification as Jews. They all felt strong emotional ties to Israel, a feeling not diminished by the Lebanon war, despite their diverse reactions to it. Nevertheless, all but three of the respondents (who were all over sixty years of age) indicated at least a concern that the federation focuses too much on Israel and not enough on local concerns. Finally, several felt that the federation was requesting a dual allegiance of them and articulated a clear discomfort about such a request. This duality entailed a competition between the Rochester community and Israel for their time and resources.

Perception of the Federation

Virtually all respondents claimed and appeared to have low information levels about the federation. Their basic perception of it was that it is an Israel-oriented fund raiser. Hence, those with some experience of the federation's fund raising activities did not see it as effectively relating to what they consider to be the two major local institutions: the Jewish Home and Infirmary and the Jewish Community Center.

Lay Leadership of the Federation

Most of the respondents thought that the lay leadership was overwhelmingly preoccupied with Israel, treating local matters—other than fund raising—with only marginal concern. Furthermore, they saw the lay leadership as a clique, admission to which is a function of how much money one gives and can induce others to give. Finally, there was a widespread belief that there is an insufficient flow of new blood into the leadership, and that what exists is recruited on the wrong basis.

The Solicitation Process

Almost all of the respondents had been substantially offended by the solicitation process at one time or another. Both younger and older respondents agreed that the old techniques rooted in peer pressure, guilt and obligations will be increasingly ineffective with the newer generations, that is, those aged under fifty and even many of those between fifty and sixty. In addition, the respondents articulated a recurrent theme that solicitation ought to be done on a more professional basis.

Among those respondents who had some substantive experience with the federation, all agreed that any and all involvement with it ultimately costs them money. Some regarded that with good humor and thought it necessary. This tended to be the case with the older respondents. Nevertheless, there was a widespread desire that the federation convincingly communicate an appreciation of people for what they can deliver beyond money.

Response of the Federation

It should be noted that in the six years following the completion of this study (1982–88), the Rochester federation has addressed virtually all of these issues in a very substantial manner. Much greater emphasis is now given to local needs. Ties with the Jewish Home and Infirmary and Jewish Community Center have been strengthened. In addition, a great deal of effort has gone into the training of solicitors. Finally, recruitment onto the board has been broadened and a process for continually bringing in "new blood" is evolving.

Discussion of the Basic Findings

Respondents and Identity

Except for those respondents in their seventies, most see themselves as an integral part of the larger Rochester community and not one bit less Jewish as a result. They are ardent Zionists who have a realistic view of Israel. Many have visited and have sent their children there. However, Rochester is their home and their community. Local problems and local Jewish problems take precedence. This is exemplified by the following comments:

> For a long time, I have felt that I am basically a member of this community, but that the federation's central business is not this community.
>
> —Respondent in mid-forties, Group I

> I make my living in this community. My clients are not Jewish. My employees are not Jewish. Most of my contributions are through my corporation's foundation. I am much more comfortable justifying those contributions when they deal with local needs.
>
> —Respondent in sixties, Group II

> I support Israel. I have been to Israel many times. I believe that Israel can and should learn to support itself. There are Jews in this country with more dire need and they should be getting much more support from the federation than they are now.
>
> —Respondent in mid-sixties, Group III

Perception of the Federation

These respondents see the federation essentially as a fund raising organization focused on Israel. They think their individual roles mean little to the federation except as sources of money. They believe that sound advice, free labor, and the spreading of good will are all almost worthless to the federation, except when accompanied by large amounts of money. One respondent captured the essence of the matter with these words:

> You can work hundreds of hours, give of your heart and your mind, jeopardize your relationship with your family, take vital time away from your business—all to serve the federation. And when the day finally comes that you want to hold high office in the federation—YOU WILL HAVE TO BUY IT!
>
> —Respondent in forties, Group I

Lay Leadership of the Federation

This set of findings was the least favorable to the local federation, inasmuch as it precipitated the most bitterness in the responses. While it was generally acknowledged that in such an organization those who give large amounts of money necessarily have large leadership roles, the claim is made that it is different now from the way it used to be. The flavor is perhaps best conveyed by the following two comments:

> The people who run the federation, with a few exceptions, have large egos, and their federation activity is an ego trip. It's sort of a clique. In fact, I was in the clique at one time. The only thing that is discussed is who pressured whom into giving how much. After a while I couldn't stand myself—so I left.
>
> —Respondent in mid-forties, Group I

> My people didn't have money. We were poor. What I have, I made. But we always gave—and more each year than the year before. Now I give thousands each year. But it's a closed shop. When I go to meetings, I'm ignored. At get-togethers, my wife is ignored. So I give. But why should I be involved?
>
> —Respondent in mid-fifties, Group III

In other words, fund raising is an isolated activity for them. This is in marked contrast to findings of other groups involved in philanthropic endeavors, where fund raising is either embedded in the sacred life of the community (see Heilman, chapter 8) or as some sort of "club" (see Chiswick, chapter 1).

The Solicitation Process

There are two aspects to the solicitation process: the cost of abrasions and the diminishing efficacy of guilt.

The respondents produced a history of abrasions and resentment when probed on the solicitation process. Most had direct experience with both strong-arm tactics and insensitivity; the latter was resented much more than the former. The following three examples illustrate this point.

In one case, a respondent's wife had died of cancer. Afterwards, he went through family counseling with his children to cope with the trauma of their loss. Not only had their financial burden been very large, but the respondent was also distracted from his business, which, in turn, showed a significant reduction in his personal income. The solicitor had brushed all of this aside as "[the respondent's] problems," pointing out to him that his problems did not diminish the needs of Israel, and that therefore he was morally obliged to give at least as much as he had the year before.

In the second instance, a normally large donor had a very bad financial year. He requested a reduction in his financial commitment. The solicitor, a friend, told him that was absolutely unacceptable. Consequently, this particular respondent made the requested pledge by borrowing the money to meet it. He subsequently learned that the solicitor, a substantially wealthier man than he was at the time, had made a far smaller pledge.

Finally, one respondent made a large contribution out of gratitude to the Jewish Family Service and later regretted it. This particular man benefited from their assistance when he was relatively young and without much money. He later raised his pledge to rather more than he could afford, and he met that commitment. However, a year afterward he became very ill. He was hospitalized for a long time and then had a long recovery period, all of this to the detriment of his income. The federation solicitor, an ostensible friend, dismissed both his argument that the previous year's level of giving was intended as a one-time special gift of gratitude and the claim that he was in extreme financial distress at the time of solicitation. The respondent made the pledge by borrowing the money to meet it and never spoke to his "friend" again.

In each of these three examples, the respondents are currently wealthy men. All are estranged from the federation.

In addition to the insensitivity of the solicitor, respondents elicited guilt as a basis of obligation to the federation. This was mentioned and rejected by most of the respondents. All raised the topic without being probed; all explicitly rejected vulnerability on that basis. These respondents are a post-Holocaust generation. They have not had to cope with the knowledge that relatives and friends perished. Moreover, they are resistant to guilt induced about their status. As one respondent said:

> I don't feel guilty. I was brought up to feel guilty, but I have outgrown that. I believe that my family and I are entitled to certain things that we have earned. That comes first.
> —Respondent in mid-forties, Group II

This is also manifested in their attitudes toward federation solicitation, which several respondents thought was relatively unprofessional, as illustrated by the following comment:

They should learn what everybody else knows—you get more with honey than with vinegar. Let them come, like everybody else, and explain what the need is, why it is deserving, and even, if they wish, what they hope that I will give. But don't tell me that I "owe." I don't "owe" anything. And like universities, and hospitals, and everyone else, let them accept what I give with a smile, a handshake, and sincere thanks.

—Respondent in seventies, Group III

Parents and Children

Although the study design did not specifically examine intergenerational differences, the interview process sometimes afforded some remarkable insights. On one occasion, a respondent's father participated in the interview. While there were substantial differences between father and son, the two exhibited a great affection and mutual respect for each other.

During many interviews with older respondents, they took the opportunity to comment on the differences between themselves and their children with regard to giving. In these instances, too, the parents were sympathetic toward their children's perspectives. The following two comments go to the heart of the matter:

My son cannot know what I know and cannot feel what I feel. I do not need an accounting from the federation—what it has done with the money—what it plans to do with the money. For me it is enough that I must give—for all those who are not here to give. This is from the *kishkes* [guts]. My son—he is giving from the head, even from the heart, but not from the *kishkes*.

—Father of Group II Respondent

When we came to this country we had nothing, but we made our pledge to the UJA—as much as we could possibly manage. And we met that pledge; even if we didn't buy clothes that year, we met our pledge. It was at the top of our list. Our children have different lists—different priorities. They give to federation, and to United Way, to colleges, to medical research, to many, many things. They also belong to country clubs, take vacations, and plan for the future. Federation is one item among many for them and definitely after the country clubs, the vacation, and the investment planning.

—Respondent in late sixties, Group III

Conclusion

Despite our small sample size, the findings should be regarded as suggestive of the attitudes and perceptions of many "undergivers." The similarity of their views is substantial. At their core, these attitudes and perceptions seem to suggest the following.

Tactical

First, at the very least, the federation needs to generate much greater publicity on what is done at a *local* level. Second, it must recognize the peer pressure, guilt-based strategy of solicitation is becoming less and less effective and more and more counterproductive. Third, people whose primary focus is local should be recruited into leadership positions. Federations should make them feel efficacious and appreciated.

Fourth, the two most visible local Jewish institutions in Rochester are the Jewish Home and Infirmary and the Jewish Community Center. The federation must demonstrate a positive relationship with them. Finally, the federation must emerge as the leader and coordinator of a set of community-valued programs, rather than as a fund raiser for programs valued by its leaders.

To its credit, the Jewish Community Federation of Rochester has already acted successfully on each of these points.

Strategic

While the Rochester federation has acted on each of these findings with commitment, its annual campaign moves ahead slowly. This may in part be due to the time it will take for new leadership channels to mature. We believe, however, that strategic changes in perception and values must occur in the campaign area.

Three points of strategic impact have emerged repeatedly in these interviews: (1) the changing form of communal membership from being a member of the Jewish community of Rochester to being a Jewish member of the Rochester community; (2) guilt being rejected as an acceptable basis of behavior; and (3) giving being seen as charity, as distinct from *tzedakeh*. Taken together, these three points go beyond the tactics and methods of solicitation and foci of public relations. They speak to the core of belief systems.

After years of struggle for acceptance, third-generation Rochesterians see themselves as members of the Rochester community, rather than members of the Jewish community of Rochester. With that comes an allegiance and commitment to that larger community. This is essentially inflexible.

In addition, guilt is rejected as a basis for decision making in regard to giving. The guilt "earned" by Holocaust survivors should not be wished upon anyone, and inculcations with guilt have usually had more negative than positive consequences on American-born Jews. As a result, this point, too, is intractable.

Finally is the issue of charity versus *tzedakeh*. The younger generation of affluent forty- and fifty-year-old Jewish businessmen speak of giving in terms alluding to Calvinism. This suggests how "American" they have become, and coincides with the finding that they see themselves primarily as Jewish members of the Rochester community rather than as members of the Jewish community of Rochester. We also believe that this suggests a serious failure of Jewish education. As a consequence, *tzedakeh* means charity for this group. It is a gift from those who had the "right stuff" to those who did not quite "have what it takes." For previous generations of Jews, *tzedakeh* meant justice and was rooted in the assumption that, given the requirements of righteousness, it was not likely that the righteous would be wealthy. While this error of understanding can be rectified among the young, it will take time and effort.

Bibliography

Chiswick, Barry R. "An Economic Analysis of Philanthropy." In *Contemporary Jewish Philanthropy in America,* edited by Barry A. Kosmin & Paul Ritterband, pp. 3–15. Savage, Md.: Rowman & Littlefield, 1991.

Heilman, Samuel. "*Tzedakah:* Orthodox Jews and Charitable Giving." In *Contemporary Jewish Philanthropy in America,* edited by Barry A. Kosmin & Paul Ritterband, pp. 133–44. Savage, Md.: Rowman & Littlefield, 1991.

Tobin, Gary A., and Sylvia B. Fishman. *A Population Study of the Jewish Community of Rochester.* Unpublished manuscript, Center for Modern Jewish Studies, Brandeis University, Waltham, Mass., July 1987.

11

The Bottom Line: Major Gifts to Federation Campaigns

Norbert Fruehauf

During 1987, in the annual Jewish federation campaigns of North America, approximately 1.2 percent of the givers provided approximately 60 percent of the total contributions. In contrast, approximately half of all contributors made donations of under $100, providing only about 2 percent of the total. In real numbers, this translated into 13,000 givers contributing $400 million compared to 450,000 givers contributing $15 million.

Is this a healthy and desirable situation? Many would say it was fantastic. Isn't there a rule of thumb that says 90 percent of the funds raised comes from about 10 percent of the givers? Certainly, that reflects economic reality and the bias in the overall distribution of wealth in the country. Furthermore, 1987 data provided by the Council of Jewish Federations (to be discussed below) indicate that about one-third of all U.S. Jewish households give to federation campaigns: 869,000 gifts were received from the 2.3 million estimated Jewish households.

This raises a key question: Can federations continue to depend on a very small segment of the North American Jewish community to provide the major wherewithal for our Jewish communities both to flourish and to provide aid and assistance overseas, including Israel?

Should they not aim to expand the base both in terms of total funds raised and numbers of givers?

Compared to other fund raising drives in the United States, the Jewish federation campaigns are generally considered premier campaigns. This is especially true in terms of the yearly achievements, the total amounts raised, and the average gift size. Certainly capital fund campaigns—one-time gifts associated with universities and museums—can report more sizable achievements, but they are not sustained efforts. Many businesses would be pleased with yearly sales increases of 5–6 percent. What then are the trends and indicators that would give us cause for hope or worry?

In order to answer these questions, let us refer to three old United Jewish Appeal (UJA) stories that serve to illustrate some issues and are appropriate for this discussion.

> Two men survived a shipwreck and were abandoned on an island. One, a Jew, was relaxed; the other, a Protestant, was nervous, pacing up and down, certain that he was not going to survive. He asked the Jew why he was so relaxed and the latter said, "Because this is December; it's UJA time in my community and they always find me."

Unfortunately, given today's circumstances of our knowledge of who is in some of the Jewish communities, he may not last long enough for his federation to find him.

> Sam Cohen, a diligent worker on behalf of the campaign, volunteered to take the card of Sinclair Miller, whom he felt quite sure was Jewish, but had never given to the campaign. After introducing himself to Mr. Miller, Mr. Cohen indicated that he was representing the federation, raising money for Jewish causes at home and abroad. Mr. Miller interrupted him and said, "I don't know why you're seeing me. I'm not Jewish, my wife is not Jewish, my children are not Jewish, my father was not Jewish and my grandfather, *olov ha shalom*,* was not Jewish either."

This story is relevant for it asks how many people there are whose relationship to the Jewish community is minimal, whose sense of belonging and association are something of the past, and whose identification with things Jewish is no longer pertinent.

> This same Sam Cohen went to see Mark Bernstein for his pledge to the campaign. He started to discuss with Mr. Bernstein the pressing needs of

---

*Hebrew: May he rest in peace.

the local community, of the people in need, and the issues facing Israel, when Mr. Bernstein interrupted. "Look, I have a wife who is quite ill; my son is on drugs and is in a rehabilitation hospital; my daughter is married to a no-goodnik and she's looking to me for support; my mother is in a nursing home; and my brother-in-law is unemployed." Whereupon Mr. Cohen said, "Well, I certainly can appreciate the burden of those obligations on you." Mr. Bernstein interrupted and said, "You're wrong. I don't help them so why should I help you?"

Taken together, these three stories, though humorous, describe the conditions many federation campaigns now face: There is little outreach, which is further compounded by a lack of identity and commitment on the part of significant segments of North American Jewish communities. Simply stated, then, what are Jewish people's understanding and commitment to principles of *tzedakah*?

Our purpose here is to discuss the place that major givers have in the funds raised by federations; the federations' significant dependence upon them; the chances of replenishing and increasing this giving population in the future, both in numbers and in the amounts they contribute; and the issues that confront federations in making that a reality.

Tables 11-1 and 11-2 show a seven-year analysis of major federation campaign achievements for the years 1981 and 1987. Almost every community raising over $2 million is included in both years. Table 11-1 shows gifts at various levels, the number of gifts (one gift may represent more than one person), the proportion of those givers of the total, the total dollar amount contributed by them, what proportion that represents of total contributions, and the per capita gift of the contributors. Table 11-2 gives the same information plus the percentage increase in that seven-year period. The total amount raised by the federations cited in this report was $526.2 million in 1981 and $710.5 million in 1987.[1]

The data revealed by these two tables indicate the following salient key factors relative to major gifts (givers of $10,000 +):

1. In 1981, there were approximately 9,000 gifts of $10,000+ that represented a little over 1.1 percent of the total givers. They contributed $273 million or 52 percent of the campaign with an average per capita gift of about $30,000.
2. By 1987, the number of $10,000 + givers had increased by 42 percent from 9,000 to almost 13,000, and they had increased

Table 11-1. *Trends in Major Gifts to Federation Campaigns, 1981*

1981	No. of Gifts	% of Total Gifts	Contribs ($000)	% of Total Contrib	Per Capita Gift ($000)
Under $100	448,264	55.99%	14,545	2.8%	0.03
$100–$999	270,841	33.83%	70,586	13.4%	0.26
$1,000–$4,999	64,345	8.04%	112,182	21.3%	1.74
$5,000–$9,999	9,200	1.15%	55,753	10.6%	6.06
$10,000–$24,999	6,066	0.76%	83,567	15.9%	13.78
$25,000–$49,999	1,751	0.22%	54,463	10.4%	31.10
$50,000–$99,999	749	0.09%	49,393	9.4%	65.95
$100,000 + Over	467	0.06%	86,097	16.4%	184.36
Total $10,000 +	9,033	1.13%	273,520	52.0%	30.28
Total $1,000 +	82,578	10.31%	441,455	83.9%	5.35
Total Campaign	800,598		526,170		0.66

Source: This analysis is based on the Council of Jewish Federations' Annual Survey of Campaign Statistics. Information is from 124 cities in 1981 and 125 cities in 1987. All major cities are included in both years with some variation in the smaller cities.

Table 11-2. *Trends in Major Gifts to Federation Campaigns, 1987*

1987	No. of Gifts	% of Total Gifts	% Incrs Total Gifts	Contribs ($000)	% of Total Contrib	$ Incrs Contr	Per Capita Gift ($000)	$ Incrs Per Capita
Under $100	452,036	51.96%	0.8%	14,792	2.1%	1.7%	0.03	0.8%
$100–$999	315,705	36.29%	16.6%	82,341	11.6%	16.7%	0.26	0.1%
$1,000–$4,999	77,017	8.85%	19.7%	137,102	19.3%	22.2%	1.78	2.1%
$5,000–$9,999	12,371	1.42%	34.5%	73,881	10.4%	32.5%	5.97	−1.5%
$10,000–$24,999	8,631	0.99%	42.3%	114,403	16.1%	36.9%	13.25	−3.8%
$25,000–$49,999	2,450	0.28%	39.9%	75,525	10.6%	38.7%	30.83	−0.9%
$50,000–$99,999	946	0.11%	26.3%	58,001	8.2%	17.4%	61.31	−7.0%
$100,000 + Over	809	0.09%	73.2%	154,462	21.7%	79.4%	190.93	3.6%
Total $10,000 +	12,836	1.60%	42.1%	402,391	56.6%	47.1%	31.35	3.5%
Total $1,000 +	102,224	11.75%	23.8%	613,374	86.3%	38.9%	6.00	12.2%
Total Campaign	869,965		8.7%	710,506		35.0%	0.82	24.3%

Source: This analysis is based on the Council of Jewish Federations' Annual Survey of Campaign Statistics. Information is from 124 cities in 1981 and 125 cities in 1987. All major cities are included in both years with some variation in the smaller cities.

their share of the total proportion of contributors to 1.6 percent. They contributed over $402 million, representing almost 57 percent of the gifts with an average per capita gift of about $31,000.

3. While there is a 42 percent increase from 1981 to 1987 in the percentage of all givers contributing major gifts of $10,000+ (9,033 in 1981 to 12,836 in 1987), their contributions represent a 9 percent rate increase in their share of all contributions (52 percent in 1981 to 56.6 percent in 1987). In other words, if we factor in the relationship between inflation and increased contributions, the numbers of givers increased significantly, while their share of the total dollars contributed increased moderately. The average size of their gifts declined in all categories except the $100,000+ bracket.

4. This is contrasted with those giving under $100 where the total contributions increased by only 1.7 percent. In fact, their proportionate share of total givers dropped on two counts: from about 56 percent in 1981 to 52 percent in 1987, contributing 2.8 percent in 1981 compared to 2.1 percent in 1987 of all the funds raised.

5. Over the seven campaign years, major gifts increased in value by 47.1 percent. The annual average increase among all the major gifts over the seven-year period was 6.7 percent. The cities included in this analysis increased their total campaign by 35 percent, or by an annual increase of 5 percent, which is in line with the consumer price index for the period. However, the ability of federations to maintain results at about the inflation rate was made possible mainly because of increases in the $100,000+ bracket of gifts. In other words, we have been standing still in economic terms.

6. In each of the major giving brackets, the per capita gift decreased, except the $100,000+ bracket. However, the increase in the per capita gift at the top was only 3.6 percent—indicative of these major givers holding their gifts at previous year levels.

7. In the 1974 "banner year" (the Yom Kippur War Campaign) there were 8,614 major gifts of $10,000+ totaling $343.5 million, contributing 51.4 percent of the campaign.

8. This decreased in 1977 to 6,600 giving units of $10,000+ totaling $207.5 million providing 45.6 percent of the total campaign. We should point out, however, that the period 1974–77 saw unusually high inflation rates for the United States.

9. In 1981 major gift units accounted for 52 percent of the total revenue, similar to the 1974 proportion, but the total dollars contributed were $273.5 million, $70 million less than 1974, not taking inflation into account.

10. By 1987, federations became increasingly dependent on $10,000+ givers. They numbered approximately 13,000 gifts to provide for approximately 56.6 percent of the campaign total, or about $402 million. However, if dollars were held constant to 1974, the amount contributed would be drastically less and about equal to the 1981 rate.

In comparison with other brackets of giving, the total campaign results for 1981 and 1987 show:

1. A 9 percent increase in total number of gifts, much less than the percent of increase for major gifts of 42.1 percent.

2. The per capita gift for all givers increased from $660 to $820, a 24.3 percent increase in per capita giving. The reason for this large per capita increase is that the dollars contributed by the $100,000+ givers increased by 79 percent, while the total number of gifts only increased by 8.7 percent.

3. The contributions among those giving under $1,000 increased by 14 percent over the seven-year period. Those between $1,000 and $10,000 increased their total contributions by 26 percent over the same period, while gifts of $10,000+ increased by 42.1 percent.

4. Several other conditions seem to be operative:
   a. Priority efforts are made to upgrade gifts of $5,000+ from one level to another; and
   b. The brackets broaden at a faster rate as giving increases, e.g., the $100,000+ bracket increased by 73.2 percent, whereas the giving under $1,000 group went up by only 0.7 percent.

These data demonstrate the validity of the theories put forward by Silberstein, Ritterband, Rabinowitz, and Kosmin (1987). In that study, Silberstein et al. categorized fund raising campaigns into three types based on the nature of both the givers and the beneficiaries: (1) elite givers to elite constituents, such as individuals giving to universities and museums; (2) philanthropies with mass support that provide a broad range of services for many, such as the United Way; and (3) philanthropies that raise money primarily from a few but offer services to many, such as the federation campaigns. Hence, in a very positive sense federations typify the "progressive" nature of their campaigns.

In order to understand why federations are so dependent on major gifts, we need first to understand the nature of their annual campaign. The campaign is the primary instrument for the support of each federation's system of organizations and institutions in their community. The successful campaign is more than the achievement of a specified dollar amount. It is the sustained building of a community and an understanding of its needs and purpose. It involves maximum coverage and involvement of people, and maximum giving in relation to the resources available in the community. It is a vehicle for community building and a means to enhance the community's self-image so it can identify and address its own needs, establish collective responsibility, and provide for its future.

Federations recognize that a small proportion of givers provide the necessary wherewithal. However, it has always been the case of voluntary financial efforts in the Jewish community that a small minority supports the majority of the effort. This is in sharp contrast to broad social welfare campaigns such as the United Way. Nevertheless the current figures available indicate that the Jewish communities' enterprises may not be viable in the long term if they continue to depend so exclusively on a small number of givers.

In order to be successful the federation requires not only a select group of donors who give large amounts of money, but also a significant involvement by many in the activities of Jewish life. The latter would help generate more contributions that, in turn, would provide brain power for the creative survival of Jewish life. In communities where such participatory leadership is absent, the evidence points to lack of campaign success in both dollars raised and respective share of the total campaign. Furthermore, this absence leads to community and federation "stagnation."

The need for personal involvement conjures up additional issues. These include a strong sense of Jewish association and of belonging, a Jewish knowledge base, a sense of community and communal responsibility, concern for other Jews and at a level of altruism that does not require plaques and names on buildings. However, as we enter the 1990s, we increasingly note a discrepancy between the number of people living a life style that is commensurate with this orientation and those who simultaneously have the financial wherewithal to make those types of commitments.

Both the "well running dry" thesis put forward by Ritterband and

Cohen (1979) and Tobin (1986b) and studies conducted by local federations (see, for example, New York 1981; Rappeport and Tobin 1987;
Tobin 1986a), have indicated that lack of Jewish wealth is not the issue.
Estimates have been made that there are more than one hundred
thousand Jewish millionaires. The threat to the future of federation
campaigns lies elsewhere. As Goldberg and Mayer suggest in chapters
9 and 10, wealth may provide a challenge to federations and may
require changing the entire way in which major gifts are acquired.

Lay and professional campaign leaders indicate that major givers
have a tendency to insulate and protect themselves and to put a cap on
their giving level. They simply want to make a gift and not become
involved. For example, some contribute significantly to their local
federation's endowment in the form of a philanthropic fund (donor
recommended fund), but then let the federation determine its distribution. An examination of recent practices indicates that federations do
not convey an urgency of need to major contributors. They, in turn,
do not see the needs of the Jewish community as real and pertinent.
While they have a sense of responsibility to help their fellow Jews,
they are simultaneously engaged with nonsectarian causes that meet
pressing societal needs. Hence, the spirit to help others may be there,
but targets of charitable acts have broadened.

Other demographic changes have resulted in federations becoming
increasingly dependent upon major gifts. There are several reasons for
this. First, there is growing evidence of positive philanthropic responses that are not made under the federation umbrella. Organizations such as the B'nai B'rith Anti-Defamation League, Simon Wiesenthal Center, New Israel Fund, and American friends groups of Israeli
universities all report significant increases in their campaigns. Even
within the federation network, which reports declining or stable Jewish
populations, there have been increased numbers of gifts in the seven-
year period cited in this chapter, from 800,000 givers to 870,000. While
total dollar contributions to Jewish life have not decreased, their
expressions and targets have changed, and this has affected the federations' market share.

Second is the question of mobility and dispersion. Jewish people are
migrating throughout broader metropolitan regions and are no longer
concentrated in Jewish neighborhoods. Consequently, a sense of community is diminishing in these areas in much the same way as it is
absent in new growth areas in the Sunbelt. This affects community life
and, in turn, affects people's sense of Jewish identification and association. Since the Jewish tradition of *tzedakah* is rooted in community,

it follows that philanthropy should diminish with the erosion of tradition, dispersion of the population, and feelings of anomie.

Finally, it is becoming more difficult to locate individual Jews. This is a result of the drop-off in affiliation, friendship circles not being exclusively Jewish, and intermarriage. The last factor, even with conversion, results in diminishing loyalties (Tobin 1986a, 1986b; Tobin and Rappeport 1987) since friendships broaden to include non-Jewish circles, one's relatives are not all Jewish, and their children have mixed experiences.

Taken together, all of these changes indicate that it is expedient, cheaper, and in the short term, a more cost-effective strategy to rely on the same people to give more. This is evidenced by the increased share of responsibility that campaign elites assume. They go to the same people for more resources as manifested by the small increase in number of givers but increase in their giving levels (for $10,000+). Federations need to ascertain, among other things, whether the increasing number of $10,000+ givers constitute a "reserve" for future expansion and development that augurs well for the future or if it represents an older generation that potentially will not be replicated.

Two recent studies might shed some light on current campaign patterns and what federations will have to do in order to accommodate the changing marketplace. A marketing analysis of $10,000+ givers conducted by the New York UJA–Federation (UJA 1988) indicated that the primary reasons for maintenance of major givers had to do with their recognition and association with their Jewish heritage, commitment to perpetuate the Jewish community and Jewish life, concern for Israel, keeping the U.S. Jewish community strong, and a sense of social responsibility.

The analysis also found that one-half of those giving in the $10,000+ bracket were over sixty years of age. More than three-quarters of them belonged to a synagogue. However, the religious motivation for giving was held by only 10 percent. Finally, the study revealed that major givers got into the system and gave at their level primarily as a result of their association with Jewish business groups, immediate family, relatives, and Jewish friends.

While this study was confined to the New York metropolitan area, its findings are representative vis-a-vis most major givers and adherents to federations. The New York UJA–Federation study also reported that nongivers are younger, less likely to belong to synagogues, and less likely to have personal contacts within the Jewish community. Their key "Jewish concerns" are antisemitism and disadvantaged

Jews. Israel is as important for this population as it is for givers. However, since they are less likely to feel that Israel's needs are urgent, they rate charitable giving to Israel lower down on their priority scale.

An unpublished study on marketing strategy conducted by the Federation of Jewish Agencies of Philadelphia in 1987 analyzed its own market in terms of future giving potential by means of a creative market identification study. This study provided a market segmentation spectrum through a typology that hypothesized a rationale for philanthropic behavior. It defines a spectrum of givers ranging from the purely voluntary-intellectually motivated to those who are obligatory-externally motivated. The findings indicate that major givers to federations seem to fall into more than one category. These are characterized as (1) those who feel required to make a gift (to belong to a certain country club or because of their firm's policies); (2) those who feel prompted to make an economic investment (to generate business); (3) those who seek status (for prestige and recognition among peers); and (4) those who are motivated by Jewish tradition.

Tactics for attracting these populations include the use of ratings, card assignment strategies, card calling, two-on-one solicitations, and missions. However, those who are interested in giving because of altruistic or specific cause-related reasons are not responsive to these traditional federation campaign tactics. In fact, many of these tactics seem to alienate this subset of givers. There are exceptions, as evidenced by "Operation Moses" (a special campaign to finance the resettlement of Ethiopian Jews in Israel) and Chicago's "Operation Ezra" (a local outreach program to poor and near-poor Jews after the Reagan administration began major cutbacks in federal assistance and the economic downturn began in the early 1980s). Respondents to these specialized campaigns also answer nonsectarian calls concerning protection of the environment or providing shelter for the homeless.

The findings presented from these studies thus pose new problems for federation campaigns. They need investigations to determine if the omnibus campaigns have hit a plateau in market penetration, if their current strategies and tactics reach as many people as they possibly can, and how they can increase total numbers and levels of contributions.

Currently, annual fund raising messages do not convey urgency or pressing needs. They focus on community building and enhancement of Jewish life. This theme of the usual, regular and sustaining is illustrated by the 1988 UJA advertising messages.

At the UJA, we're thankful that it's the daily emergencies that need your help more than ever.

No dangerous airlifts. No invading enemies. No starving immigrants. Just the boring old stuff.
And those who receive our help every day will always be thankful that you continue to remember.
United—It's what we are and what helps us continue to be.
Jewish—It's belief and responsibility and action.
Appeal—We ask so that we may be able to give. (UJA 1988)

In fact, very often the needs are ignored by solicitors who rely on the principles of "people give to people;" or "you can afford to give more." A priori these do not convey urgent, pressing needs to the noninvolved or uncommitted. It's a message for the already initiated. It appeals to those involved and immersed in the federation system, not to the uninvolved. Hence, we can predict the response rate.

While federations have been fortunate to maintain campaigns at present levels, they continually go to the same people and ask for more. In reality, the circle of the wagon train is getting tighter. Besides trying to find new givers to replace those who died or moved, they can no longer afford to take safe, incremental measures. Rather, they need to think strategically in the long term to effect change.

First, the system has to be more creative in presenting its cases with more urgency. Second, federations need to identify key segments of their communities for special attention, special treatment, education, and involvement. They then have to devote significant resources to that effort. Third, the system cannot continue treating the whole continent uniformly without differentiating among regions or communities. They must create new approaches to appeal to a great variety of subgroups. Finally, the federation umbrella has to change color from black to a color spectrum that encompasses more variety and allows for greater pluralistic expression.

Serious and careful attention needs to be addressed to targeted giving. It has the potential of presenting serious dilemmas to local federations as the central planning and fund raising organizations of their respective communities. Nevertheless, if handled carefully and correctly, it might provide new and innovative opportunities for increased involvement by major contributors and produce increased revenue. Needless to say, all of this requires a capacity for comprehensive financial planning that would establish community priorities based on needs and established by community consensus in each federation.

Federations need to become more creative and less time demanding with their top lay leadership. They must become more effective in involving Jews from business and professional elites in areas pertinent, significant, and worthwhile to them. Such involvement needs to be regarded as important in their own eyes, not just the federations'.

The potential for expanding the numerical base and increasing the number and size of major gifts exists. However, to realize that potential, federations will need to take major steps and invest significant energy in the following activities and initiatives. They will need research and development, especially in regard to current and potential major contributors, more and better qualified professional staffs, an increase in investment expenditures, and changes in the modus operandi of the federations. Above all, they will need to think and act over the long term and not just over an annual cycle.

Note

1. The total dollar achievements for all federations, nearly two hundred, in North America (Canada and the United States) was $579,761,000 in 1981 increasing to $778,691,000 in 1987.

A Note on Endowments

While this chapter has focused primarily on giving to the annual campaign, it is important to note that major contributors also play a key role in federation planned giving programs, viz., endowment development. During approximately the same time frame for which campaign data are presented, endowment contributions in the form of bequests, philanthropic funds, lifetime gifts, and charitable trusts have increased by 158 percent—from $135.5 million to $344 million. Around 10 percent of the federation annual campaign contributions now come from their endowments. Federations' endowment fund grants in fiscal year 1986–87 to agencies of the federation and others (nonbeneficiaries) totaled approximately $236 million.

These endowment developments suggest that federations may well explore some new strategies in approaching major gift contributors. Rather than viewing a prospect from three perspectives, i.e., his potential and interest in giving to the annual campaign, capital development, or endowment, federations may initiate approaches to prospects on a more interrelated basis. There seems to be a national trend in fund raising in the general community whereby planned giving techniques and capital fund development are merging with regular annual giving efforts. These trends were reported recently by the American Association of Fund Raising Councils from an opinion survey of member firms (AAFRC 1987). The report indicated that "Capital campaigns, endowment development and annual giving, once distinct operations are now increasingly tied together. Previously, the ventures were kept separate to ensure that regular annual giving would maintain its standing against the larger capital campaigns." To this, we would add endowment funds.

Bibliography

[AAFRC]. *Giving USA*. New York: AAFRC Trust for Philanthropy, 1987.

Annual Survey of Campaign Statistics. New York: Council of Jewish Federations, 1987.

Federation of Jewish Philanthropies of New York. *The Jewish Population of Greater New York*. New York: Federation of Jewish Philanthropies of New York, 1981.

Rappeport, Michael, and Gary A. Tobin. *A Population Study of the Jewish Community of MetroWest New Jersey. 1986*. East Orange, N.J.: United Jewish Federation of MetroWest, April 1987.

Ritterband, Paul, and Steven M. Cohen. "Will the Well Run Dry? The Future of Jewish Giving in America. *Response*, 12 (1979): 9–17.

Silberstein, Richard, Paul Ritterband, Jonathan Rabinowitz, and Barry A. Kosmin. *Giving to Philanthropic Causes: A Preliminary Reconnaissance*. New York: North American Jewish Data Bank, 1987. (Originally published in *1987 Spring Research Forum: Working Papers*.)

Tobin, Gary A. *Human Service Delivery in the Baltimore Jewish Community*. Baltimore, M.D.: Associated Jewish Charities and Welfare Fund, July 1986a.

———. *Jewish Wealth and Philanthropy. The Myth of the Well Running Dry*. New York: Council of Jewish Federations, November 1986b.

[UJA]. [Background paper on marketing strategies]. Unpublished memo. New York: United Jewish Appeal, 1988.

12

Havurah Jews and Where They Give

Bethamie Horowitz

Joke: A Jew is found on a deserted island. He gives the guy that finds him a tour of the island on which he has been living for several years. There is not one, but two shuls [synagogues] on the island. Why two? "This is the shul I go to, and that is the one I wouldn't set foot in!"

The joke about the two shuls is about the subtle sets of distinctions that make a person feel part of one subgroup, yet alienated from another within the Jewish world. As such, this joke is not only funny but also relevant because it highlights a neglected aspect of the social scientific study of the American Jewish community: the images and preferences that underlie people's affiliation with various substreams of Jewish life and life in the American context. In terms of the issues of philanthropy and American Jews, these images and attitudes are crucial to our understanding of how different groups of people relate to the philanthropic enterprise. In other words, to understand "who gives where and why" we must take stock of the socio-psychological climate within which a person enacts choices about giving money to one cause but not to another.

The existing body of social research about American Jewry does not explain the particular choices people make when they decide to donate money to one cause and not to another. The bulk of the data about Jewish giving is in strictly sociological terms such as age, occupational status, schooling, etc. In this paradigm the person is defined as a bundle of demographic characteristics, and the Jewish community is conceptualized in aggregate terms (in other words, as a sum of the millions of individual parts). Thus from these data we know, for instance, that the occupational structure of American Jewry is shifting from largely entrepreneurial to a more professional profile, and that younger people (the current 25–40-year-olds) give less than their parents did. While these sorts of correlational analyses indicate the broad trends, they offer little sense of either the context or the content of people's lives—the "why" and "how" of giving. This gap hampers our ability to take stock of the changing dynamics of philanthropy in the American Jewish community.

The statistics about American Jewish philanthropy paint a bleak picture of a younger generation of American Jews: they appear to be less connected to the Jewish world and they give less money than their parents. However the statistics don't tell everything. Anecdotally we know that there are "pockets of energy," other subcultures of young people who are involved and affiliated, albeit through channels other than the usual organizational ones. One such subculture has been called the Havurah world, the "new Jews," or the "Jewish Catalog culture." I want to focus on this subgroup within the American Jewish scene because it stands in contrast to the worrisome outlook suggested by the statistical trends. Within this subculture there appears to be a strong and serious commitment to *tzedakah* or philanthropy, and although it may be insignificant in quantitative terms, it is worth examining because in this realm the Havurah world offers an important counterexample to the overall picture of American Jewish philanthropy.

Furthermore, the study of where people in the Havurah world give *tzedakah* illuminates the nature of the subculture itself, which, because it is a social circle rather than a formal organization or denomination, is not easy to track down via the large-scale survey techniques so often used to study the American Jewish community. By examining the causes supported by people in the Havurah network, we will arrive at a fuller understanding of how this world is situated in the American Jewish scene.

Finally, this study of patterns of giving within a subculture is presented as a proposal about an alternative mode of research within the Jewish community. It suggests the importance of including other levels of analysis in the description of American Jewish life, beyond simply "the Jewish community" and "the individual."

Defining the Subculture: Who or What Are the Havurah Jews?

An interesting feature of this subculture is its lack of a simple name—there is no one term adequate or agreed upon for describing it. Thus, at various times and places, this nebulous thing has been called the "new Jews," the "Havurah movement," the "Jewish countercul- ture," the "Jewish Catalog culture," the "Jewish revival," and the "new Jewish culture." In fact, it usually takes about a paragraph to convey what is meant by this topic, for example:

> the Jewish Catalog culture [is] an emerging style of Judaism that is difficult to define, but increasingly visible on the American Jewish scene. An outgrowth of some of the *chavurot* [sic] of the late 60s and early 70s, it has no organizational or theoretical structure, but borrows freely from each of the other branches. It has been influenced by the liberalism of Reform, the social relevance of Reconstructionism, the intellectualism of the Conservative movement, and the traditionalism of Orthodoxy—as well as by the spiritual energy of Chassidism. (Baltimore *Jewish Times* February 26, 1982)

We have before us an object that defies simple description. That we cannot pin it down reflects the nature of the subculture itself: the Havurah world is not defined by a coherent ideology or institutional structure. It is more loosely organized; it tends to fall between the institutional cracks. This between-categories quality of the Havurah world also underscores the inadequacy of relying mainly on organiza- tional and institutional concepts to describe new developments in the Jewish community. But concepts such as these, which do not easily capture such emergent phenomena, are the ones most often applied to the American Jewish community. Thus, using a distinction like denom- ination (Reform, Conservative, Reconstructionist, Orthodox, or "just Jewish") to locate this subculture would not be sufficient.

The sociological literature offers an alternative conceptual frame- work for finding and defining the new Jewish culture: the concepts of social network and social circle. Whereas organizations are formal social systems with explicit mandates, leadership structures, and mem- bership boundaries, networks and social circles refer to looser entities.

They are more emergent and flexible, and tend to be invisible because they fall between the categories carved out by formal structures. Circles in particular have characterized such processes as culture production systems (Coser, Kadushin, and Powell 1982; Kadushin 1976), the diffusion of new ideas and innovation (Coleman, Katz, and Menzel 1957; Crane 1969), the small world phenomenon (Milgram 1967; Travers and Milgram 1969), the American intellectual elite (Kadushin 1974). These are all cases where common sense (and journalists!) tells us that such things as "the new Right," the "New York School," or "the glitterati" exist, but that, in organizational terms, tend to be invisible. They can hardly be tracked down simply by writing to the head of an organization because no organization "covers" the phenomenon. Yet there is a known core of people and activities that make up each of these circles, and this is certainly true for the new Jewish culture or Havurah world as well.

How to Find the Havurah/New Jewish Culture

If there is no central address for locating the Havurah world, no particular set of demographic characteristics that uniquely defines this group of people, how does one identify it? The study of social networks involves starting from the "inside" and identifying or tracking the patterns of interaction among participants in the network—a kind of sociometry of "who relates to whom" that generates a map of the culture's structure as it goes along.

Following a strategy much like that of the naturalist who locates a watering hole in the bush, we begin by identifying locales or activities that would bring participants in the network together. In New York City, people in this network would be more likely to *daven* (to pray) in one of the *minyanim* (prayer groups) at Ansche Chesed[1] than they would at Lincoln Square[2] (or at a *shtibl* [Hassidic conventicle]), and they would be less likely to be found at Park Avenue Synagogue[3] or at the Stephen Wise Free Synagogue.[4] We would probably find people in this network at the Association of Jewish Studies, but not at the Jewish Educators Assembly. They would be more likely to turn up at the Coalition on Alternatives in Jewish Education (CAJE) conference or at the National Navurah Conference, but probably not at meetings of Hadassah or B'nai B'rith. They would tend to be involved in Peace Now, but less likely in the World Zionist Organization. Fifteen years ago we would have found them on the subscription list of (and among the contributors to) *Response Magazine* or *Genesis II,* and perhaps more currently among the readership of *Tikkun* (although this is hardly the "insider's" journal).

Taken together we can think of these settings as "items which imply interaction" of the subculture as an entity, expecting from the outset that such characteristics need not be true for every individual in the network, but will tend to be true for the thing-as-a-whole. We expect a different pattern of interaction to characterize this subculture compared to other groups in the Jewish world.

An intriguing way of tracking the Havurah subculture is to map out where people in this network give *tzedakah.* The assumption here is that the places people choose to support not only reflect their personal and individual convictions and values, but taken together, provide evidence of the images shared within the new Jewish culture as a whole.

The Pilot Study

In this chapter I report on a pilot study of the Havurah world and its relationship to *tzedakah.* The goal of this study was to explore the issue and practice of philanthropy within the Havurah network by interviewing people from the core of the network about these concerns and then analyzing the findings for patterns that could be said to characterize the network as a whole.

For this study I identified a list of people with longtime involvement in the Havurah world—many were founders of the New York and Boston Havurot nearly twenty years ago. These were, with two exceptions, people whom all would agree are well-connected "insiders" in the social network.[5] Current membership in a *havurah* or *minyan* was not required;[6] having been a "fellow traveler" was. Twenty people were interviewed, most of whom today reside in New York City. Aside from longtime involvement in "the movement," a practical criterion for inclusion in this exploratory study was easy accessibility.

If we were to describe the people interviewed in demographic terms, they would be part of the category of young, urban professionals, and might be expected to have less connection to the Jewish life than they in fact do. As it turns out, more than half the people interviewed are professionally involved in the Jewish world (as academics or communal professionals), nearly everyone else works in the nonprofit world. In terms of Jewish education this is a literate group, partly as a result of long-term involvement in a subculture that values ongoing study. This is a group of people who are actively reading and writing, especially about Jewish things: ten are authors of books related to Jewish life and letters.

Nearly everyone interviewed has an active connection to Israel: they make regular visits in the summers or during sabbaticals, or for work-related projects, and many people maintain relationships with Israeli friends and relatives.

The interview, which lasted approximately half an hour, was informal, although it was framed around a set of basic topics. A prime concern was to learn where people gave *tzedakah,* Jewish and otherwise. Some people preferred to read a list from their tax returns, while others recollected where they gave. People were encouraged to comment as they went along about why they gave to certain places, to explain what it meant to them. In addition, I asked whether or not they contributed to the United Jewish Appeal (UJA) and why, and whether there were places to which an individual actively refused to contribute.

A second area of inquiry involved practices, customs, or routines associated with the giving of *tzedakah:* Did a person give donations at particular times during the year? Were there special customs or habits of giving? Were there special customs or habits of giving? Were there special personal, family, or community rituals or practices associated with *tzedakah?*

Findings

One thing that stands out about giving among the Havurah Jews is the seriousness and mindfulness with which people treat the idea of giving. This is not an unexamined concern in people's lives. People give money and time (volunteer), and they view these donations as obligatory. They use the term *tzedakah* rather than "philanthropy," a difference in language which conjures up an act that for some may be different from simply donating money to a cause. For instance, one person explained that to him, *tzedakah* involves *gmilut hesed,* which he translated as "bearing witness": he understood this to mean that it must have an aspect of personal involvement, as well as being oriented to social change. Other people mentioned the notion of *tikkun olam,* "repairing the world," underscoring their commitment to a certain orientation to making the world a better place through giving. Regarding personal involvement, I was struck by the numbers of individuals who said that they gave support to individuals that they came to know about—one teacher and her husband support a college student from a disadvantaged background, another couple gives directly to people they know about in Israel, one person gives through a rabbi he knows, and there are several other cases of personal, most often anonymous, *tzedakah*.

In addition to a shared outlook or approach to *tzedakah,* many people in this crowd have carefully worked out systems for distributing their own *tzedakah*: one person has decided to give to anyone that asks (either by mail or to beggars on the street); another makes a master list of all of the places he plans to give—and each Friday he writes a check, until all of the names have been checked off. At the completion of this cycle of a year or so, he begins a new list. A third gives *tzedakah* whenever she completes a business deal. In addition, when she works with others she often includes in the business arrangements an understanding that her colleagues donate money to one cause or another as part of doing business with her. Most of the people interviewed give *tzedakah* before the Jewish holidays, on *yahrzeits* (anniversary of the death of a relative), and in honor of life cycle events. Several people explained that they set aside envelopes to causes they want to support, and pay these when they pay the bills (one woman pays before she pays her bills).

Most people seem to have an amount in mind when they allocate their [limited] funds. Many people I interviewed spoke about *tzedakah* in terms of the biblical injunction to set aside tithes; many people attributed the magic number of "10 percent" of their income to this biblical concept. Finally, most people spoke about feeling guilty that they don't give enough—for instance, one couple was told by their accountant that they were giving more than they could afford and would have to cut back, and they still felt they were not giving enough. As one person said, "we live in New York, and you can't walk around New York today without feeling that you're privileged [in relation to the poverty on the streets]."

Thus, this is a very self-conscious group in terms of giving, which is characteristic of most other aspects of their Jewish practice. What is noteworthy is the extent to which the giving of *tzedakah* is a private act, and not really discussed or displayed within the communal setting.[7] Most people said they did not discuss the giving of philanthropy (decision-making) with their friends; although they could guess, they didn't really know where other people in their world gave.

Where They Give

There is a clear pattern of giving among people in this social network that is built upon a shared set of positive images about how to be Jewish in America. These positive images can be divided into two types: "What is worthwhile supporting in the Jewish world" and "What Jews should support in the world-at-large." This is by way of saying that for the Havurah Jews, *tzedakah* includes both Jewish and non-Jewish causes. As one person explained to me: "I give a healthy chunk to Israel, a healthy chunk to places I'm involved in, and one-quarter to general non-Jewish" (see table 12-1).

Non-Jewish Causes

It is obvious that people give to things in which they are involved—Jewish and non-Jewish—be it their synagogue, their children's schools, their friends' organizations, and in support of their local community's

Table 12-1. *Where People Give*

1. *"Insider":* Ansche Chesed, Ziv Tzedakah, Project Ezra, Havurah Committee, Heschel School, Project Dorot, *Shalom Center

2. *"New Age"* Jewish: Jewish Fund for Justice, American Jewish World Service, *Jewish Hospice, *New Jewish Agenda

3. *Other Jewish:* UJA, Soviet Jewry, Hillel, Righteous Gentile, Ethiopian Jews, National Foundation for Jewish Culture, *YIVO

4. *Israel:* New Israel Fund, Peace Now, American-Israel Civil Liberties, Interns for Peace, AIPAC, *Labor Israel, *Mercaz

5. *Local (NYC) Life:* Fresh Air Fund, Public television and radio, Museums, Coalition for the Homeless, Central Park Conservancy, Police Athletic League, Alumni Funds (college, professional school, Camp Ramah)

6. *World-at-Large:* Medical research, United Way, Amnesty International, Oxfam, Anti-nuclear, Sierra Club, Wildlife, Abortion rights, NOW, MADD, Orphans and children, Refugees, Blind and deaf, Hospitals, Food for Survival, Legal Aid, ACLU, Handgun control, NAACP, Prison reform, *Klanwatch, *Native Americans, *Planned Parenthood, *Battered Women, *People for the American Way, *Gay Men's Task Force, *War Resister's League, *Appalachian Mountain Club

*Mentioned by one person only (out of twenty).

quality of life. They give to public television, public radio, the public library, and the public parks and museums because they have benefited from these institutions and want to show their support. Similarly, they tend to support their colleges and professional schools, as well as Camp Ramah (if they attended).

Beyond the local scene, the Havurah network supports causes of a particular type that could be described Left-Liberal: concerned with social change and the environment, civil liberties, homelessness, hunger, and human rights. There is nothing on the Right here, nor too far Left. In addition, nearly everyone supports some sort of medical research (cancer, M.S., etc.). Abortion rights and the National Organization for Women (NOW) have strong support, too.

What I have termed the "New Age" Jewish funds, which combine a Jewish outlook or auspices with attention to various Left-Liberal causes in the national or international scene, hold a ready appeal to the Havurah Jews. For instance, the American Jewish World Service supports projects that deal with poverty, hunger, and disease all over the world. These "New Age" funds provide a new gloss on Y. L. Gordon's *haskalah* (Enlightenment) formulation of Jewish and general identity. Gordon wrote, "Be a human being in the world, and a Jew inside your home," the the Havurah network support of the "New Age" Jewish funds suggests that people want to act in the larger world as Jews, without keeping that identity as a private, internal matter.

So far, the pattern of giving we find among people in the Havurah network is probably not significantly different from the rest of their American Jewish demographic cohort. When we turn to the places they support in the Jewish world, we find a more distinctive pattern of giving.

Jewish Causes

The pattern of giving to Jewish causes among people in the Havurah network is characterized by the clear likes and dislikes vis-à-vis various parts of the Jewish world. In addition to being simply a list of causes supported or avoided, the pattern of giving can be read as a "cognitive map" of affiliation with various parts of the Jewish world. For Havurah Jews there is a positive and a negative image of the Jewish world: "The Jewish world I belong to," and "the Jewish world I wouldn't set foot in."

First of all, the Havurah Jews support their own institutions—the *minyanim,* the schools, and the projects that friends direct. Insofar as certain projects and causes are seen as "insider" projects, serving interests of people who participate in the network, people support these even when they are not particularly close with the organizers. It is not so much a matter of friends as a matter of supporting their own: without internal support by the Havurah network, many of the projects and nascent institutions (e.g., Ansche Chesed, the Heschel School[8]) would not have come about.

Second, they support a variety of smaller, targeted funds in Israel. Aside from the concrete problems these funds address, they also sustain a particular image of Israel that appeals to the Havurah network's Left-Liberal concerns: the advancement of civil liberties, support services for battered women, pluralist vision of religious life in the state, Arab-Jewish cooperation, and a desire for peaceful relations. This group advocates through their giving to Israel a set of values that is consistent with what they support in the world-at-large. What is interesting is that many people say that they are interested in using their limited funds to support smaller, newer projects that would not be likely to get mainstream funding. They see themselves as supplying seed money for new ideas. "Alternatives" could be the code word for this culture on some level: alternative visions of Jewish life.[9]

The tensions between the need for alternative channels and mainstream involvement emerge when we examine the Havurah world's relationship to the Jewish communal apparatus. There are three modes of relating to the United Jewish Appeal (UJA) among these people: the people who never give to UJA, those who give minimally, and those who give generously to UJA (see Appendix for verbatim comments). People in each of these three modes seem to be responding to different aspects of what UJA means.

Those who don't give to UJA can be thought of as exercising a "protest vote" (Cantril 1958). This term was used to refer to people in postwar Europe who voted for the Communist Party, although they were not members of the party, because they were discontented with the overall system. Of course, the Jewish community does not hold elections, and in a way that is precisely the point: people with this outlook (more than a third of the people interviewed) feel alienated from the UJA policy about Israel and about the way the system is set up. They see it as too monolithic and bureaucratic, without any room for dissenting opinions. When asked to give money, these people have in mind the Israel side rather than the domestic side of UJA/Federation.

One way to understand this group's separateness from UJA is in terms of their independent relationship with Israel. Insofar as the UJA operates by making a concrete connection between American Jewish donors and Israeli life (via UJA missions and projects like Project Renewal), the people in this network don't need the UJA to give them a personal connection to Israel. These people have a view of Israel in particular that is based on sources of expertise and information that are independent of the mainstream organization. Every one of the people who spoke about not giving to UJA has had an ongoing relationship with Israel. These are Hebrew-speakers, people who keep up with developments in Israeli life. Instead of giving to the UJA, these people give to the New Israel Fund, to Ziv Tzedakah,[10] and to other small, independent projects.

Those who give only minimally to UJA constitute about half of the pilot group. They describe themselves as giving "to pay Jewish taxes." These people have mixed feelings about the UJA. While they support the local communal work carried out by federation, they are unhappy about the nature of UJA support for Israel, echoing the concerns of those who never give to UJA, particularly the worry that their donation to UJA will be taken as unqualified support for the Israeli power structure. If anything, they are motivated to give because of local federation activities, and are not inclined to support the UJA's Israel-related activities. They, too, support the New Israel Fund and other smaller Israel-related projects.

Finally, a few people in this group have a generous and wholehearted attitude about giving to UJA. Most people in the pilot study work professionally in the Jewish world (eleven out of fourteen households); they all have ongoing professional involvement with the mainstream communal organizations. They view their donations to the UJA, which they offer without reservation, as a demonstration of their commitment to the American Jewish community. It is not that they are uncritical of aspects of UJA; rather, for them these criticisms can be expressed through means other than withholding money. In fact, one of them commented to me that he thought a better way for a "protest voter" to protest UJA policy would be for such a person to send a letter to UJA indicating that "unless x, y or z policies are changed, the sum that I am setting aside will be donated to another Israel-related cause." Incidentally, most people in this category of wholehearted givers do not give to the New Israel Fund (although they support other Israel-related projects of various sorts).

The interviews suggest that as some people in this network move into regular professional contact with the more mainstream organizations (e.g., federation-affiliated agencies, Hebrew Union College, Jewish Theological Seminary), they tend to give or give more (and with a more wholehearted attitude) to UJA than they did when they were younger or otherwise employed. This change is correlated with their professional integration into the UJA-Federation world, as one person put it, "I want to sit at the table, to be able to influence that world."

Where people say they will never give money is as revealing of the outlook of the Havurah Jews as are the causes they are inclined to support. These causes represent aspects of the world that this group of people rejects for various reasons. In table 12-2 I have arranged the numerous causes rejected by people in the Havurah network according to five types of reasons.

First, nearly half of the people queried refuse to give to the ultra-Orthodox (in Israel and in the United States). These are not simply "blanket" refusals, since some people will give to yeshivot once they

Table 12-2. *Where People Won't Give (excluding "UJA")*

1. *"I won't give to anyone who would spit on me if I walked into the room."*

   • the Orthodox
   • the ultra-religious
   • Satmar or right-wing Yeshivas (esp. in Israel)
   • Lubavitch

2. *Israel-related*

   • America-Israel Public Affairs Committee (AIPAC)
   • Jewish National Fund
   • Zionist Organization of America

3. *Places which encourage Jewish paranoia*

   • Simon Wiesenthal Center
   • Anti-Defamation League

4. *The Right*

   • the Right (Jewish or secular)
   • Meir Kahane
   • Republican Party

5. *Places I used to support but about which I am now disillusioned."*

   • ACLU—"due to Nazi march in Skokie"
   • Certain groups in the Black community

have investigated who sponsors a particular institution. People seem to reject these sorts of causes because, as one person explained, "I won't give t
o anyone who would spit on me if I walked into the room." In other words, people in the Havurah network reject this part of the Jewish world because they see it as excluding the Havurah Jews (and others) as legitimate participants in Jewish life, and because the ultra-Orthodox are seen as representing an intolerant way of religious life.

Second, more than half of the group said they would not give to certain Israel-related organizations, especially to the America-Israel Public Affairs Committee (AIPAC). Many offered reasons that included policy related concerns: "They (AIPAC) are too ready to toe the right-wing line in Israel"; "I don't agree with their policy"; "[the Jewish National Fund (JNF)] won't plant trees in Arab communities." But more predominant was a concern that these organizations represent a myopic and constrained view of Israeli interests: "[AIPAC] is blind to things other than Israel in evaluating the congressional record of elected officials"; "[the AIPAC] supports the Israeli government irrespective of Israeli politics. Therefore it espouses a political point of view in Israeli life"; "It's an agent of the Israeli government in its explicit support (unlike UJA's implicit support)."

Third, people in this network bristle in the face of causes that they see as encouraging Jewish paranoia. The rhetorical aspect of the messages of these organizations does not go over well among people in this network. Most often mentioned was the Simon Wiesenthal Center, about which one person said, "They make it sound like the Holocaust will happen again unless you give money." Moreover, people feel that the substantive message is not on the mark. Organizations like the Anti-Defamation League (ADL) and the Wiesenthal Center are seen by some as encouraging Jewish self-righteousness, or as emphasizing "Jewish survival above all," instead of other more positive Jewish values. Thus, one person commented, "I prefer to support the recognition of Righteous Gentiles, because we can learn from the Holocaust." Or, "I prefer to give out of love, rather than fear. But these are fearful times."

Less often mentioned than these first three types of rejects were causes on the Right and a few people who mentioned causes on the Left. "The Right" refers to the Jewish/Israeli Right (e.g., Kahane, and the Israeli ultra-religious, for some). A few people mentioned both Jewish and general concerns, and two people specifically named the Republican Party. These causes are rejected because they are seen as dangerous or contrary to the basic values held by the people who mentioned them.

On the other hand, several people said that they used to give to old-time Left causes, like the American Civil Liberties Union (ACLU), but no longer do (in the aftermath of "the Nazi march"). Two people expressed frustration at what they perceive to be the lack of active, positive causes to support in the Black community: "I'd like to give to something in the Black community that has a vision beyond simply fighting discrimination. No one seems to be dealing with the lack of leadership." In these cases, people reject particular causes that they had once supported because they are perceived as no longer working effectively towards the issues people care about, or because the organization's aims are perceived as diverging from people's core concerns.

Conclusions

Taken together, the objects of *tzedakah* among Havurah Jews offer us the makings of a "cognitive map" of the shared images underlying this subculture. These include an image of Jewishness that allows for a rich and active Jewish expression in all aspects of living without a parochial and exclusive stance that holds the world-at-large as either foreign or forbidden. It also diverges from an image of Jewishness that is based only on ethnicity (indexed by "just Jewish" in some recent surveys).

The Havurah subculture is characterized by a pattern of philanthropic affiliations that distinguish it from mainstream establishment Jewish life. First, the Havurah network is an American Jewish subculture that takes personal philanthropy seriously. In this regard it resembles the pattern of giving among the Orthodox, and stands in contrast to the broad trends seen in American Jewish life. Like the Orthodox, the havurah network includes a cadre of people that is highly identified and highly educated in Jewish terms, and these factors help explain their strong commitment toward giving. Unlike the Orthodox who support the orthodox Jewish world almost exclusively, people in the Havurah world are prepared to give to the world-at-large as well as to a range of Jewish causes.

Second, just as Havurah Jews pray in their own *minyanim*, they give money through different channels (often of their own creation) and have an outlook about "how to be Jewish" that they perceive as an alternative stance to what mainstream American Jewish establishment puts forth. They seem to need channels for giving that are not omnibus, but rather are particularly targeted. These sorts of "boutique" funds seem to engage people more actively than the "department store" approach.

Although this subculture is distinct, it is not self-sufficient or isolated. It has points of integration and involvement with the mainstream organizations, particularly in terms of funding, employment, audiences and forums for books, speeches, and ideas. Rather than viewing these alternative approaches to philanthropy as a threat or a challenge to mainstream channels, these funds can be considered as a way of expanding and changing the overall American Jewish philanthropic pie.

Appendix
Comments About Giving to UJA

"No, I don't (or won't) give to UJA"

—"Normally, no, and on principle. But this year I'm involved due to the West Side Y. I don't give because of the things they support in Israel; it sends the wrong message to the Israeli government, a waste of money."

—"No, there's no dialogue in the UJA, not enough consultation or dialogue about the priorities in Jewish life. While cohesiveness is important, the community is too focused on cohesiveness, and it leaves no room for dissent or dialogue. My personal values aren't reflected. The money needs to go to HaTikvah, not to the West Bank infrastructure. The issue of bureaucracy is not so important now (it once was)."

—"I care too much about Israel to throw my money away [on bureaucratic structure]. I give to smaller places that are more accountable."

—"Thank God they don't ask me! I don't know where the money goes."

—"I used to give [to Federation] when I lived in California, but here they are combined. UJA supports things in the West Bank, at least in terms of freeing up monies. I also no longer support the JNF because they do not plant trees in Israeli-Arab communities.''

—''The UJA is not a bad thing, but there are projects that UJA won't support. There are small projects that need the attention of others—of 'those who will be mindful of them'—not apparatchnikim, but committed people. I prefer direct giving, rather than the bureaucracy.''

''Yes, I give to the UJA''

—''I give despite great reservations. They give to so much. I feel they do enough good things to warrant my contribution. You pay your financial dues to the American Jewish community. But I give less than I used to.''

—''I do give to UJA, but a minimum amount. I'm not supporting it for Israeli policy. I am supporting it for local Jewish life. I feel I should give [something] to UJA, but I'd rather give to small groups that would benefit more.''

—''I give very little to UJA. Although it's administration-heavy, mainly I give only a minimum because too much goes to the Jewish Agency. Therefore it supports the Israeli political establishment—in particular the Orthodox parties. It's a form of political patronage.''

—''We give a nominal amount to UJA, enough to cover us getting *The Jewish Week*. We've always given, but only a small, symbolic amount.''

—''I was not always a contributor—I have strong views about Israel and peace. But I got a raise, and [my boss] solicited me. I want to sit at the table, to influence people in that world.''

—''Historically UJA has been our largest gift each year. It involves communal discipline. It was regarded as the enemy, but they do a lot of good.''

—''It is our largest gift now. When I began working in the [mainstream] Jewish world, I was solicited at work. It's a form of taxes.''

—"We've always given a major amount to UJA. It's like paying taxes."

Notes

1. Ansche Chesed is a synagogue located on New York City's Upper West Side. It was rejuvenated in the early 1980s when members of several independent *havurot* and *minyanim* joined the aging congregation of the neighborhood synagogue. Cowan (1982, 212–17) describes this process.

2. Lincoln Square is a modern Orthodox synagogue located on New York City's Upper West Side.

3. The Park Avenue Synagogue is a mainstream Conservative synagogue located on the Upper East Side of New York City.

4. The Stephen Wise Free Synagogue is a Reform congregation located on New York City's Upper West Side.

5. Of course, a full study of this network would involve a more extensive "snowball" sampling procedure to empirically map out the participants in the network. One would be able to sample and compare people at the "core" and at the "periphery" of the network.

6. In fact membership in a *havurah* is besides the point, since the whole thrust of this inquiry is to get at the underlying subculture that produced the phenomenon of the *havurah,* among other things.

7. Several people mentioned that they participate (or have participated) in a *tzedakah* collective (see Strassfeld and Strassfeld, 1980, 31–32 for a fuller description), but this does not constitute the bulk of their giving.

8. The Abraham Joshua Heschel School is a nondenominational Jewish day school located on the Upper West Side of New York City that sees its pedagogical outlook as informed by the approaches of progressive education.

9. In this regard it is interesting to note that CAJE, the Coalition for Alternatives in Jewish Education, founded over a decade ago by havurah-oriented educators, has now become a major organization in the mainstream Jewish education establishment. It is not surprising in light of CAJE's status that recently the word "alternatives" dropped out of its name, and it is now called the Coalition for the Advancement of Jewish Education.

10. Ziv Tzedakah is a fund directed by Daniel Siegel, who has acted as a *tzedakah*-agent in Israel on behalf of friends and acquaintances since the early 1970s. It targets modest worthy projects and activities in Israel. See his "1979 Tzedakah Report" in Strassfeld and Strassfeld, 1980, 26–28.

Bibliography

Cantril, Hadley. *The Politics of Despair.* New York: Basic Books, 1958.

Coleman, J., E. Katz, and H. Menzel. "The Diffusion of Innovation among Physicians." *Sociometry* 20 (1957): 251–70.

Coser, L., C. Kadushin, and W. Powell. *Books: The Culture and Commerce of Publishing*. New York: Basic Books, 1982.

Cowan, Paul. *An Orphan in History*. New York: Doubleday, 1982.

Crane, Diane. "Social Structure in a Group of Scientists: A Test of the Invisible College Hypothesis." *American Sociological Review* 34 (1969): 335–52.

Kadushin, Charles. "Networks and Circles in the Production of Culture." *American Behavioral Scientist* (July/August 1976): 769–84.

———. *The American Intellectual Elite*. Boston: Little, Brown, 1974.

Milgram, Stanley. "The Small World Problem." *Psychology Today* 22 (May 1967): 61–67.

Strassfeld, S., and M. Strassfeld. *The Third Jewish Catalog*. Philadelphia, Penn.: Jewish Publication Society, 1980.

Travers, J., and S. Milgram. "An Experimental Study of the Small World Problem." *Sociometry* 32 (1969): 425–43.

13

The New Jewish Philanthropies

Ira Silverman

During the last decade a half-dozen or so new Jewish philanthropies have been founded and have flourished. All seem to represent a trend, characterized by internal structures that are participatory, informal, small, and internally democratic, and a public posture that is "liberal" or "progressive." This leftward political shift is not unrelated to the *havurah* movement in general and their style of giving in particular (see chapter 12). Indeed, these new Jewish philanthropies represent an outward expression in the voluntary sector of the fellowship of Jews that the *havurah* movement has created.

Simply stated, organizations such as the New Israel Fund, the Jewish Fund for Justice, the American Jewish World Service, and *Mazon* (sustenance), taken together, espouse a world view based on what they claim are the tenets of the universalist tradition in Judaism. Within the new philanthropies themselves, this "progressive" mode of operation in both their external politics and their internal styles probably represents a reaction against the thrust and style of the mainstream, established Jewish charities, even as the new philanthropies abjure explicit "anti-establishment" motivation.

These new philanthropies are direct descendants of the late 1960s counterculture that challenged the established Jewish charities of that period. Symbolized by demonstrations at General Assemblies of the Council of Jewish Federations, calling for more emphasis on Jewish education, they led to significant community change. Consequently, as reflected in community federation budgets, Jewish education *has* been accorded a much higher priority. Similarly, young leadership groups have flourished, academics and Jewish organizational professionals have been given more visible platforms, religious rituals have been incorporated into previously "secular" meeting agendas, and informal groups such as *havurot* have been encouraged.

Despite these marked changes, a number of Jews of that counterculture generation, now mostly in their thirties and forties, have remained critical of aspects of the major Jewish philanthropies, that is, their (understandable) reliance on and obeisance to major donors; their emphasis on (necessary) organizational maintenance and (valuable) community welfare agencies rather than social change; their sheer size, leading to formality, rigidity, slowness, alleged secrecy, etc. Allocations within Israel, through Keren Hayesod and the Jewish Agency, have received the sharpest criticism.

These new philanthropies were founded against this backdrop. While we do not wish to suggest here that either their founders or a majority of their current supporters voiced any of these specific criticisms, a substantial portion of their backing has been facilitated by general dissatisfaction with the major charities. As mentioned above, the development of these new funds should be seen in the context of the *havurah* movement, specifically the National Havurah Committee.

In addition, it is also related to other new political or religious phenomena, such as *Tikkun* and *Lilith* magazines, the (influential but now defunct) Radius Institute, *P'nai Or* (a fellowship committed to Jewish renewal, study, and prayer led by Rabbi Zalman Schacter-Shalomi in Philadelphia), the Shalom Center and New Jewish Agenda, as well as a plethora of small organizations whose raison d'être is Israeli-Palestinian relations. These organizations, devoted to social change with emphases on such matters as women's rights, nuclear disarmament, and civil liberties, have begun to constitute something of a "movement" that provides a context for the activities and support base of the new philanthropies discussed in this chapter.

While it has been suggested above that these new groups evolved naturally enough out of the counterculture roots, their current directions seem contradictory to their original goals. For example, the late 1960s challenge to the federation called for a deepening of Jewish sensibilities and Jewish priorities with emphasis on greater ritual observance, kashrut, Jewish education, work for Soviet Jewry, etc. Now the new philanthropies seem to stress a more universalist orientation, such as relief assistance to the poor living in both the United States and the Third World, regardless of religion or ethnic background. Nevertheless, many supporters of these new groups see their organizations' missions as arising out of a particularly Jewish mandate, albeit universalist rather than particularist.

This suggests the need for an examination of several questions, including:

1. To what extent do Jewish community philanthropies, new and old, reflect Jewish community interest? Specifically, how do they achieve balance between competing good interests, e.g., Jewish and universal, Israel and American Jewry, national and local?
2. How well does the established philanthropic structure permit and encourage new ideas and new people to emerge, and do these new philanthropies do any better?
3. How well do the new and old philanthropies interact? Is there a problem of competition or duplication?
4. What are the costs and benefits of these new philanthropies, and their implications for the future, particularly with respect to motivating a new generation of givers?

While there are literally dozens of Jewish charitable organizations formed in the last decade, including some of those mentioned above, for the purposes of this chapter four key "new philanthropies" are emblematic: The New Israel Fund, the Jewish Fund for Justice, the American Jewish World Service, and *Mazon*.

The commonality of these four groups is not only their newness but also their differentiation from the other new religious and political groups and publications: these are "funds," that is, charities that collect money from donors and dispense them to an array of other groups, including other organized charities; they are not direct service providers. In that respect, these new philanthropies are organized, on an extremely smaller scale, along the lines of federations.

The New Israel Fund

The New Israel Fund (NIF) was founded in 1979 by Jonathan Cohen and Eleanor Friedman, then of San Francisco. With the benefit of inherited wealth from her family (of the Levi-Strauss Haas and Friedman families) and connections to other wealthy Bay Area young people, the two launched the NIF to create a new means of contributing to Israel.

The New Israel Fund's main purpose was twofold: (1) to support projects that advance social justice and democracy in Israel, and (2) to involve American Jews deeply in that process. In both respects they imagined that the NIF would differ from the established philanthropies, particularly UJA-Federation. NIF-supported projects would be progressive, innovative, and unlikely to be in the network aided by the Jewish Agency with UJA receipts. Furthermore, the involvement of donors, particularly in selecting and evaluating recipient projects, would be greater and in more regular partnership with Israelis.

In the almost ten years since its establishment, the New Israel Fund has grown and evolved in several ways. It has, nevertheless, maintained its commitment to support progressive projects by providing money and technical assistance to over 130 Israeli voluntary organizations working principally in five fields: (1) fostering pluralism, including bridging gaps between Orthodox and non-Orthodox Jews, and between Ashkenazim (Jews of European descent) and Mizrahim (Jews of North African and Middle Eastern descent); (2) encouraging cooperation between Jews and Arabs; (3) promoting the rights of women; (4) protecting civil rights and civil liberties of all citizens, but particularly of the disadvantaged, of minorities, and of children; and (5) strengthening community action, for the improvement of neighborhoods, including housing, employment, municipal services, youth work, etc.

The beneficiaries of the largest NIF grants over the years have been the Association for Civil Rights in Israel, Neve Shalom, and the Israel Women's Network. NIF has also created and supported a small number of its own special projects, most notably a Leadership Fellows Program to provide work or study opportunities for selected promising young Israelis and *Shatil* (a Hebrew acronym for "Support Project for Voluntary Organizations"), which fosters voluntarism and helps non-profit social change groups in Israel. NIF also sponsors study tours to Israel.

As for its other goal of fostering deep involvement of donors in the philanthropic process, in partnership with Israelis, NIF has provided such opportunities to the donors who have served on its various governing and advisory boards. NIF has an overall board of directors that includes both North Americans and Israelis who work together. Other committees and advisory boards function separately, but include meetings both in the United States and in Israel. The "partnership" seems to work, but whether it is deeper than that which characterizes key UJA donors is open to question. Moreover, as NIF has grown, now having thousands of donors, the depth of involvement is necessarily less uniformly intense.

NIF's 1987 budget was $2.5 million. All of its income came from contributions, and $1.9 million of that was disbursed to Israeli beneficiaries. The balance covered management and overhead costs. Since its founding, some 7,500 people have contributed to NIF, in annual amounts ranging from $200,000 to $5. Its 1989 (volunteer) president was Mary Ann Stein, and its executive director during that period was Norman Rosenberg. It has offices in New York, Toronto, and Jerusalem.

The Jewish Fund for Justice

The Jewish Fund for Justice (JFJ) was founded in 1984. Among its initiators was Si Kahn, a civil rights worker, folksinger, and general social activist. The son of a distinguished rabbi, the younger Kahn was motivated to integrate his Jewish values with his devotion to aiding the poor, particularly in the United States. Several people created a board and small staff, and raised some money to launch the JFJ.

The JFJ, in its promotional material, calls itself

a new grant making institution through which American Jews support social and economic justice efforts on the part of America's poor and disenfranchised. Through its grant making and technical assistance, JFJ supports community advocacy and organizing efforts that seek to break the cycle of poverty . . . to change the circumstances that keep people poor . . . and nurture independence and self-sufficiency.

The JFJ further describes its purpose as threefold: (1) to bring new resources to the struggle to combat poverty and to create a more just society; (2) to provide American Jews with an institution through which individuals could express their concern for the well-being of all Americans and do so within the context of Jewish life; and (3) to provide a Jewish presence in coalitions of religious and ethnically based philanthropies. In this way, JFJ resolves the seeming contradiction between particularist (i.e., Jewish) giving with universalist disbursing. Recent examples of recipients of JFJ support include:

Navajo/Israeli Technical Assistance Project, Flagstaff, Arizona. With an Israeli agronomist as resource person and teacher, Navajo farmers adapt Israeli drip irrigation techniques in order to increase their crop yields and build economic self-sufficiency.

Greater Bridgeport Interfaith Action, Bridgeport, Connecticut. Ten churches and synagogues organized this coalition to address issues of concern to low-income residents of Bridgeport. The coalition has most recently been focusing on housing development and displacement issues.

Youth Action Program, New York. This East Harlem organization builds the self-confidence and leadership skills of neighborhood youth by assisting their efforts to plan and implement their own community improvement projects.

Jonah, Jackson, Tennessee. Jonah is a community organization in rural western Tennessee enabling its low-income, predominantly black membership to gain improved access to local government policymaking. Members have had success in public education, health care delivery, and public services.

In its guidelines for grant applicants, the JFJ outlines the need for the prospective recipient to combat poverty, benefit and involve the poor, enable the poor to change the conditions that limit their lives, etc. In addition to those kinds of criteria, JFJ also declares its interest in projects that

> encourage greater Jewish involvement in efforts to combat the causes of domestic poverty; this includes greater financial involvement, greater involvement as activists or volunteers and greater involvement by other Jewish organizations; . . . [and that] take an approach or address an issue which is not yet attracting substantial financial support from the Jewish community.

Since its founding, the JFJ has disbursed $250,000 in grants. Si Kahn continues to chair the organization; its professional staff, led in 1989 by Marlene Provizer, is based in New York City.

The American Jewish World Service

In 1985, the American Jewish World Service (AJWS) was founded by a group of prominent rabbis, scholars, and Jewish communal and business leaders. They were all galvanized by the vision and energy of Lawrence Phillips, chief executive officer of the Phillips-Van Heusen Company and an activist in several Jewish community organizations.

The AJWS founders raise and give money to aid Third World development out of a Jewish sensibility. As Elie Wiesel said at the founding press conference, "As Jews we must show that our suffering has produced a tremendous cry against moral numbness. When I needed people to come and help, nobody came. Therefore, today, I must come, I must help."

The AJWS calls itself a nonpolitical organization that is dedicated to alleviating poverty, hunger, illiteracy, and disease among the people of the world, regardless of religion. It is an organization that will allow American Jews to act upon—within a Jewish context—their own "deeply felt and long-cherished impulse to improve the quality of life for all people."

In its five years of service, the AJWS has focused on both emergency disaster relief and long-range problems in the areas of agriculture and health care. Its major projects include relief and reconstruction following disastrous mud-slides in Colombia; famine relief aid and pharmaceutical and medical services in Mozambique; emergency medical aid in the aftermath of the lake bed volcanic eruption in Cameroon; development of revolutionary mobile plastic grain silos (with Israeli technical assistance) in Togo, Sri Lanka, and the Philippines; market cooperatives and other agricultural aid in the Philippines; and other similar projects in El Salvador, Mexico, and Ecuador.

The AJWS board, comprised of prominent individuals and chaired by Lawrence Phillips, has more of an "establishment" complexion than the other new funds and has been more rapidly successful in raising desired amounts. Contributions in 1986 totaled $860,000 and in 1987, $1.5 million. The professional staff is based in New York City and was led in 1989 by Andrew Griffel.

Mazon

Mazon: A Jewish Response to Hunger was founded in 1985. It was the brainchild of Leonard Fein, who was then the editor of *Moment* magazine. The organization was launched after *Moment* published a series of articles about domestic and international hunger, providing a novel approach to addressing the problem. Fein had noted that many Jews expressed concern about the excesses of costly Jewish catered "affairs" and wondered if some of that money could be given to the hungry.

Mazon, then, offers American Jews "a vehicle through which they

may add a rich dimension of public service to their private celebrations
(bar or bat mitzvahs, weddings, birthdays, or anniversaries) as an
offering to feed the hungry.'' The assembled board of directors,
including people drawn especially from the denominations of Jewish
religious life, has been used to spread the word and encourage the
participation of synagogues and other groups.

While nowhere near 3 percent of the estimated $500 million ($15
million) a year spent on celebrations has yet to be received by *Mazon,*
the level of donations is now about $1 million annually. *Mazon* gives to
a mix of projects addressing hunger among Jews or non-Jews as a
compromise on what they see as a divisive issue. Recent recipients
included Jewish Family Services of San Diego, Prairie Fire Rural
Action in Iowa, Westside Food Bank in Santa Monica, Philadelphia
Hunger Reduction Team, National Council of Negro Women, Metropolitan New York Coordinating Council on Jewish Poverty, New York
Coalition for the Homeless, Mother Waddles Perpetual Mission in
Detroit, Institute for the Advancement of Education in Jaffa, American
Jewish World Service, and several other groups.

Lee Javitch, past president of the American Jewish Congress, serves
as chairman of *Mazon*'s board. The staff, based in Los Angeles, is
headed by Irving Cramer.

Discussion

While the development of these organizations both separately and
as a collective phenomenon is impressive, it is still small. Taken
together, they raise over $6 million a year and support several hundred
recipient agencies. They draw from over 20,000 donors. But, inasmuch
as their foundings were to some degree in opposition to mainstream
philanthropies and based on constituencies who were marginal in
relation to organized Jewish life, we must ask to what extent they
reflect Jewish community interests.

Short of major survey research, we have no way of measuring that
reflectiveness. Nonetheless, a review of the donor base suggests that it
is wide, geographically well dispersed (not, for instance, just an East
or West Coast phenomenon), and Jewishly pan-denominational.

Indeed, these new organizations—by their very existence—have
turned the reflectiveness question on its head. Hence, while the mainstream philanthropies obviously have a broad base, the new philanthro-

pies ask if the former are not skewed in such a way as to reflect inadequately the interests of the Jewish community.

The main critique of the established organizations is that they pay insufficient attention (and give insufficient money) to universal causes, favoring only Jewish recipients; or conversely, that they support "Jewish" hospitals and social service agencies that really have little or no Jewish content, and fewer than ever Jewish clients. Another issue is the level of Jewish philanthropy sent overseas, particularly to Israel, while significant Jewish needs (e.g., Jewish education) remain unmet at home. Local donors and agencies cry out for more dollars for their programs, and resent the siphoning off of so much for national purposes.

While it is difficult to assert what the "right" balance on this issue should be, the extremely broad base of donors who voluntarily continue to give what they do provides a tolerably good reflection of their preferences, which is a manifestation of the "democratic" way of defining the Jewish "community interest." That is not to deny that some individuals think that they can better prescribe that interest, based either on true expertise or on sheer *chutzpah* (nerve). The principal caveat would be if there were such rigidity in the philanthropies as to preclude shifting preferences, responsiveness to new events, or new recognition of needs.

That leads to another question: How well do the established philanthropies permit and encourage new ideas and new people to emerge? The very founding of these new philanthropies demonstrated that the mainstream groups have been limited in their ability to shift direction to meet newly voiced calls for action. The activities underwritten by these new groups are not, by and large, supported by the mainstream organizations. However, they are not antithetical to the established interests either and, if the big groups were so inclined, could have been incorporated within their scope. Lack of inclination cannot only be interpreted as a principled decision to stick to ongoing activities, but also reflects an inertia based on less conscious, simple resistance to change. Plainly, these big organizations do suffer from the endemic institutional reluctance to modify, diversify, decentralize, and innovate.

Moreover, despite professed organizational goals of "outreach," most large organizations find it difficult to accommodate new people in their structures unless they either have extraordinary wealth or status, or are prepared to "start from the bottom" as volunteers. The notable exceptions have been the highly successful leadership development groups, particularly of UJA-Federation, which have managed to confer a sense of worth and excitement on relative newcomers with promise of future leadership. The founders of all four of the new philanthropies discussed here would probably have been welcomed in the more established organizations, but would have met (or did meet) with significant resistance to their calls for shifting priorities.

The net result—four new groups—may indeed be the most effective way to address the problems they seek to solve. Whether a degree of new philanthropy competition and duplication with the mainstream groups is really the best outcome, however, is another matter.

Since their foundings, all four of these organizations have expressed concerns about antagonizing the "establishment" with competition or duplication. There is a range of opinion within the leaderships of these new groups; some are troubled by the prospect of such antagonistic relations, others want to compete with the big groups.

The New Israel Fund, for example, is not really a David taking on a Goliath of UJA. The NIF cannot even lift a slingshot. In actual dollar terms, there is no question of real competition. Even if some people do reduce UJA contributions in order to give more to NIF, the dollar shift is infinitesimal. Hence, whatever antagonism does exist stems from a matter of principle. UJA stands as the all-embracing community fund in support of Israel; for some, it is an affront to encounter a new group making competing claim for support, implying, albeit unwittingly, that UJA funds do not do the job well enough.

The NIF leadership has been sensitive to the issue, and has consistently urged donors to support NIF *in addition* to UJA, rather than instead of such support. Nonetheless, the impatience of some American Jews with Israeli government policies regarding Arab-Jewish relations, civil liberties, and Jewish religious pluralism has produced a shift of donors from UJA to NIF though the amounts are trivial in actual dollar terms. In addition, NIF-supported projects are indeed substantially different from those supported by the Jewish Agency with UJA funds. Consequently, there is really no question of duplication in the program area.

The duplication question has been raised, though, in the case of the American Jewish World Service. After establishing itself as a Jewish organization that uniquely supports Third World development, it received protests from the American Jewish Joint Distribution Committee (JDC). The JDC has long been engaged in international relief efforts, although principally in support of imperiled Jewish communities, and occasionally providing needed disaster relief to others. However, the AJWS is distinct from the JDC since the main mission of the former is the long-term economic development of Third World peoples, regardless of ethnic or religious background. While AJWS funds are small compared to JDC's, the competition/duplication issue arises and persists.

The Jewish Fund for Justice and *Mazon* offer less direct competition or duplication with older or bigger agencies, but they, too, have occasionally been criticized for diverting attention or money from the centrally important Jewish community agencies. In many instances, there have been meetings to explain positions and smooth relations. Currently, the new philanthropies have good relations with the established groups, perhaps due in large part to the fact that they really pose no serious threat as competitors for big dollars.

Finally, there is the question of the costs and benefits of these new philanthropies. There is some degree of competition and duplication of no real consequence with older organizations, but it is small in the scheme of things. Similarly, the marginal (additional overhead) cost of maintaining new offices, staff, etc. amounts to some $1–2 million, but that seems to be justified by the marginal benefits obtained by them in the form of new funds otherwise unraised. In the minds of some, the new philanthropies pose a moral cost by calling into question the adequacy of the older organizations.

That, however, would also appear on the benefit side of the ledger because a major contribution of these groups, in addition to the real substantive work they do, may be precisely in calling into question what the community is doing, in breaking the inertia, in catalyzing new developments. The existence of the New Israel Fund, for example, may not actually have had anything to do with the decision of the Jewish Agency to allocate a new fund of $1 million for "innovative and creative" projects, but that new program is already informed by what NIF has been initiating.

Another already clear benefit of the new philanthropies has been their attracting significant numbers of younger donors to participate in Jewish life. All four of these programs have many people in their twenties and thirties in volunteer leadership and staff positions. These groups seem to be motivating a new generation of givers as a result both of their programs and freshness. As a guide to overall community philanthropic planning, this suggests that their programmatic directions might be copied or expanded, and their freshness pursued by more consciously spinning off still new groups, which in their very newness will appeal to newer or younger—and maybe even older—

donors. In the calculus of late twentieth-century *tzedakah,* their benefit
will outweight their cost.

Bibliography

Horowitz, Bethamie. "Havurah Jews and Where They Give." In *Contemporary Jewish Philanthropy in America,* edited by Barry A. Kosmin and Paul
Ritterband, 187–204. Savage, Md.: Rowman & Littlefield, 1991.

Part 4

The Clients

14

The Changing Client System of Jewish Federations

Donald Feldstein

In February 1942, the Council of Jewish Federations met in General Assembly to consider the impact of World War II and its aftermath on federations. Among its conclusions was the following: "Our plans will have to take into consideration a sustained interest in *the great society* which we hope will have been created by the peace."

In order to understand the changes in the client system in Jewish philanthropy, we have to appreciate some of the special complexities of that system. In its older forms Jewish philanthropy consisted of a few responsible well-to-do Jewish leaders creating a service system to meet the needs of the poor, unwashed masses of Jews who needed these services. The clients were clearly the ultimate consumers of the service. Even today, most nonprofit hospitals conceive of the patients as the client. Thus, marketing departments are integrated inside hospitals with planning or public relations departments, aiming their efforts at potential patients.

In business as well, the client or consumer system consists of the consumers or purchasers of the service or product that the business offers. A group of managers or directors of the business makes decisions for the business, but that group is never confused with the clients.

219

220

Once a philanthropy begins to depend on a mass base, however, the system is changed radically. In United Ways, and even more dramatically in Jewish federations, there are really two sets of clients. There is the traditional, final consumer of the product or service of the organization, but there is also the large group of thousands of individuals or households who have to decide whether and how much to contribute to the organization. In a sense, they have to "buy" the service themselves, at least the idea that the service is important and worth supporting. Therefore, in Jewish federations, marketing tends to be related to campaign departments rather than to planning departments. It is intended to reach a broad constituency that has to be sold on the idea that it is "buying" something worthwhile with its contribution, and these "sales" are needed to keep the organization going.

For some time now, Jewish philanthropy has operated with at least an implicit recognition of the reality—that there are two distinct client systems. In examining the question of how changes in the client system have implications for Jewish philanthropy, we must look at changes in each of the two client systems described, and the interaction between these systems.

Community Building

The most fundamental change in Jewish philanthropy that affects the client system is the shift in the very mission of the federations from fund collecting and allocating to community building. Faced with the emerging welfare state to care for many basic needs, having largely "made it" on the American scene by the late 1960s, facing the breakup of the old liberal/labor/black/Jewish coalition, coming to grips in 1967 with the reality that the destruction of Israel was an intolerable possibility, the North American Jewish community made an about-face in the basic direction of its entire philanthropic endeavor. It shifted from a primary focus on helping American Jews to integrate into American life successfully to a basic concern with maintaining and enhancing their Jewish life in the face of the "threat" of freedom in North America. The building and enhancement of community itself became the primary mission of the federation. Fund raising and allocating become only one of the primary tools in accomplishing that mission. Federations became less federations of agencies and more federations of the entire Jewish community. Functions of synagogues and social agencies began to be blurred. Leadership came from all sources because their agendas had largely merged and radical shifts were made, however gradually, in the funding of Jewish community services. Funding shifted from the hard social services to community-building activities in Jewish education, in Jewish informal education, in college campus programs, community relations, etc. At the same time, the state picked up the tab on social services (e.g., Medicare/aid, services to the poor and disabled, etc.).

From the mid-1970s to this day, federations engaged in writing by-laws or developing mission statements have universally redefined themselves from being a fund raising and allocating organization to an institution for the creative survival of the Jewish people. With this new reality, the difference between the two kinds of clients described above becomes inextricably blurred, with important consequences for how the operations of the institution must be viewed. If a charitable institution is supported by a few elite wealthy people serving the masses, the distinctions between the two client systems are easy to make. However, when the donors are themselves a significant percentage of the Jewish community, providing services to ensure the Jewish identity of *their* own children, *their* families, *their* neighbors of every economic class, as well as poor Jews, then the distinctions crumble. We are clients in a new way. We are members of a kind of voluntary quasi-socialist society, creating and maintaining institutions that we believe are necessary for the common good, whether or not they can be supported by the users.

The client is not simply the troubled individual or family—the collectivity of the Jewish community is the client. What is also new is the provision of service ("outreach" we call it) to people who never asked for it. It is one thing to guarantee that no parent is prevented from educating his child Jewishly because of poverty. It is another thing to convince a parent that the child needs a Jewish education. Yet it is this latter kind of activity that consumes more and more of our time and resources, and to which we ask people to contribute.

Actually, the modern welfare state is similarly all-encompassing. Consider the following example.

A veteran, an individualist opposed to government intervention, returning from the Korean war went to college on the GI bill, bought his house with an FHA loan, saw his kids born in a VA hospital, got electricity from the TVA and, later, water from an Environmental Protection Agency project. His parents retired to a farm on Social Security, got electricity from the Rural Electrification Administration and used soil testing from the U.S. Department of Agriculture. When the father became ill, the family was saved from financial ruin by Medicare, and a life was saved with a drug developed in the National Institutes for Health. His children participated in the School Lunch program, learned physics from teachers trained in the National Science Foundation program, and went to college with guaranteed student loans. He drove to work on the interstate and moored his boat in a channel dredged by army engineers. When floods hit, he took Amtrak to Washington to apply for disaster relief and then spent some time in the Smithsonian museum.

As with social welfare, so with Jewish philanthropy. Try the following analogy:

When the Jewish Community Center invited Elie Wiesel to lecture, the auditorium was filled with seven hundred people. Nonetheless, the stirring lecture incurred a deficit of $850. The federation, which funded that center program, thought the money was well spent as a form of adult Jewish education. Now the same federation spends thousands of dollars on outreach and leadership development so that large numbers of Jews, not otherwise identified or affiliated with any Jewish organization or causes, vote to declare their membership in the Jewish community by contributing to an annual campaign. This effort incurs a good deal of cost. Is this "fund raising cost" or "administrative expense," or is it an equally legitimate expense for informal Jewish education? If community building is the mission, engaging people with the community is a community service to a group of *clients*.

Mass-based philanthropy has always had a two-client system, the ultimate consumer of the philanthropic service and the contributor. But with the change in mission in Jewish philanthropy, those two client systems have become in many ways one, and serving them just different aspects of one network of community services.

The fundamental blurring of the old distinction between the two client systems is that the consumers or users of the services of the federation and its agency system and the bulk of contributors to that system are one and the same group. There is still an elite group of large contributors who are not heavy users of the system, and this phenomenon has to be dealt with separately. But in large part and increasingly, this union has taken place. These are some of the consequences of this fundamental change that are discussed here:

1. The users of services, like the North American Jewish Community itself, are an increasingly affluent group.

2. The users of the services are not only also the contributors, but

as a result of that, this same group are the evaluators of the services, the ones who make planning decisions about which services should be increased or cut. The system is impacted by the desire for more participatory input in philanthropy by the donors.

3. As this merged and blurred client group becomes more like its North American general community, it is increasingly affected by a regressive image of philanthropy being developed in the larger society.

Above I described a watershed change. In the remainder of the chapter, I shall touch on three other changes in the client system, changes related in part to the change in mission, changes with particular importance for Jewish philanthropy. The changes are (1) the growing affluence of the North American Jewish community; (2) the impetus for participatory input in philanthropy by donors; and (3) the increasingly regressive image of philanthropy being developed in the larger society.

The Affluent Community

A significant, small percentage of Jews, particularly in the large cities, continues to be in poverty and demand priority attention from the Jewish philanthropic establishment. None of this contradicts the reality that the Jewish community in North America is probably the most affluent Jewish community in the history of the Diaspora, and that Jews are remarkably affluent even when compared with other affluent ethnic groups.

There are a number of implications which flow from this reality:

1. Jewish social services are increasingly services for the entire community—rich, middle class and poor.

2. The best way to serve the poor is in the context of services that are open to and actually utilized by all elements of the community. They tend to be better services, serve people with greater dignity, and do more good. By contrast, "services for the poor are poor services." Therefore, the trend toward universalizing Jewish social services is a healthy one.

3. Outside of the very largest cities, Jewish federations and agencies have probably not kept up with the need to continue to be aware of

and to serve the poor. In community after community, the established Jewish agencies tend to proceed as though, except for some individual cases, there are no Jewish poor, no special services that have to be mounted, no outreach that has to be done. It would be tragic if Jewish philanthropy moved to serve the total community at the expense of the poor.

4. In serving the Jewish aged and disabled, federations and their agencies are beginning to discover the ways in which services can be mounted to these groups aimed at the broad range of economic levels and how this improves the service for all classes. Traditionally, for instance, housing for the elderly has been provided through government-supported programs for the elderly poor. However, eligibility requirements have become increasingly stringent, leaving out a large bulk of lower middle-class and upper lower-class Jewish elderly who are too "wealthy" to qualify. In fact, in some communities, it has become difficult to maintain a high percentage of Jewish clientele in the face of these eligibility requirements. Communities have just begun to learn how to use syndication (until the newest tax law) and nonprofit bond issues to finance such programs. Such approaches make it possible to offer better housing to Jews with a sliding scale so that the affluent can pay their way with a little bit toward the financing of others. There can be a wide range of economic classes served in the project and the poor can be served in dignity in a first-class facility with the deficit being funded through the federation.

Similarly, one of the needs that has come to the fore lately has been the need for small permanent group homes for retarded Jews, who have been cared for by their parents but whose parents are now aging and worried about the future of their children. Affluent parents (whose anguish at the prospect of leaving a child uncared for is no less awful than that of the poor) are able to help endow such facilities. These endowments, over time, can build a base of support to make such an expensive community service possible and available, and over decades able to throw off funds to start other such institutions. It is these creative approaches that are possible in a variety of community services once we commit ourselves to a universalist approach, and that are denied as long as we think of ourselves as charitable institutions for the poor alone.

5. Most services will go to most Jews who are not poor, and this is appropriate. Jewish philanthropic campaigning has simply not adapted

to marketing the campaign as one by the Jewish community, of the Jewish community, and for the Jewish community. Marketing and solicitation continue to rely on old stereotypes. When push comes to shove, we trot out the same photograph of the elderly woman moved from a ghetto apartment to a new housing development under Jewish auspices. We simply have not found a way to educate, interpret, or inspire people around a proud community, creating an exemplary network of human services for all its members, as a way of developing its own survival and enhancement.

I know that in Israel there was a good deal of resentment a few years ago at an advertisement that urged people to contribute to UJA/ Federation and showed an Israeli child on crutches. The implication that the proud nation of Israel could not afford to provide crutches to all its young people who needed them was demeaning and insulting. We have barely scratched the surface in how to educate for support of nation building, partnership, working together as equals for the enhanced continuity of the Jewish people at home and in Israel. However, our client system of donors is increasingly sophisticated. These people know that, if they really wanted to, deeply, most families could pay for the Jewish education of their children or for their marital counseling. They need to be inspired about outreach, but instead we help them raise questions about services to the nonpoor. An improvement in marketing, I believe, is one of the major challenges facing the Jewish community.

6. A subsidiary, but an important challenge of affluence, is the whole problem of fee-setting and scholarships. If fees are set too low, the Jewish community is being unfair to itself and its donors by not challenging participants in the community enterprise to pay their fair share. People who could pay for and need the service stay away because it becomes labeled, in their minds, as being for "poor people." If fees for services are set too high, then a large percentage of Jews are forced to seek scholarships and helped to feel pauperized, and perhaps to abstain from using the services. We have not applied our creativity, our ability to innovate, and our intelligence to solving these problems for intelligent fee setting for all the services in the Jewish community, from Jewish education, to family treatment, to participation in the ballet class at the Jewish community center.

All of the above problems are ones that are solvable if we turn our attention to them in our desire to serve all Jews in the Jewish community living in a generally affluent society.

Demands for Greater Participation, Input, and Designation

We have discussed two-client systems; we are learning that the client system composed of the donors is uneasy about the lack of opportunities for participation, input, control over where their contributions are going and how they are being spent.

Nonetheless, we have simply tended not to market our campaigns dramatically or based on targeted specific goals with which people can identify. The idea of "giving to Israel" or giving to support your local Jewish community is a noble one, but even if it succeeds in achieving a contribution, it is not likely by itself to inspire increases. Neither for Israel nor locally do we tend to target certain dramatic goals or needs of the community that must be achieved, and can only be achieved with additional contributions. This has nothing to do with designated giving. It has to do with each community setting certain objectives to energize its campaign.

If a community does a study of needs and decides that it is imperative that at least one of every three Jewish adolescents spends a summer in Israel, and that one way or another it must be possible to make this financially feasible, then programs can be designed and financial targets set. It can be made clear to the contributor why the campaign must have 13.5 percent more money this year than last. Or if the government decides that in Israel some regional industrial park or Dead Sea canal must be built, and that everything raised nationally beyond what was raised a year before will go toward that project for the next two to three years, that lends itself to a dramatic campaign. It takes some kind of drama to energize and galvanize a community around commonly felt needs and priorities. We simply have not done very much of this, and in that sense we are very primitive in our approach to our client system of contributors. We simply ask for a tax increase each year.

Particularly for those people who do need to feel a more personal connection to what they contribute to, we also need to replicate the Project Renewal model. There are pieces of Jewish Agency programs, there are elements in our communities that can become the responsibility of certain communities or subgroups within a community.

We can even live with designated giving, so long as it is the community, rather than the individual, who does the designating. One can select a number of priorities, programmatic or capital in nature, and invite contributors, particularly major contributors, to do extra giving for those causes. Some communities have already begun experimenting with such an approach. However, we have not organized ourselves yet in any consistent or comprehensive way to take advantage of the impetus to do good in projects for which we have a particular affinity without undoing the community basis for federated giving.

Designated giving, as it has been thrust on the United Way system by political pressures, could be the undoing of federated philanthropy in the Jewish community as it has begun to hurt the United Way. If individuals contribute to any one of a list of agencies or causes and then it is distributed by the federation, then the federation is nothing more than a bank or temporary holding company for contributions. The distinction is subtle but critical. On the one hand, we have a variety of techniques that personalize input and decision-making and choice in contributing around priorities and needs established by a community process. On the other hand, we have an invitation to designate by each individual contributor, which completely undoes the notion of citizen planning and decision-making on priorities. We need to define ways to exploit the former without falling into the latter.

The General Attitude toward Philanthropy

Jewish philanthropy in North America exists as part of a larger system and is inevitably influenced by that system. In the last eight years, we have witnessed a growing meanness of spirit about mutual aid and the worthiness of the needy. We have experienced a de-education of the public in the nature and meaning of philanthropy. Charitable impulses still exist but are exploited in primitive ways. Is there a problem of hunger? Let there be some giant rock concert and the problem will be relieved. Are there homeless? Let all Americans hold hands in a chain stretching from the Atlantic to the Pacific oceans and we shall have dealt with the problem of homelessness. These quick-fix throw a penny in the *pushka* (charity box) approaches to philanthropy have grown immeasurably in the last eight years without any serious examination of what percentages of dollars raised reach the target groups or how relevant private philanthropy can be to the dimensions of the problem.

At the same time, there has been a regression in some basic attitudes toward philanthropy. For generations, it seemed that philanthropy would grow more universal, depending on mechanisms that helped all people and the poor along with them in a dignified manner (like Social Security) rather than relying on old-fashioned charity, which depended on proving how beaten down and needy you were in order to qualify for aid. This has all changed. More and more, social planners advocate means-tested programs to pinpoint scarce dollars on target populations.

The last eight years has seen a massive shift toward the privatization of community services. Hospitals, mursing homes, child care centers, even prisons are run by corporations for profit, intruding on what had once been an almost exclusively voluntary charitable or state domain. And even while this trend has developed, there has been an unprecedented attack by business on the nonprofit sector, trying to narrow its scope, reach, and definition in ways that are reminiscent of the last century. Attacks are made on the tax-exempt status of voluntary agencies.

The Small Business Administration, citing supposed abuses of or failure to pay unrelated business income tax by some voluntary agencies, tries to define unrelated business in ways that may be crippling to the voluntary sector. While national leaders wax eloquent about voluntarism, tax incentives for charitable contributions have declined significantly in recent years in a number of ways.

A Jewish community center lost its exemption from real estate taxes because it did not serve exclusively poor and indigent people at no fee. We hear much about a "kinder, gentler America" and "one thousand points of light," but apart from the gap between the rhetoric and reality, the most serious problem is the presentation by national leadership of the government as the enemy. We are told that we must not "throw money" at problems, that government programs only make social problems worse, and that the only hope is what can be done by voluntary groups, preferably small and local. The truth, of course, is that the major social problems in the United States, from earliest times through Social Security and Medicare and Medicaid, could only be addressed by significant and major government programs. The elderly used to be the largest group in the poverty population. Improvements in Social Security, SSI, Medicare, and Medicaid have turned that around significantly. Today, the United States is the only modern country in the world that does not have some kind of children's allowance or similar program, and children are now a large and growing group in the poverty population.

Government programs often fail, but without government programs there really can be no significant progress in the most significant social problems we face. Similarly, without a turnaround in current attitudes, the voluntary sector cannot perform its role in the national society that it needs to perform.

In order to justify their continuation as charitable organizations, they are called on from time to time to prove that they serve the poor exclusively, that they charge no fees, that they conduct no operation that in any way, shape, or form could overlap with any part of the profit-making sector. All of this is simply bad public policy.

I would hope that most of us do not want to return to the days where the poor were served only in separate, exclusive services for the poor. I would hope that most of us see as progressive the development of sliding scales and inviting people to participate in their own helping process to the extent that they are able even while maintaining an open door to all. Yet, counter trends to these developments are strong, and in some ways the whole voluntary system is beleaguered and defensive. Our own voluntary leaders are infected by some of these attitudes. Our ability to meet the needs of our client systems will in large part depend on our ability to turn around these larger trends and to return to the road on which we were traveling for at least half a century before this change. That road sees philanthropy as part of a larger society committed to mutual aid and participation by clients in that aid, a society that builds dignity and universal inclusion: in short—the great society.

15

Israeli Society and Diaspora Philanthropy: How Well Does the Gift Perform?

Israel Katz

The complex relationship between Diaspora giving and Israel has been marked by a curious trait for years. Considerable effort has been invested in understanding how the money is raised, but much less effort has been expended on evaluating how it is spent. This is particularly true of the largest Israeli recipient of Diaspora philanthropy, the Jewish Agency. Since 1948, American Jews have donated over $5.5 billion to the Jewish Agency through the United Jewish Appeal–Federation system.

In this chapter we would like to focus on the neglected aspect of this system—the performance side of the gift—using insights and theories from social welfare and organizational analysis. To illustrate our findings, we shall draw on the Katz et al. (1988) study of the Jewish Agency Department of Immigration and Absorption, which was conducted in 1987 by the Center for Social Policy Studies in Israel. Needless to say, our conclusions do not necessarily apply to all types of Diaspora philanthropy in Israel. There are considerable differences between the UJA-Jewish Agency system and free-loan funds for yeshiva students in places such as B'nai Brak, not to mention the "American Friends" organizations of Israeli universities and hospitals.

Although we are concerned mainly with the goals of philanthropy and their implementation, these must be understood as part of a comprehensive philanthropic or voluntary system of organization. This system comprises donors, allocators, implementors, and beneficiaries. Our approach is based on the assumption that the process of implementation of the goals of a philanthropy cannot be properly understood unless they are seen as part of a broader system of interacting components.

For many years, the philanthropic system encompassing Israel and the Diaspora has operated on the premise that the job of Diaspora Jews is primarily to raise as much money as they can to "help Israel" on the assumption that the Israelis would know how to put it to good use.

Nevertheless, more than forty years have passed since these views were formed. We need to ask certain questions: Does doing good for the noble cause guarantee that the work will be done well? Does the exalted nature of the cause ensure that the overall mission of the philanthropic or voluntary organization will remain consistent with its operative objective? Under what conditions are these objectives implemented as intended, and under what conditions will they fail to be carried out? This chapter will attempt to grapple with such questions as they concern the Jewish Agency and its Department of Immigration and Absorption.

Philanthropy in the Diaspora and Israel

Philanthropic activity in various forms has been a prominent feature of Jewish society and religious life throughout the ages, as both a personal mitzvah and an obligation of the community as a whole. American Jewish philanthropy has continued this tradition on an impressive scale that is often held up as an example to both other Diaspora communities and to the non-Jewish world. American Jewish philanthropy has helped Jews the world over—in the past, in the present, and so it would seem, in the future as well.

In Israel, the voluntary social welfare system is extensive and may be relatively larger than in other countries. Indeed, it may even be said that the State of Israel was established largely by volunteers and by voluntary, nonprofit organizations. The basis for Israel's public social services—in social security, housing, health, education, and employment—was laid by voluntary bodies before and after the establishment of the state.

Today Israel's voluntary system or "third sector" (after government and business) continues to expand significantly. It employs more than one in every nine employees and accounts for more than one in every twelve shekels of gross national product. Over the past decade, Israeli society has become more dependent on the third sector: its share of the GNP has grown from about 6 percent, between 1955 and 1975, to about 8 percent during 1975–85. If the activity of volunteers, which is quite impressive but is not reflected in the GNP, were added to the figures on employment and output, then the third sector's weight in the social and economic life of Israel would increase even further (Roter et al. 1984).

American Jewish philanthropy has made a significant contribution to Israel's development, both before and after 1948. These donations made possible the immigration and absorption of close to two million immigrants and the establishment of hundreds of towns and rural settlements. Moreover, in its early years, when the state was faced with severe economic, security, and social burdens, American Jewish philanthropic aid was especially vital and provided a major source of foreign currency (see tables 15-1 and 15-2).

Table 15-1. *Israel's Exports and U.I.A. Transmittals (in millions of $)*

Year	Exports	U.I.A.
1951	46.8	50.0
1952	43.4	44.6
1953	59.6	44.2

Table 15-2. *Foreign Currency Income 1954/55 (in millions of $)*

Exports, visible	88.2
Exports, invisible	15.7
Jewish Organizations Currency	73.4
Goods	4.9
Sale of Bonds	37.9
U.S. Grant-in-Aid	44.9
German Reparations	94.7
Personal Transfers	24.2
Other Receipts	14.0
Total	397.9

Source: Council of Jewish Federations.

The more than $5.5 billion raised since 1948 by federations and the UJA represents the largest segment of American Jewish philanthropy for Israel, which has been channeled through the Jewish Agency and the Joint Distribution Committee (JDC) (see table 15-3). These funds— which now amount to about $350 million a year—are raised in local communities by federations and forwarded to the UJA. The UJA then transfers part of the money to the JDC, which runs its own operations in Israel, and the rest to the United Israel Appeal, which passes the money on to the Jewish Agency. The agency itself is run as a partnership between the major fund raising bodies in the Diaspora and the World Zionist Organization (WZO). Hundreds of millions of dollars more have been raised for Israeli hospitals, the Jewish National Fund, and Israel's universities. In recent years, it has been estimated that between $500 million and $590 million is raised each year in North America for Israeli causes of all kinds.

It should be noted that the performance of Jewish philanthropy for Israel cannot be measured solely by the relatively simple yardstick of dollars and cents. It is widely accepted that fund raising for Israel benefits the donors as well as the recipients. Among other things, it strengthens Jewish identity in the Diaspora; that is, philanthropy for Israel contributes to a reinforcement of the identity and image of being Jewish. It also symbolizes American Jewry's concern for the security and well-being of Israel and expresses the community's desire to exercise political influence in the wider American milieu. The "missions" of American givers are a central focus of the UJA operation. Site visits to facilities reward the giver emotionally and hope to inspire further philanthropy when reinforced by access to the Israeli political elite who emphasize their important role as "Jewish leaders."

The Department of Immigration and Absorption

The Jewish Agency's Department of Immigration and Absorption, which we shall refer to henceforth as "the department," provides a good illustration of some of Israel's problems as a welfare state and some of the problems of Diaspora philanthropy for Israel. In recent years the department has had a budget of $100 million, out of a total agency budget of close to $420 million.

Before 1948, the agency and WZO acted as "the state in the making," by carrying out the political tasks of the Zionist movement and by providing services for immigrants. When the state was estab-

Table 15-3. *UIA Remittances to the Jewish Agency (UJA Funds), May 5, 1988*

Fiscal Year	Total	Fiscal Year	Total
1948	$ 41,600,000	1970	$ 120,043,000
1949	64,600,000	1971	159,308,000
1950	50,700,000	1972	175,681,000
1951	44,300,000	1973	232,310,000
1952	48,100,000	1974	449,574,000
1953	42,700,000	1975	205,706,000
1954	40,700,000	1976	279,676,000
1955	30,300,000	1977	209,793,000
1956	36,600,000	1978	250,243,000
1957	48,200,000	1979	256,549,000
1958	49,800,000	1980	260,998,000
1959	37,300,000	1981	268,919,000
1960	46,200,000	1982	266,433,000
1961	39,100,000	1983	329,445,000
1962	36,028,000	1984	303,020,000
1963	27,954,000	1985	346,782,000
1964	27,737,000	1986	337,034,000
1965	34,435,000	1987	317,553,000
1966	40,784,000		
1967	37,614,000		
1968	196,521,000		
1969	111,999,000		
Total:			$5,902,339,000

Source: Council of Jewish Federations.

lished, the government took over some of the agency's previous functions, leaving it with the tasks of immigration and absorption, Youth Aliya, rural settlement, and cultural and educational work in the Diaspora. The agency's relation to the government was grounded in a special "Status Law" and given formal expression in a covenant signed by representatives of the two bodies in 1954.

In 1968, the government decided to take over immigrant absorption from the agency and to establish a new ministry for this purpose, called the Ministry of Immigrant Absorption. The government leaders at that time felt that the agency's handling of absorption left much to be desired, especially concerning newcomers from Western societies. They also acted on the assumption that since this area of activity was central to Israel's national life, it should come under the government's direct responsibility. It was also argued that since most aspects of immigrant absorption—housing, employment, and education—were handled by government ministries, it would be best to have a government ministry, rather than a nongovernmental body, coordinate these services.

The agency vehemently objected to being stripped of its responsibility for the care of newcomers, and sought to overturn the government's decision. It is not hard to understand the agency's motives in this case since absorption had been one of its historic preserves. No less important, however, was the reaction to the government's decision by the American Jewish fund raising establishment. The UJA–UIA leadership strongly protested this move, since they felt it would "jeopardize the fund-raising structure in the U.S." (Stock 1984, 191; see also Horev Report 1976, 10). Taking absorption away from the agency would have removed one of the UJA's most effective fund raising appeals, which was that the contributions were needed to help "needy immigrants and refugees" (Stock 1984, 191).

These appeals and protests led the government to significantly modify its original decision. Prime Minister Eshkol announced that the agency would retain responsibility for caring for "needy immigrants and refugees, a field which has for the most part been the responsibility of world Jewry" (Stock 1984, 191). He noted that when the Ministry of Absorption would be established, its functions would be defined in accordance with this principle. The agency thus continued to provide services to all immigrants in absorption centers, hostels, and kibbutz ulpanim (Hebrew language schools) and to provide welfare services to those in need. At the time, the Absorption Ministry expected that this unclear division of responsibility and functions would be merely temporary.

Since then many people in Israel, including immigrants and former immigrants, have reached the conclusion that the way responsibility for absorption was split up in 1968 between the government and the agency was both harmful to the newcomers and wasteful of resources. This was, in fact, one of the main conclusions of Katz et al. (1988). The blurred lines of responsibility and accountability frequently forced immigrants into a bureaucratic runaround between the two agencies, and different standards of treatment were sometimes applied. Some immigrants found that the system retarded their integration into Israeli society and made it harder for them to learn how to fend for themselves. Some observers have argued that the problems of the absorption system as perceived abroad actually became a deterrent to *aliya* (immigration).

One is left with the strong impression that in this case, the resources mobilized from Jewish philanthropy, which could have been used to serve other vital needs of Israeli society, were not utilized effectively. Moreover, in their insistence on preserving the agency's role in absorption, the American fund raising leaders seemed to be more concerned about the needs of the fund raising system than about the needs of the agency's clients—the new immigrants.

Indeed, the question being raised is essentially what should be the Jewish Agency's role in absorption vis-à-vis the role of government. The agency should continue to deal with absorption in the role of a nonprofit organization that supplements the work of the public system and its responsibility. Hence, the current trend is in this direction as the State of Israel prepares to respond to the challenge of a hopeful "mass" immigration from Eastern Europe.

There were many shortcomings in its structure and operations. It was found, for example, that the department and its various units lacked clearly defined objectives and modern tools of planning, management, and control, and that criteria of performance and measures of effectiveness were virtually nonexistent.

The Jewish Agency, Israel's Welfare State, and Criteria of Organizational Performance

Several policy options were recommended. The preferred course of action—which was eventually adopted by the agency board of governors—was to transfer basic absorption services to the government. This would enable the agency to provide supplementary services in the field of absorption, thus utilizing its advantages as a nonprofit organization supported by philanthropy. One of the main tasks proposed for the agency in its future role was the encouragement of a voluntary activity in the field of absorption by mobilizing veteran Israelis as well as immigrant associations. The head of the department and other officials, however, opposed the idea of transfering the basic services under their responsibility to the government. Such a reaction is, of course, natural—no one likes to give up a big piece of their turf. But on a deeper level, this reaction expressed a resistance to the notion that the agency should abandon its quasi-governmental status and assume the more limited role of a nonprofit organization. An aversion to restricting the agency's tasks to those appropriate to a nonprofit organization was to be found among other agency leaders.

The Jewish Agency as an Organization

The Jewish Agency's special legal status in Israel, and the fact that it has been entrusted with functions that are normally assumed by governments, make it difficult to put it into the same category as an ordinary voluntary or nonprofit body. Is it governmental, nonprofit, or half and half? In a strict sense, however, it is a nonprofit organization, since those who run it—the donors and the leaders of the WZO who serve on its governing bodies—are free to determine its goals and functions as long as they do not conflict with Israeli law. Moreover, it is supported by philanthropic funds.

Agency leaders, however, and some others as well, repeatedly stress the importance of its quasi-governmental status. Of course, this unique status helps the agency and its leaders cling to the aura and trappings of power by recalling the days when it was the "state in the making." (As a senior agency official once said: "In 1948 the Jewish Agency was awarded a state, but lost its status as a government.") The prestige conferred by the agency's unique status may also account for the desire of the fund raising leaders to maintain their partnership with a quasi-governmental body in Israel rather than with an ordinary voluntary organization.

The agency's desire to preserve its quasi-governmental status did not reduce the tendency for its functions and responsibilities to become blurred in relation to those of the government. On the contrary, this desire made the problems worse. The performance of the agency could improve if it redefined its relations with government as those of a voluntary organization. This applies to immigrant absorption as well as to its other activities.

It seems, however, that the preference for a quasi-governmental status for the agency is also related to how the power and functions of the state are perceived vis-à-vis the limitations placed on nonprofit organizations, in modern society in general, and in Israel in particular.

For the founding fathers of Israel, most of whom were socialists, the establishment of the state symbolized not only the beginning of a new era for the Jewish people, but also the birth of a welfare state—one is tempted to add, the first Jewish welfare state in two thousand years. The egalitarian, progressive welfare state envisioned by the founders of Israel was not only meant to carry out the universal mission of creating a just society, it was also supposed to serve as the vehicle for integrating the disparate groups of immigrants that came to Israel from over one hundred countries.

The establishment of Israel's welfare state also represented another historical transition. No longer would the traditional institutions of Jewish philanthropy play the dominant role in providing for the social needs of the community. This role would be carried out by a democratically elected government, acting through the welfare state apparatus and not through collecting charity from the wealthy and pious of the community, as an expression of the religious obligation of *tzedakah*. And if the new Jewish society of the State of Israel was still in need of Diaspora assistance, this could be provided under the banner of "partnership in nation-building," rather than as a modern form of charitable help for the needy.

For most of the period since 1948, the government's responsibility for identifying and dealing with social needs has been continually stressed, with the voluntary sector relegated to a marginal role. This tendency stems not only from the power and centrality of the state in the public life of Israel, but also from the weaknesses of most voluntary organizations. The latter were usually lacking in resources, which meant that they could not attract good professional staff and that their services were of low quality. Since they were dependent on the generosity of donors, they were also marked by a paternalistic approach and often tended to promote the interests of elite groups in the community. In a broader sense, some advocates of the welfare state argued that philanthropy conflicts with the welfare state and hinders its developments.

More recently, however, this notion that philanthropy and the welfare state are in conflict seems rather obsolete (Flora and Alber 1981; Salamon 1987). Actually, acknowledging the central role of government in the modern welfare state neither requires nor justifies the disparaging of the contributions of voluntary organizations to social welfare.

Contrary to its image in America, the welfare state in western democracies does not represent the realization of socialism. The function of the welfare state, rather, is to mediate between the democratic polity and the capitalistic market economy. Modern voluntarism also owes its origins to the tensions and interaction between democracy and capitalism (Flora and Alber 1981). Indeed, the voluntary sector has expanded greatly in the West, including Israel, in recent years because there is no intrinsic confrontation between the welfare state and services provided by nonprofit organizations. Both, in fact, complement one another (Salamon 1987).

The welfare state needs a healthy volunteer sector to cultivate the citizens' sense of social obligation and to channel the drive for active involvement inspired by this commitment. When it tries to monopolize responsibility for social services, the welfare state "nationalizes" concern for social needs, thereby denying citizens the opportunity to express their obligations to their fellowman and community. Social action undertaken by other large organizations, such as political parties or quasi-governmental bodies, can also have the same stifling effect on human concern and community initiative.

Both the Jewish Agency Department of Immigration and Absorption and the Ministry of Absorption are guilty in a way of "nationalizing" the tasks of helping newcomers, which may have discouraged voluntary initiatives among Israeli citizens in the field of immigrant absorption. By making immigrant absorption the exclusive province of large bureaucratic organizations, both the government and the agency may have left no role for those who seek to cultivate a sense of social obligation and involvement through voluntary frameworks.

Measuring Departmental Performance: The Elusive Quest for Criteria

Unless an organization has developed means for measuring its performance, there is no way it can know whether it is discharging its responsibilities properly or attaining its objectives. A business firm uses profits as a measure of performance. The performance of a human service organization, however, is clearly more difficult to assess. It is no wonder, then, that the Department of Immigration and Absorption has found its performance hard to measure, so hard that it may have stopped trying.

Organizational goals may be vague or ill-defined. Also, they may be defined differently by the various constituencies that have a stake in the organization. Furthermore, each constituency may have different standards for evaluating the services provided. Kanter and Summers (1987) have noted that the meaningful questions in performance measurement are for the most part not technical, but conceptual: not how to measure effectiveness, but rather what to measure.

Some claim that an organization's very survival may serve as an adequate measure of its performance or success. A voluntary organization, so this argument goes, would not survive if it were not functional for those who contribute to it or use its services. An organization can continue to attract contributors, however, for reasons that have little to do with its effectiveness. Furthermore, political factors may assure an organization's survival, and clients may continue to use its services because better services are not available. The department has clearly succeeded in surviving, but this is not an adequate criterion of its effectiveness.

In the case of the department, the issue of organizational performance may be explored more effectively by identifying its major constituencies and their respective expectations concerning its objectives. Three major constituencies of a nonprofit organization are relevant for this analysis: (1) the board of directors, which in this case comprises two groups who serve on the Board of Governors of the Jewish Agency, that is, the Diaspora donors and the politicians of the WZO; (2) managers and professionals; and (3) the clients or recipients of its services.

The *first group* of constituents, the directors, is primarily interested in evidence of sound performance that reinforces the legitimacy of the organization. That, in turn, enhances its attractiveness as a recipient of contributions. The organization must be seen to perform well, but not so well that it has eliminated the need for future contributions. The organization's performance must also confer prestige on its directors. In the case of the department, its "effectiveness" can usually be demonstrated to this group simply by citing the number of immigrants that have received services of various sorts. Rising numbers may serve as an indicator of "success," but declining numbers do not necessarily mean the opposite since the level of immigration to Israel is considered to be beyond the department's control.

The *second group* of constituents, the managers and professionals, is interested primarily in information that would help them identify problems in goal attainment and to adjust the organization's functions or allocation of resources in accordance with the needs to be served. The low level of professionalism in the department means that the demand for this sort of information is very limited. The managers who are political appointees are in any case not judged according to professional criteria of performance.

The *third group* of constituents, the organization's clients, has an obvious interest in the quality of its services, although considerations of efficiency, that is, the cost-effectiveness of service delivery, may be of little concern to them. For example, individual immigrants tend to evaluate absorption centers in terms of personal convenience rather than in terms of cost-effectiveness.

Kanter and Summers (1987) state that a balanced approach to organizational performance should take into account the expectations and standards of the various constituencies, so that performance information is generated that meets the needs of each group. Problems are likely to arise, however, when the multiple constituencies of an organization lack a system of balanced performance measurement.

Jewish philanthropic organizations that raise funds in the Diaspora in order to attain various objectives in Israel are clearly characterized by multiple constituencies. In this respect, the department resembles other bodies in Israel funded by Diaspora contributions. In many cases the indicators of performance sought by each constituency are disconnected from one another, which sometimes feeds tensions between the constituent groups. Furthermore, because the constituencies are geographically separated and act in different social contexts, it is all the more difficult to reach a reasonable balance between expectations of organizational performance.

In the case of the department, the inclinations of the Diaspora donors (and the WZO leadership) to perceive and articulate its goals in broad terms has influenced the approach of management. By paying lip service to vague goals that have little operational meaning, the departmental management avoids friction with the members of the agency board of governors. Donors, politicians, and managers alike seem to prefer a frame of reference that stresses the broad mission of "helping Israel," "nation-building," or "fostering Israel's security," rather than face up to the task of defining operative goals and criteria of implementation. With the exception of the organization's clients, then, whose main concern is quality, all other constituencies of the department tend to evade the practical realities of performance. In a voluntary organization, the clients' collective voice is rarely heard, and this also holds for the department. The board of governors never insisted on the implementation of a decision that called for the establishment of a council of immigrant associations to advise the department.

Our findings concerning the department confirm a tendency found in many voluntary organizations, in which the focus of interest shifts from output to input since the survival of the organization is largely determined by fund raising. Rather than concentrating on performance, service delivery, or the attainment of the organization's goals, a tendency emerges to focus on fund raising. In particular, as in the case of the department, when the realities of the organization make it difficult or depressing to confront problems of performance, it becomes more tempting to take refuge in fund raising concerns. Furthermore, because the donors have no need themselves of the organization's services, they rarely have any way of judging just how good or bad they are. Of course, management reports to them on these matters, but such reports tend to be heavily biased. These factors reinforce the disconnection between the concerns of the department's constituencies created by geographical and social distance.

The main findings of our study of the department reflect these problems: the blurred lines of responsibility and accountability, the lack of explicitly defined operative goals and policies, lack of program evaluation, etc. Such problems may have no adverse impact on the survival of the organization, especially at times when all concerned are eager to maintain peace and quiet, but the problems must eventually surface, hurting the organization and damaging the quality of its services. Furthermore, these problems engender internal political strife at various levels of the organization, and encouarge goal displacement of various sorts, which is made easier by the slack connection in any case between policy and operations. Many of these phenomena, of course, occur at the expense of the organization's clients. Under such conditions, as we have seen in the department, conflicts among the constituencies also become common, with one group inciting against the other, managers against the fund raisers, clients against managers, etc.

Under such conditions, the alienation or disconnection of the main constituencies from each other—Diaspora donors from the providers of services in Israel—becomes predictable, and both suffer the consequences. In Israel, this is reflected in the low quality of services and the inadequate utilization of philanthropic resources in relation to social needs, and in the Diaspora, by difficulties in raising funds for services that have gained a reputation for poor quality and that have become the subject of public controversy.

Summary and Conclusion

In the past, considerable emphasis has been placed on Diaspora giving, while less effort has been expended on understanding better how it is spent. This chapter has focused on the neglected aspects of the system—the performance side of the gift. However, it would be misleading to examine the performance of philanthropy only, without relating it to the other components of the voluntary system in which fund raisers, donors, allocators, implementers of programs, and beneficiaries operate. The assumption is that the realization of objectives must be perceived and related to as an intrinsic part of the philanthropic system in which other components also act and interact with each other and the total system.

On the basis of a study of the Department of Immigration and Absorption of the Jewish Agency, undertaken in Jerusalem in 1987, it was felt that the department may provide an illustration of a type of Diaspora philanthropy for, and its performance in, Israel.

The 1987 study revealed serious shortcomings as to the role, structure, and operations in the department.

Two basic and strategic failings were singled out for the purpose of this chapter due to their special relevance to other philanthropic or voluntary organizations in Israel that are funded by Diaspora or American-Jewish philanthropy: (1) the ambiguity in the role and image of the department as a voluntary nonprofit organization or a governmental public organization, and (2) the virtual nonexistence of criteria and measurements of performance and effectiveness.

The Jewish Agency is essentially a nonprofit organization. Its leadership and others, however, cling to its role as a semipublic or quasigovernmental organization. The image and behavior that evolved from this view often led to the blurring of the organization's function and responsibility in relation to those of government. The Jewish Agency's reluctance to recognize its role as a nonprofit organization may be accounted for by pragmatic reasons.

However, on a deeper level, it is also based on the misunderstanding of the respective roles of the modern welfare state, the nonprofit sector, or "Third Sector" (next to the private and public sectors). Contrary to the notion that the nonprofit sector hinders in the development of the Western welfare state, it has been increasingly recognized that they do not conflict, but can and should complement each other inasmuch as they are both associated with political democracy and the capitalist market economy.

The welfare state needs a healthy and strong voluntary sector to foster and nurture a sense of social obligation and commitment to one's fellowman and community. Experience indicates that the state does not perform this function well. On the contrary, welfare states often "nationalize" social concerns and services, thus depriving citizens of their involvement in human care in their community. This phenomenon is not conducive to the fostering of a sense of social obligation of citizens toward their fellow man and community.

Israel has nationalized much of the social concern. It is a highly overcentralized society. Overcentralization may have been essential and efficient in the early 1950s and 1960s when immigrants from more than one hundred countries confronted each other in a country that had to be built and in which a cohesive society had to be molded.

In recent years, however, centralization reduces the responsiveness of the system to change social and economic conditions. Overcentralization also results in the lack of incentives to innovate at the grass roots level. Now efforts must be made to decentralize the system so as to identify and meet the needs of the heterogenous groups and localities. Voluntary organizations can help to meet this task. Consequently, acknowledging the central role of government in the modern welfare state neither requires nor justifies the disparaging of the contribution and potential of the voluntary sector. Nevertheless, it must be borne in mind that voluntary organizations often reveal serious shortcomings such as insufficiencies of resources, paternalism and patronage, amateurism and low professional standards, etc. They do need help. Philanthropy and government must aid these organizations so that they can do what the private and public sectors cannot.

The voluntary sector in Israel, its size, scope, and activities are promising. It can expand its activities and lead to richer and greater citizen participation in Israel's concerns and services for the public good.

Such expansion is needed for strengthening democracy in Israel, and for the recruitment and activization of additional economic resources for the people of Israel.

Organizations need to measure their performance to know whether they accomplish their goals. The performance of nonprofit organizations in human services is difficult to assess. The department found its performance extremely hard to measure and perhaps because of that, stopped trying.

The problem of performance measurement is particularly complex in organizations that have many different constituencies. All such constituencies have a stake in the organization, but each may have different interests and expectations and, therefore, also different standards and measures for evaluating the service provided.

In the case of the department, like in similar philanthropic organizations, there were three or four constituencies at least with rather different expectations concerning their organization's objectives: (1)

the board of directors, (2) the managers and professionals, and (3) the clients or recipients of its services. The directors are interested primarily in evidence of sound performance that reinforces the legitimacy of the organization and enhances its attractiveness as a recipient of contributions. The managers are interested in information that helps them identify problems in goal-attainment and to adjust the organization's functions in accordance with the needs to be served. The clients have an obvious interest in the quality of the services although consideration of the cost-effectiveness of service delivery may be of little concern to them.

Hence, it seems that different constituencies prefer different kinds of performance and effectiveness measures. Kanter and Summers (1987) suggest that the performance assessment system in nonprofit organizations must acknowledge the existence of multiple constituencies and build tests of performance that balance clients and donors, boards and professionals, managers, and other constituencies of the organization.

Jewish philanthropic organizations that raise funds in the Diaspora in order to attain objectives in Israel are clearly characterized by multiple constituencies. Often, indicators of performance sought by each constituent are disconnected from one another. The main constituents are also geographically separated and act in different social contexts. It is all the more difficult to reach balanced systems that meet the different expectations of the respective groups. Many of the shortcomings and failings of the department and other similar organizations, funded in the Diaspora and active in Israel, seem to evolve from the disconnectedness among their multiple constituencies. A main challenge, therefore, for Diaspora philanthropy and its gift in Israel must be in the more active and stronger coupling between the different constituencies.

Bibliography

Central Bureau of Statistics. "Immigrants and Potential Immigrants by Period of Immigrant and Last Continent of Residence (1882–1986)." In *Statistical Abstract of Israel, 1987* (Table V/1). Jerusalem, 1987.

Correspondence between the Chairman of the Jewish Agency, Aryeh Louis Pincus and the Prime Minister, Levi Eshkol and the Minister of Absorption, Yigal Alon, following the decision of the Government to establish the Ministry for Absorption (1968, June–September).

Chusi, A. Personal communication to I. Katz, Haifa, 1965.

Data from Israel Fact Sheets, no. 3 ("The Balance of Trade"), 18.19. Cited by E. Stock, *Partners and Purse Strings*. New Jersey and Jerusalem: University Press of America, Inc., The Jerusalem Center for Public Affairs/Center for Jewish Community Service, 1987.

Eisenstadt, S. N. Introduction. In *The Welfare State and Its Aftermath,* edited by S. N. Eisenstadt and O. Ahimeir, p. 6. London and Sydney: Croom Helm in association with the Jerusalem Institute for Israel Studies, 1985.

Flora, Peter, and J. Alber. "Modernization, Democratization, and the Development of Welfare States in Western Europe." In *The Development of Welfare States in Europe and America,* edited by P. Flora and A. J. Heidenheimer, 37–80. New Brunswick, N.J.: Transaction, 1981.

[Horev Committee]. *Report of the Committee to Study Matters of Immigration and Absorption* [Hebrew]. Jerusalem: Jewish Agency, September 1976.

Jewish Agency. *Comptroller's Report for the Years 1986–87.* Submitted to the Jewish Agency Assembly, Jerusalem, June 1987.

Kanter, Rosabeth, and David V. Summers. "Doing Well While Doing Good: Dilemmas of Performance Measurement in Nonprofit Organizations and the Need for a Multiple-Constituency Approach." In *The Nonprofit Sector,* edited by Walter W. Powell, 154–66. New Haven, Conn. and London: Yale University, 1987.

Katz, I., A. Globerson, Y. Kop, J. Neipris, and J. Weinblatt. *The Jewish Agency Department of Immigration and Absorption: Options for Change 1987.* Jerusalem: The Center for Social Policy Studies in Israel, 1988.

Keyserling, L. H. *The Flow of Funds, to Date and Potential, from the U.S. and Israel, Being Primarily a Study of Fund Raising by the American Jewish Community for Jewish Causes.* Confidential report submitted to American Friends of Israel, April 16, 1956.

Roter, R., N. Shamai, F. Wood, and D. Gliksberg. "The Nonprofit Sector and Volunteering." In *Israel's Outlays for Human Services, 1984,* edited by Y. Kop, 181–229. Jerusalem: The Center for Social Policy Studies in Israel, 1984.

Salamon, Lester M. "Partners in Public Service: The Scope and Theory of Government-Nonprofit Relations." In *The Nonprofit Sector,* edited by W. W. Powell, 99–117. New Haven, Conn. and London: Yale University, 1987.

Stock, E. "The Reconstitution of the Jewish Agency: A Political Analysis." In *Understanding the Jewish Agency, A Handbook,* edited by D. J. Elazar and A. M. Dortort. Jerusalem: Jerusalem Center for Public Affairs, 1984.

"United Israel Appeal Remittances to the Jewish Agency [UJA Funds]." Jerusalem: United Israel Appeal, 1988.

Selected Bibliography

Andrews, Frank E. *Philanthropic Giving*. New York: Russell Sage Foundation, 1950.

Boskin, Michael J., and Martin Feldstein. "Effects of the Charitable Deduction on Contributions by Low-Income and Middle-Income Households: Evidence from the National Survey of Philanthropy." *Review of Economics and Statistics* 59 (August 1977):351–54.

Bubnic, A. "The Charitable Behavior of San Francisco Bay Area Physicians." Institute For Non-Profit Organization Management, Working Paper no. 5. San Francisco, Calif.: University of San Francisco, 1988.

Cohen, Steven M. "Will Jews Keep Giving? Prospects for the Jewish Charitable Community." *Journal of Jewish Communal Service, 55* (Autumn 1978):59–71.

———. "Trends in Jewish Philanthropy." In *American Jewish Yearbook, 1980*, pp. 29–51, edited by David Singer and Milton Himmelfarb. New York: American Jewish Committee and Jewish Publication Society, 1981.

———. *American Modernity and Jewish Identity*. New York: Tavistock Publications, 1983.

———. *American Assimilation or Jewish Revival*. Bloomington, Ind.: Indiana University Press, 1988.

Coles, Robert. *Privileged Ones: The Well-Off and the Rich in America*. Boston: Little, Brown, 1977.

Daniels, Arlene Kaplan. *Invisible Careers: Women's Civic Careers from the Volunteer World*. Chicago, Ill.: University of Chicago Press, 1988.

Douty, Christopher M. "Disasters and Charity: Some Aspects of Cooperative Economic Behavior." *American Economic Review* 62 (September 1972):580–90.

Edmondson, Brad. "Who Gives to Charity?" *American Demographics* 127 (November 1986):44–49.

Eisenstadt, S. N., and Ora Ahimeir, eds. *The Welfare State and Its Aftermath.* London and Sydney: Croom Helm in association with the Jewish Institute for Israel Studies, 1985.

Feldstein, Martin, and Amy Taylor. "The Income Tax and Charitable Contributions." *Econometrica* 44 (November 1976):1201–22.

[Filer Commission Report.] *The Commission on Private Philanthropy and Public Needs.* Vol. I. Washington, D.C.: Department of the Treasury, 1977.

The Foundation Directory, 11th ed. New York: The Foundation Center, 1987.

Giving USA. New York: AAFRC Trust for Philanthropy, 1987.

Gold, Doris B. "Women and Voluntarism." In *Women in Sexist Society, Studies in Power and Powerlessness,* edited by Vivian Gornick and Barbara K. Moran, 533–54. New York: Basic Books, 1971.

Goldberg, S. P. "Jewish Communal Services: Programs and Finances." In *American Jewish Yearbook.* Vol. 78. New York: American Jewish Committee and the Jewish Publication Society, 1977.

Goldin, Milton. *Why They Give: American Jews and Their Philanthropies.* New York: Macmillan, 1976.

Goldscheider, Calvin. *Jewish Continuity and Change: Emerging Patterns in America.* Bloomington, Ind.: Indiana University Press and Center for Modern Jewish Studies, Brandeis University, 1986.

Greeley, Andrew M. *Ethnicity, Denomination and Inequality.* Beverly Hills, Calif.: Sage, 1977.

Heilman, Samuel C. "The Gift of Alms: Face-to-face Almsgiving among Orthodox Jews." *Urban Life and Culture,* 3 (January 1975):371–95.

Himmelfarb, Harold S. "Measuring Religious Involvement." *Social Forces* 53 (June 1975):606–18.

Hodgkinson, Virginia Ann, and Murray S. Weitzman. *Dimensions of the Independent Sector.* Washington, D.C.: Independent Sector, 1986.

———. *Giving and Volunteering in the U.S.,* 1988 ed. Washington, D.C.: Independent Sector, 1988.

———. *The Charitable Behavior of Americans.* Washington, D.C.: Independent Sector, 1986.

Iannaccone, Lawrence R. "An Economic Model of Religious Participation," Department of Economics, Santa Clara University, November 1986. (mimeographed)

———. "A Formal Model of Church and Sect." *American Journal of Sociology* 94, supplement (July 1988):241–68.

Ireland, Thomas R. "The Calculus of Philanthropy." *Public Choice* 8 (Fall 1969):23–33.

Jakobivits, Dr. Sir Immanuel. "Women in Community Service." *L'Eylah* 23 (Spring 1987):4–6.

Karp, Abraham. *To Give Life: The UJA in the Shaping of the American Jewish Community.* New York: Schocken Books, 1981.

Kirstein, George. *The Rich: Are They Different?* New York: Houghton Mifflin, 1968.

Kop, Y., ed. *Israel's Outlays for Human Services, 1984.* Jerusalem: The Center for Social Policy Studies in Israel, 1984.

Kosmin, Barry A. "The Political Economy of Gender in Jewish Federations." *Contemporary Jewry* 10 (Spring 1989):17–31.

———. "Understanding Contemporary American Jewry: Implications for Planning," North American Jewish Data Bank, Occasional Papers no. 4. New York: CUNY Graduate Center, 1988.

Liebman, Charles S. "The Sociology of Religion and the Study of American Jews." *Conservative Judaism* 35 (May/June 1981):16–33.

Long, Stephen H. "Social Pressure and Contributions to Health Charities." *Public Choice* 14 (Winter 1976):56–66.

Mayer, Egon. "Discomforts with Jewish Philanthropy. Some Perspectives of the Children of Philanthropists." *Journal of Jewish Communal Service,* 64 (Spring 1988):223–33.

Mogulof, Melvin B. "Foundations: Their Actual and Potential Influence on Jewish Communal Life." *Journal of Jewish Communal Service* 63 (Summer 1987):283–89.

Moore, Deborah Dash. *At Home in America: Second Generation Jews in America.* New York: Columbia University Press, 1981.

Nelson, Ralph L. *Economic Factors in the Growth of Corporate Giving.* New York: National Bureau of Economic Research, 1970.

Phelps, E. S., ed. *Altruism, Morality and Economic Theory.* New York: Russell Sage Foundation, 1975.

Powell, Walter W., ed. *The Nonprofit Sector: A Research Handbook.* New Haven, Conn., and London: Yale University Press, 1987.

Rimor, Mordechai, and Gary Tobin. "Jewish Giving to Jewish and non-Jewish Philanthropy." Paper presented at conference on Philanthropy and the Religious Tradition, Independent Sector, Chicago, Ill., 10–11 March 1989.

Ritterband, Paul, and Steven M. Cohen. "Will the Well Run Dry? The Future of Jewish Giving in America." *Response* 23 (Summer 1979):9–17.

Ritterband, Paul, and Richard Silberstein. "Jewish Philanthropy in Contemporary America," North American Jewish Data Bank, Information Series no. 2. New York: CUNY Graduate Center, 1988.

Roberts, Russell D. "A Positive Model of Private Charity and Public Transfers." *Journal of Political Economy* 92 (February 1984):136–48.

Schervish, Paul G., and Andrew Herman. "Varieties of Philanthropic Logic Among the Wealthy." In *1987 Spring Research Forum: Working Papers*. Washington, D.C.: Independent Sector and United Way Institute, 1987.

Schwartz, Barry. "The Social Psychology of the Gift." *American Journal of Sociology* 73 (July 1967):1–11.

Schwartz, Robert A. "Personal Philanthropic Contributions." *Journal of Political Economy* 78 (November 1970):1264–91.

Silberstein, Richard, Paul Ritterband, Jonathan Rabinowitz, and Barry A. Kosmin. "Giving to Jewish Philanthropic Causes: A Preliminary Reconnaissance." In *1987 Spring Research Forum*. Washington, D.C.: Independent Sector and United Way Institute; reprint ed., North American Jewish Data Bank, Reprint Series no. 2. New York: CUNY Graduate Center, 1987.

Sklare, Marshall. "The Future of Jewish Giving." *Commentary* (November 1962):416–26.

Sombart, Werner. *The Jews and Modern Capitalism* (trans. by M. Epstein.) Glencoe, Ill.: Free Press, 1951.

Tonai, Rosalyn, M. "Asian American Charitable Giving," Institute for Non-Profit Organization Management, Working Paper no. 4 (March 1988). San Francisco, Calif.: University of San Francisco.

Warner, Irving R. *The Art of Fundraising*. New York: Harper & Row, 1975.

Wixen, Burton. *Children of the Rich*. New York: Crown Publishers, 1973.

Woocher, Jonathan. *Sacred Survival: The Civil Religion of American Jews*. Bloomington, Ind.: Indiana University Press, 1987.

Yankelovich, Skelly & White Inc. *A Study of Giving Patterns to the United Jewish Appeal*. New York: United Jewish Appeal, 1981.

———. *The Charitable Behavior of Americans*. Washington, D.C.: Independent Sector, 1986.

Zuckerman, Alan and Calvin Goldscheider. *The Transformation of the Jews*. Chicago and London: University of Chicago Press, 1984.

The Contributors

Barry R. Chiswick, Research Professor and Head, Department of Economics, College of Business Administration, University of Illinois at Chicago, Chicago, Illinois.

Donald Feldstein, Associate Executive Vice President, Council of Jewish Federations, New York, New York.

Arthur S. Goldberg, Director of Research, Robert F. Wagner, Sr. Institute of Urban Public Policy, Graduate School and University Center, City University of New York, New York, New York.

Norbert Fruehauf, Assistant Director, and Director of Planning and Resource Development, Council of Jewish Federations, New York, New York.

Alice Goldstein, Senior Researcher, Population Studies and Training Center, Brown University, Providence, Rhode Island.

Samuel C. Heilman, Professor of Sociology, Queens College of the City University of New York, Flushing, New York.

Bethamie Horowitz, Senior Scholar, Center for Jewish Studies, Graduate School and University Center, City University of New York, New York, New York.

Israel Katz, Director, Center for Social Policy Studies in Israel, Jerusalem, Israel.

Barry A. Kosmin, Director, North American Jewish Data Bank, Graduate School and University Center, City University of New York, New York, New York; Director of Research, Council of Jewish Federations, New York, New York.

Egon Mayer, Professor of Sociology, Brooklyn College of the City University of New York, Brooklyn, New York; Senior Research Fellow, North American Jewish Data Bank, Graduate School and University Center, City University of New York.

Rela Geffen Monson, Dean for Academic Affairs, Gratz College and Center for Jewish Community Studies, Melrose Park, Pennsylvania.

Mordechai Rimor, Research Associate, Maurice and Marilyn Cohen Center for Modern Jewish Studies, Brandeis University, Waltham, Massachusetts.

Paul Ritterband, Professor of Sociology, The City College of the City University of New York, New York, New York; Director, Center for Jewish Studies, Graduate School and University Center, City University of New York, New York, New York.

Ira Silverman, Director, Institute of Human Relations; formerly Executive Vice President, American Jewish Committee, New York, New York.

Gary A. Tobin, Director, Maurice and Marilyn Cohen Center for Modern Jewish Studies, Brandeis University, Waltham, Massachusetts.

Madeleine Tress, Senior Scholar, North American Jewish Data Bank, Graduate School and University Center, City University of New York, New York, New York.